To Alan -

In friendship &

with appreciation

Michael

LOUIS FINKELSTEIN AND THE CONSERVATIVE MOVEMENT

Conflict and Growth

LOUIS FINKELSTEIN AND THE CONSERVATIVE MOVEMENT

Conflict and Growth

Michael B. Greenbaum

Academic Studies in the History of Judaism
Global Publications, Binghamton University
2001

Library of Congress in Publication Data

Michael B. Greenbaum, *Louis Finkelstein and the Conservative Movement: Conflict and Growth.*

ISBN 1-586840-96-7

Published and Distributed by:
Academic Studies in the History of Judaism
Global Publications, Binghamton University
State University of New York at Binghamton
Binghamton, New York, USA 13902-6000
Phone: (607) 777-4495 or 777-6104; Fax: (607) 777-6132
E-mail: pmorewed@binghamton.edu
http://ssips.binghamton.edu

Academic Studies in the History of Judaism

Publisher: Global Publications, State University of New York at Binghamton
Address: SSIPS, LNG 99, SUNY Binghamton, Binghamton, N.Y., 13902-6000

To Cindy

ושלל לא יחסר

(Proverbs 31:11)

Table of Contents

Preface

The relationship of the Seminary and its chancellor to the Conservative Movement has long been a subject of debate, if not a source of tension, among the national organizations of the movement as well as its rank and file. This is no less true today than it was eighty years ago. Understanding the source(s) of this issue and the efforts from inside and outside the Seminary to grapple with it seemed necessary if one was to understand the nature of JTS and the movement today. To what extent is the JTS–Conservative Movement relationship particular to JTS or similar to that of other seminaries and the religious movement with which they are connected? I puzzled over the apparent systemic nature of this tension, wondering why a generation of leaders before my contemporaries and me had not been more successful in ameliorating these differences. The past few decades have born witness to the struggle of religiously affiliated institutions of all kinds to define themselves both within the academy and with their religious group. The results have been uneven as many chose to all but separate themselves from their faith group while others have come perilously close to compromising the values of the university world.

I undertook this study in the hope that I would come to better understand the current state of JTS and the Conservative Movement, and, as a result, similar institutions would benefit from its findings, making it easier for them to navigate their struggle over mission-conflict.

As I began this project, I viewed the idea of mission-conflict as "black or white," meaning that it was possible to separate out the mission or identity or values of the religious body from the character of the academic institution. One of Finkelstein's coworkers had thought so, too, as reflected in the following statement:

> In Dr. Finkelstein's concept, the Seminary is to build bridges not only between Jews and members of other faiths but between various groups in Judaism. It is possible, of course, that instead of building bridges, the Seminary may turn into a third party.[1]

For Jessica Feingold, the Seminary's mission remained an either/or situation: either the Seminary would be a "bridge builder" in the broader community, which meant that it could not get too close to the religious movement with which it was philosophically linked, or it would become a third party—that is, an ideologically identifiable branch of Judaism, but it seemingly could not attempt to be both. In view of the results of this study, one must now conclude that Feingold's characterization of the mission is an oversimplification. In truth, the relationship of the academy with the religious body makes a separation of their two missions virtually impossible.

Witness the fact that in the almost thirty years in which I have been a participant in the effort to write an institutional mission statement for the Seminary, the outcome has always been a two-pronged statement attesting to the Seminary's mission as both an academic center and a spiritual and religious center. So, JTS's current mission reads, in part:

> The Jewish Theological Seminary of America, the intellectual and religious center of Conservative Judaism:
>
> 1) Serves as the preeminent center for the academic study of Judaica outside of Israel, as one of the preeminent centers world-wide, and as a training center for scholars to advance the study;
> 2) Educates Jewish professionals and lay leadership in the spirit of Conservative Judaism for the total

[1]Jessica Feingold to Frieda Schiff Warburg, 12 May 1947.

community through academic and religious programs, both formal and informal.

Perhaps mission-conflict in religiously affiliated institutions should be understood as a polarity that needs to be managed, rather than as a problem to be solved.[2] Instead of viewing it as an either/or situation requiring institutions to choose one side over the other, religiously affiliated institutions and their religious bodies would be well served to view it as a both/and situation, requiring that all parties recognize that the educational institution cannot possibly function well if it is forced to choose the academy over the religious body, or vice versa. The two sets of values are interdependent, precluding choosing one at the expense of the other. Moreover, the problem will not end by limiting the institution's mission to following only the values of the academy or the values of the religious group with which it is affiliated.

In short, the conflict of mission or identity is intrinsic to religiously affiliated institutions with elitist goals, perhaps making such institutions "bi-missional." Accordingly, the issue before religiously affiliated institutions of higher education is not whether they can rid themselves of this tension between the values of the academy and the values of the religious body; but rather, the need for them to acknowledge that the tension may be appropriate, and to learn to live with it in a positive and creative way, giving support to both the values of the academy and of the religious group with which it is associated.

The publication of this book is the culmination of almost two decades of work. First conceived as a doctoral dissertation in 1981, it was approved by my doctoral committee at Teachers College, Columbia University, in 1994.

---

[2]Johnson, 1992, pp. 81ff.

The study was of necessity limited in scope, concluding in 1955 at the midpoint of Louis Finkelstein's presidency. Subsequently, I have documented and analyzed the remaining years of his presidency (1952–72) in "The Finkelstein Era," published in *Tradition Renewed: A History of the Jewish Theological Seminary of America*, vol. 1, edited by Jack Wertheimer, in 1997. There are a number of essays in that publication that elucidate subjects and events that I could not address in detail. Marsha Rozenblit's chapter, "The Seminary during the Holocaust Years," is but one example.

This long and often arduous journey would not have been possible without the help of so many people, each of whom enabled me to persevere in the course of numerous highs and lows that I encountered all the way.

Without the encouragement, in the mid-1970s, of Roberta Kiel, then director of personnel at the Seminary, I probably would not have undertaken the pursuit of a doctoral degree in higher-education administration. Her instincts, as always, were on the mark. My thanks also to Professor Douglas Sloan for appreciating the value of this research project when it was but an idea and taking me on as his advisee, and to Professor Sharon McDade, without whose strong guiding hand and upbeat encouragement this study would have remained unfinished.

The long hot days in the dusty and overcrowded Seminary attic locating and then reading through some thirty drawers of uncatalogued files were made a bit easier thanks to the help of Seminary students Michael Finkelstein, Ed Snitkoff, and Jodi Futornik. My thanks also to Arielle Jarmuth and Suzanne Kling for their help with the footnotes.

I am particularly grateful to my friend and colleague Rabbi Neil Gillman for the frank conversations in which he convinced me that I absolutely had to complete the dissertation and, more recently, for his encouragement to publish it. My teacher and friend, Dr. Maurice Wohlgelernter, professor emeritus of English at Baruch College, was always there for me, making sure I never gave up, and so much more.

The long and lonely days of my initial research and writing were made bearable thanks to the support and guidance of my friends Professors Benjamin Gampel, Jack Wertheimer, and Raymond Scheindlin.

Of course, without the support, encouragement, and understanding of the Jewish Theological Seminary, beginning with Chancellor Gerson D. Cohen and now Chancellor Ismar Schorsch, this project could never have been undertaken. The completion of this dissertation and its subsequent publication only further deepens my debt to this institution, to which I already owe so much. "Making the time" to complete this study would not have been possible without Chancellor Schorsch's indulgence, understanding, and encouragement. He will be my teacher always.

My deep appreciation goes to my colleague Rabbi Benjamin Scolnic for bringing my work to the attention of Professor Jacob Neusner, and to Professor Neusner for his belief in the study. To my assistants Faith Monkarsh, Sharon Pollack, and Benedict Hughes, whose efforts on the computer brought the text to life goes my unbounded gratitude, as it does to Kelly Washburne and Janice Meyerson, whose careful reading of the text and preparation for publication have made for a vastly more readable volume. I am appreciative of Rachél Fester's work in preparing the index. My thanks also to Rabbi Judah Nadich and Marjorie Wyler for their valuable comments and insights.

Finally, I shall remain ever grateful to my beloved family. Cindy and our wonderful children, Yonatan, Yael, Etan, and Michal, have been so understanding over the years as Abba always seemed to be working. They are my treasure.

Chapter 1
Academy or Fountainhead?

> Religiously affiliated institutions often experience a tension between the values of the academy and the needs of the religious body with which it is identified. This tension can be particularly acute when resources are limited. The Jewish Theological Seminary is an example of an institution that has lived with this tension. Various studies of religiously affiliated institution have tried to understand the complex nature and characteristics of these kinds of institutions.

The Jewish Theological Seminary of America is an institution that has struggled, and continues to struggle, with the conflict between being a religious and an academic institution. Whose mandate—that of the religious body's or that of the school's—is the institution to follow? This book examines the mission of this institution as it was formulated, expressed, and reformulated during the tenure of one of its most important presidents, Dr. Louis Finkelstein. When did it limit its perspective to that of an academy and when did it reach out beyond its students to serve American Jewry at large? What were the issues, problems, and circumstances that guided Finkelstein to pursue one or the other of these paths during his presidency? What happens when an institution is further stressed by inadequate financial resources?

Today, there are more than 750 colleges and universities in the United States that acknowledge one or another kind of affiliation with a religious group.[3] These colleges constitute about 20 percent of all American colleges and universities and an even larger segment of private colleges and universities. This is a significant contribution to the educational diversity

---

[3]Rodenhouse, 1999, pp. xlvii–xlviii.

for which American higher education has become distinguished.

Some work has been done on the nature and organization of such institutions.[4] However, these studies have been few in number and, for the most part, simplistic in their analysis.[5]

Typology of Religiously Affiliated Institutions

Of greater use is Cuninggim's taxonomy for the church-related sector.[6] He identified three groupings of religiously

---

[4]Riesman, 1980; C. R. Pace, 1972; Anderson, 1977; Baldridge et al., 1978; Patillo and MacKenzie, 1966; Parsonage, 1980; Cuninggim, 1978; O'Brien, 1994; Stoltzfus, 1992.

[5]One study suggests that evangelical colleges are representative of all religiously affiliated institutions of higher education (Riesman, 1980). Two other studies glossed over the differences between religiously affiliated institutions and secular institutions, not to mention the differences that exist within the group of religiously affiliated colleges and universities (Pace, 1972; Anderson, 1977). In other studies, religiously affiliated institutions of higher education are grouped with all other independent institutions of higher education (Baldridge et al., 1978). These attempts to understand and analyze religiously affiliated colleges and universities have also led some to posit an "ideal type" of institution. This ideal type is used as a way of evaluating all religiously affiliated colleges and universities as being more or less religiously affiliated (Patillo and MacKenzie, 1966; Pace, 1972). This ideal type includes such outward signs as the election of a larger number of trustees by the religious body, the presence of a significant number of members of the sponsoring denomination in the faculty and in the student body, compulsory attendance at worship, and so on. This ideal type is predicated on the assumption that these "indispensable marks" of religious affiliatedness can be definitely identified. The difficulty with this ideal type is that it may or may not have much to do with reality since the characteristics on which the evaluations are made may be quite arbitrary and the differences of history, tradition, and mission among religious bodies tend not to be considered in such an approach (Parsonage, 1980, p. 113).

[6]Cuninggim, 1978. See also Cuninggim, 1994, where he addresses the nature of the relationship of the college to the church and how their relationship has been undergoing change.

affiliated colleges: the "consonant," the "proclaiming," and the "embodying." These three types can be placed along a continuum ranging from those institutions having close ties to the religious body on the one extreme (the embodying college to those exercising considerable independence from the religious body on the other (the consonant college)

> The "consonant college" is an institution that, feeling independent in its own operation, is committed to the tradition of its related church and to a consistency with that tradition in its own behavior. Its values are in the main its denomination's values. They are taken seriously and are evident in the life of the college and the lives of the alumni/ae.[7]

The major difference between this type and the other two is the way it attests to its status. It affirms its relationship to the religious body quietly as an unassertive ally would do (for example, Haverford, Salem College, and Carleton College). In such colleges, it usually matters little, if at all, to the college or the denomination, whether or not there are particular forms of organizational structures, organic ties, or religious requirements.

The proclaiming college is an institution that announces its affiliation with its sponsoring denomination at every appropriate occasion. It practices in its programs what it proclaims to be in ways that are approved by the worlds of education and religion.

> These ways differ from college to college and from church [religious body] to church [religious body]. No one form of structural tie, no one provision for religious nurture, curricular or extracurricular, no one pattern of faculty, student or trustee composition is requisite.[8]

---

[7]Parsonage, 1980, p. 113.
[8]Parsonage, 1978, p. 34.

The proclaiming college is its own master in deciding what it shall be and do, both academically and religiously. As a college, it is in confederation with the religious body and readily admits it (for example, Notre Dame and Southern Methodist University).

The embodying college is one whose allegiance is to the tenets of its religious group with educational overtones, whereas the proclaiming college is one whose allegiance is to the norms of higher education, but with some ecclesiastical overtones. "It is the mirror, almost the embodiment, of the denomination to which it gives fealty. Whether forced or unforced, it is the Reflection of the church."[9]

Mission/Identity Conflict

This taxonomy acknowledges the diversity that exists within the religiously affiliated sector and the complexity of the college relationship underlying that diversity.[10] It is that diversity and the complexity of the relationship between the religious body and the academic institution that is most often responsible for the conflict over missions presently existing in most religiously affiliated colleges and universities. Most students of higher education acknowledge that one of the organizational characteristics that delineate academic institutions is ambiguous goals. This characteristic is all the more trenchant among religiously affiliated institutions because "adding to the goal ambiguity of an institution of higher education is the ambiguity of the relationship with the religious body."[11]

It is difficult for religiously affiliated institutions to deal with these ambiguities, particularly at times of limited

---

[9]Ibid. p. 35.

[10]This diversity is further illustrated by R. T. Sandin, 1990.

[11]Baldridge et al., 1978.

resources.[12] The two missions often have different priorities, though some overlap may exist. They are based on a different set of values.[13] When a surfeit of students and available funds exist, a religiously affiliated school might well serve both the needs of the religious body and those of its immediate academic constituency.[14] However, during periods of declining enrollments and spiraling costs such as occurred in the 1970s and early 1980s, many such schools were severely challenged to be able to meet the needs of both groups.[15] In those instances in which the school was unable to serve fully both constituencies, it was further challenged to find ways to determine whose needs should receive priority.

There have been a number of studies detailing the different approaches to this matter of identity. Patillo and MacKenzie have focused on those features of religiously affiliated institutions that distinguish them from their secular counterparts while other writers "address the issue of

---

[12]For example, the number of Catholic colleges and universities has declined from 309 in 1965 to 222 today. Hunt and Carper, 1996. See also Burtchaell, 1998, p. 823.

[13]One observer notes that whereas church-related institutions could once rely upon their faculty to share its values with students, the newer faculty members, having been trained in the "value-free" education of the public university, could no longer be expected to fill this role. Arthur J. DeJong, 1990. See also Burtchaell, 1998, p. 850.

[14]See, for example, Douglas Sloan, who explores "the ways in which mainline Protestant churches did, and did not, deal with the faith-knowledge relationship" (Sloan, 1994, p. viii).

[15]Too many religious colleges and universities have lost their sense of mission. In these tight economic times for higher education, people have to find value in that mission and be willing to pay for it. Hunt and Carper, 1996. "The 'market' or 'consumer' mentality is a strong driving force in determining the missions of theologates; to ensure enrollment, schools must try to provide programs that are responsive to the needs and goals of the bishops and religious supervisors who support them, not always the same programs that faculty and administration believe are the best preparation for ministry" (Schuth, 1989, pp. 47–48).

direction for church-related colleges."[16] One of these writers suggests that a religiously affiliated institution has to choose between being a religious body and a college.[17] Indeed, it has been suggested that their academic programs "too often reflect a research university model" and that it is imperative that they "retain their sense of autonomy. Critical decisions concerning curriculum, faculty credentials, and educational philosophy must be influenced by their own mission."[18] Still others, such as the Lutheran colleges in America have chosen to address the potential conflict in mission through examining their institutional image, noting that a college's conflict over mission has much to do with the way the institution is perceived by its constituencies. Most recently, Catholic colleges and universities have been forced to reconsider their mission and identity by the Vatican's issuance of *Ex Corde Ecclesiae* in 1990, requiring that those schools be more accountable to the Roman Catholic Church. The U.S. Catholic Bishops Conference was charged by the Vatican with responsibility for drafting a policy that would define this new relationship. In 1999, it produced a document that set forth a new set of criteria with which Catholic institutions will have to comply in order to satisfy the wishes of the Vatican.

It may well be that a conflict of missions or identities is intrinsic to religiously affiliated institutions. Perhaps they are by definition "bi-missional" and, although at times either mission will prevail, the two—that is, the needs of the religious body and the needs of scholarship—can never be so completely separated as to eliminate one at the expense of the other. Thus, the real issue for such institutions is whether the conflict between missions is permitted to be a destructive

---

[16]Bruning, 1975, p. 27.

[17]Sherry, 1967.

[18]Richard L. Noftzer Jr. in Guthrie and Noftzer, *Agendas for Church-Related Colleges and Universities* 79 (fall 1992): 86.

element within the organization, or whether it is turned into a creative tension.

In addition to religiously affiliated schools, that tension is apposite to other kinds of institutions—for example, a research hospital such as the Memorial Sloan-Kettering Institute. Such institutions are torn between their goal of conducting the finest medical research possible and their mandate to serve the public. In order to service the large community with distinction, Sloan-Kettering must maintain its high level of research and scholarship; otherwise, it might be just another cancer-care facility. Its scholarship and research are what enable it to meet the community's needs; yet largely because it serves the community, it can conduct its exceptional research. In essence, the relationship between scholarship and community is a symbiotic one, wherein both missions are necessary for either to survive.

The Jewish Theological Seminary

This relationship between scholarship and community also exists at the Jewish Theological Seminary of America. The Seminary is a prime example of a religiously affiliated institution that has grappled throughout its history with the central issue concerning academic goals and service to a burgeoning and changing constituency. It must balance these two sometimes conflicting missions, especially during this period of mounting deficits and limited resources. Should it concentrate on fulfilling its role as the religious center for the Conservative Movement, creating new programming to reach out to the laity in order to meet their spiritual, communal, *and* academic needs? Or should it be directed toward fulfilling its role as the academic arm and spiritual center of the Movement, mandated to train functionaries and scholars to serve the larger community?

The Jewish Theological Seminary stands today as both the academic and the religious center of the Conservative Movement, the largest denomination of synagogue-affiliated Jews in America. As we shall see, it is unique among all religiously affiliated institutions, as well as among its own Jewish counterparts. Unlike, for example, its Reform counterpart, the Hebrew Union College–Jewish Institute of Religion, the Seminary was not founded by a lay body, but was itself the founder of the United Synagogue of America, the lay group of the Conservative Movement with which Conservative synagogues are affiliated. Furthermore, unlike its numerous Orthodox counterparts, all of which can confer rabbinic ordination, the Seminary until 1996 was the only institution in the world where one could be ordained as a Conservative rabbi. Even today, the overwhelming number of individuals ordained as Conservative rabbis are graduates of the Seminary.

With five schools at its New York campus (the List College of Jewish Studies, the Graduate School, the Rabbinical School, the H. L. Miller Cantorial School, and the William Davidson Graduate School of Jewish Education) and a sixth school in Israel (the Schechter Institute), the Seminary now has a student body exceeding 750, and a faculty of some one hundred full- and part-time scholars. The Seminary is accredited by the Middle States Association of Colleges and Schools and is chartered by the Regents of the State of New York. It offers the degrees of Bachelor and Master of Arts, Master and Doctor of Philosophy, Doctor of Hebrew Literature, and Bachelor and Master of Sacred Music. To these degree-granting programs, the Seminary admits qualified applicants without regard to race, color, religion, or national or ethnic origin, with the exception of applicants to its rabbinic and cantorial programs, who must be of the Jewish faith.

The Seminary is also the religious center for the members of some 790 synagogues in North America, Canada, Europe, South America, Asia, and Israel, the whole of which constitutes the United Synagogue of Conservative Judaism (formerly the United Synagogue of America). Since its founding, the Seminary has ordained some 937 rabbis who are among the fifteen hundred members of the Rabbinical Assembly—the Movement's organization of Conservative rabbis.[19] In addition, other constituent organizations of the Conservative Movement, such as the Women's League for Conservative Judaism, which represents local sisterhoods in each congregation, and its male counterpart, the Federation of Jewish Men's Clubs, depend on the Seminary for religious guidance.

Among these programs, one should be aware that the Seminary also provides the religious and educational supervision for a network of overnight Jewish educational camps in North America that serve over 7,500 young people every summer It operates the Department of Community Education, through which it reaches a nationwide audience. Through its Finkelstein Institute, it engages in interfaith work and through its Melton Research Center, it develops curricular material for the Jewish school.

Academically, the Seminary today is both an institution committed to the perpetuation of Conservative Judaism and a university affirming the critical and dispassionate study of all religious texts in an atmosphere of academic freedom and pluralism. Conservative Judaism is that branch of American Judaism that seeks to "accommodate Jewish tradition to the new conditions and insights of the modern age, while preserving intact the structure and content of traditional

[19]The other six hundred rabbis are graduates of other non-Conservative institutions who have been admitted as members in the Rabbinical Assembly.

Jewish observance."[20] In its attempt to grapple with the tension between tradition and the open society, it is distinct from Reform, on its left, which abandoned any commitment to Jewish law , and from Orthodoxy, on its right, which refuses to consider modifying Jewish law.

The Seminary was founded in 1886 as a school for the training of teachers and rabbis, and reorganized in 1902 to include the task of laying the foundations for the development of a knowledgeable Jewry, that is, traditional in its observance but American in its behavior. It was this group of Jewry that was later to coalesce into the Conservative Movement. The Seminary, therefore, has been committed to a dual mission for most of its 114 years.

Louis Finkelstein

To understand Finkelstein's work, a brief review of the administrations of Dr. Solomon Schechter and Dr. Cyrus Adler is required. An outstanding scholar in Cambridge, England, Schechter was invited to America by the Seminary's lay leaders in 1902 to head the reorganized Seminary. Schechter's close associate, who was to succeed him as president of the Seminary upon his death in 1914, was Dr. Cyrus Adler. Even in these early years, there was a struggle between those Seminary leaders who wanted to build a movement around the Seminary and those who saw the Seminary's purpose only as an outstanding center of Jewish scholarship.

However, the most significant period in the Seminary's history in terms of this "mission conflict" was during the administration of Louis Finkelstein (1940–72). It was during his administration, and particularly the first fifteen years, that the program of the Seminary and the size of the Conservative

---

[20] *Emet ve-Emunah: Statement of Principles of Conservative Judaism*, 1988, p. 8.

Movement grew significantly, adding to the "creative tension" that was then played out to its fullest. *Therefore, that era will be the major focus of this book.*

Marshall Sklare wrote that Finkelstein was a "school man"[21] and that under his leadership, the Seminary saw itself only as a school for the training of rabbis, cantors, teachers, and academicians to serve the Jewish community. That position is underscored by the way his administration handled matters pertaining to the interpretation of Jewish law for the larger community. It will be shown later how the Seminary's faculty abdicated its role as the arbiters of Jewish law for the community to the movement's rabbinic group. Jewish law was therefore studied only in an abstract, or pure, sense, and was not used, as it might have been, to meet the needs of the community. In that area, it is fair to say that Finkelstein limited the Seminary's role to that of an academy, rather than making it the spiritual fountainhead of a religious movement.

However, in matters outside the area of Jewish law, Finkelstein was far from being a "school man" in the narrow sense that Sklare uses the term. Finkelstein, like Schechter before him, sought to mediate the Jewish tradition to the broader community, including the community of Conservative Jews. He believed that society could be improved by bringing people to the study of Torah, in the broadest sense. The Institute for Religious and Social Studies and the Conference on Science and Religion, for example, were clearly founded with this belief in mind. In 1939, Finkelstein did what no other previous religious leader had been able to accomplish, namely, to gather under one roof representatives of differing Christian faiths together with Jews for the purpose of searching for solutions to society's moral

[21]Sklare, 1955, p. 185.

and ethical dilemmas. He considered that to be an integral part of religious learning

In studying how the Seminary under Finkelstein mediated its dual mission of academy and fountainhead, one begins to realize that the two missions of scholarship and communal service are not easily separable, nor can they necessarily work in tandem free of tension and ambiguity. Furthermore, specific programs and activities cannot be labeled easily, let alone definitively, as serving one mission more than the other. Thus, one begins to discern a new, albeit complicated, role for the church-related institution of higher education: that of the broker that bridges authentic scholarship with the needs of the people.

Chapter 2
Solomon Schechter (1902–15)

Solomon Schechter headed the Seminary as it was reorganized in 1902, transforming it into a center of scholarship and expanding its role into the larger community. He gave the institution its ideological and philosophical foundations. Seeking a base of financial support for the Seminary, he created the United Synagogue of America.

The Reorganized Seminary

The Seminary was established in 1886 by a leadership that wanted to stem the rising tide of Reform Judaism. He believed that a traditional Jewish institution would appeal to the Jewish immigrant population and provide them with a school to train their religious leaders. However, by the end of the 1890s, the early Seminary was faltering. Key academic and rabbinic leaders had died, and those remaining were aging. Given the absence of strong rabbinic leadership, lay support deteriorated. Most significantly, the number of students in the institution was very small. In 1901, Joseph Blumenthal, who had been president and a pillar of support of the Seminary, died. The institution was near bankruptcy and was forced to seek loans using as collateral its property on Lexington Avenue in New York City.

If the Jewish Theological Seminary[22] was to have a future, a bold step would need to be taken by those for whom this institution represented the future of American Judaism. Such

---

[22]Its name was changed to include "of America" when the founding Jewish Theological Seminary Association merged with the newly formed "The Jewish Theological Seminary of America" on 30 March 1902. For a full description of the early Seminary (1886–1902), cf. Fierstein, 1990; and Davis, 1963.

a step was indeed taken and is described anecdotally in Cyrus Adler's[23] autobiography, *I Have Considered the Days*. He relates how, in a conversation with Jacob Schiff at a party at the home of Isidor Straus, he had remarked how unfortunate it would be for the largest Jewish community in the world not to have an institution of higher Jewish learning. Schiff became interested in the Seminary and, together with Louis Marshall and others, committed himself to the saving of the Seminary.

This group of wealthy and distinguished laymen most of whom were Reform Jews, took up the banner of the Seminary in order to preserve traditional Judaism in America. They had little hope in Reform Judaism's accomplishing the task at hand because of the religiosity of the immigrant group. They saw the graduates of the Seminary, who were traditionally observant, as the only ones who had a chance of Americanizing the Eastern European immigrants.[24] These immigrants were of two kinds: deeply religious, retaining the ways of the *shtetl*, that is, an Orthodoxy that was alien to the American environment; or politically radical and secular, having thrown off the yoke of Judaism to embrace new "anti-American" ideologies. The former certainly would not be attracted to Reform Judaism, with its numerous breaks with the tradition, and although the latter group wanted no part of organized religion, they would never come to see Reform Judaism as authentic Judaism under the best of circumstances because Reform had rejected many of the core beliefs of traditional Judaism. Given an increase in anti-Semitism, and with acculturation the watchword of established American Jewry, this immigrant population was a threat to the Americanized, sophisticated lifestyle of the Reform and

---

[23]Adler served as chairman of the board from 1902 until 1905 and as president of the Seminary from 1915 until 1940.

[24]Davis, 1963, pp. 322–23.

German Jewish population that had settled in America earlier, and was by now comfortably acculturated. These Jews felt that it would be in their best interest to see to the Americanization of this immigrant population. It was from this belief that their support for the Seminary grew.[25] Sol M. Stroock, chairman of the Board of Directors of the Seminary from 1929 to 1941, remarked that these founding lay leaders realized that "the Seminary must be national in character, that no 'pent-up Ithaca' should restrict its powers, and that the whole broad continent must be inspired through its influence."[26] Thus, the Seminary was seen by its lay leaders as the institution that could "create a bridge between the cultural and religious backgrounds of the newcomers to the American environment.[27]

In the months that followed the discussion in Straus's home, those laymen who had expressed an interest in saving the Seminary developed a financial plan for its reorganization. As part of that plan, efforts that had been ongoing for some time were intensified to hire Solomon Schechter of London, for all concerned believed that he was the most appropriate person to lead the new Seminary. Schechter had both a traditional Jewish education and classical university training. Prior to his coming to New York, he was a reader in rabbinics at Jews' College in London, and subsequently received an appointment as a reader in Talmud at Cambridge University. By the time of this appointment to Cambridge University in 1894, his scholarly reputation was significant. But his greatest scholarly achievement was yet to come. In 1896, he identified a treasure trove of Hebrew texts in an ancient Egyptian synagogue in Cairo. Although the existence of this *genizah* (hidden room) had been known, the

---

25 Robinson, 1989, p. 369.

26 Adler, 1939, p. 155.

27 Parzen, 1964, p. 28.

documents that Schechter identified had a significant impact on Jewish scholarship for decades to come. Judge Mayer Sulzberger, believing that the time was right to build a knowledgeable Jewry, identified with Schechter's scholarly capabilities.[28] Adler saw Schechter as someone capable of cultivating the support of wealthy community leaders and philanthropists such as Jacob Schiff .[29]

Even before being approached by those desirous of reorganizing the Seminary, Schechter had expressed strong belief in the school and its role in the perpetuation of Judaism. In 1893, he wrote to Alexander Kohut, a leading figure in the institution's early years:

> What is your college doing? America must be a place of Torah, because the future of Judaism is across the seas. You must make something of your institution if the Torah and wisdom are to remain among us. Everything is at a standstill in Germany; England has too few Jews to exercise any real influence. What will happen to Jewish learning if America remains indifferent?[30]

Little did he know then that only a few short years later, he would be in the position to carry out his own words. Schechter's decision to come to America and to become the head of the Jewish Theological Seminary of America came only after a long courtship by the leaders of the Seminary in New York. A voluminous correspondence together with personal visits by Adler and others eventually came to convince Schechter that if he came, he would have, among other things, the appropriate title that he deemed necessary to

---

[28]Sulzberger was a jurist in Philadelphia and an outstanding leader in the Jewish community. He was deeply involved in the early Seminary and, in 1902, gave his unique collection of rare Hebraica to the reorganized Seminary. In addition, his collection of Jewish ceremonial objects formed the core collection of the Seminary's Jewish Museum.

[29]Karp, 1969, 5:126.

[30]Ibid., 5:112.

exercise the authority to run an academic institution.[31] While he was promised the title he sought, he was concerned about having to share authority with Adler, whom the Board wanted in charge of the institution's day-to-day administration. Here again, Schechter demonstrated his concern for the powers and perquisites of his office, in expressing the hope that "the sphere of work duties and rights [are] described and delineated in such a way as to make collision [between him and Adler] impossible."[32]

It is clear from the correspondence between Schechter and Judge Sulzberger that Schechter was interested in coming to America to run a school and to build a center of Jewish learning. He was not interested in building a movement or in establishing a denomination. Early in this correspondence (1896), Schechter wrote, "It is not Orthodoxy which I wish to preserve but Judaism."[33] In 1900, he put the matter more succinctly:

> The real question is whether you [Sulzberger] think it desirable, both for the Seminary and myself, that I would accept the offer; that is to say whether the Seminary can be arranged in such a way as to become a centre of Jewish Wissenschaft pure and simple.[34]

Still later (1901), he expressed his concern over the makeup of the Seminary's Board of Trustees:

> The great point is that the whole power and authority of selecting teachers, examining and awarding degrees are vested in the Seminary itself—and that is also the rule in Berlin, Vienna and Budapest—*not* in an advisory board consisting of Rabbis as they have in New York. I

---

[31]A complete picture of the process to bring Schechter to America is found in Karp, 1963, pp. 42–62. See also Ben-Horin, 1963.

[32]Solomon Schechter to Judge Mayer Sulzberger, 21 July 1901 (Ben-Horin, 1963).

[33]Solomon Schechter to Judge Mayer Sulzberger, 10 April 1896, ibid.

[34]Solomon Schechter to Judge Mayer Sulzberger, 5 March 1900, ibid.

> do fear that this Board may be troublesome in time....If you do not want the Seminary to be too much of a party affair you will have to do something to meet this difficulty—the less Rabbis meddle with us the better for the cause. We must be quite independent of them.[35]

The details of his position having been worked through and the arrangements for his coming to America having been made, Schechter arrived on these shores in the spring of 1902. It was in March of that same year that the old Jewish Theological Seminary Association was merged with the new Jewish Theological Seminary of America Corporation. The board leaders of the old Association were replaced by the men who had committed significant sums of money to the Seminary's financial reorganization. Given the Association's lack of funds, its leadership had no choice but to relinquish control of the institution to those who were now prepared to fund it. The board was changed from one that was elected biennially to a self-perpetuating one An endowment fund in excess of a half million dollars was established, without which Schechter would not have agreed to come. Once on the scene, he immediately proceeded to raise the academic standards and engaged a full-time faculty of noted scholars. To successfully launch the "new" Seminary, Schiff agreed to a new building near Columbia University, which he funded. Among other things, this new building enabled the institution to house the rare books and manuscripts recently donated to the Seminary by Judge Mayer Sulzberger.

---

[35]Solomon Schechter to Judge Mayer Sulzberger, 28 July 1901, ibid. Schechter was also concerned that a rabbinical board would be unable to draw the necessary financial support. (Bentwich, 1964).

Building the Nondenominational Academy

Schechter came to America to establish a center of Jewish learning. His dream was to build "a Jewish Academy with regular academicians, which by reason of its authority and scientific work, [w]ould give Jewish opinion the weight and importance in all matters relating to Hebrew learning."[36]

In his inaugural address, he described his mission as "to create a theological centre which should be all things to all sections of the community."[37] According to Adler,

> Dr. Schechter...held the view that the Seminary must always shelter men of different types of mind...[and] that the greatest hope for Judaism would be a combination of the rationalist and the mystic, and that any generation which could produce such conditions would indeed produce great men and rabbis.[38]

Schechter set the direction in which the Seminary was to proceed for decades to come. As Adler noted, Schechter gave the Seminary "our ideal":

> [t]he creation of a conservative tendency, which was almost entirely absent or lay dormant in this country for a long time. Its aim was to preserve and to sustain traditional Judaism in all its integrity and by means of the spoken or written word, to bring back to the consciousness of Jewry its heroic past, which must serve as a model if we were to have a glorious future, or any future at all; but at the same time, to remain in touch with our present surroundings and modern thought, and to adopt what was best in them and above all, to make use of modern method and system.[39]

---

[36]Lewis Strauss, "Speech at the Adler Memorial," 1950. Cyrus Adler Papers.

[37] Schechter, *Seminary Addresses*, p. 11.

[38]Adler1933.

[39]Ibid.

Just a few months into Schechter's presidency, a Chicago Jewish newspaper captured the essence of the character that Schechter wanted the Seminary to have. The Seminary is, "in the fullest sense of the word, a Seminary for America, that represents all types of Jews and it is even more emphatically American by its conservative tendency."[40]

Schechter wasted no time in transforming the Seminary from merely a school to prepare rabbis to a center for Jewish learning that reached out to the larger community. One of his first steps was to gradually change the Seminary into a postgraduate school by requiring all students to have completed college before entering the Seminary.[41] In 1909, he established the Teachers Institute (T.I.), realizing that a school that trained only rabbis was insufficient to have any significant impact on the American Jewish community. It was largely through the Teachers Institute and its related programs that the Seminary in its early years reached beyond its scholarly walls to the broader Jewish community.

While Schechter acknowledged his conservative tendency, he told Adler that he strongly believed that "if the Seminary is to become a real blessing, it must not be degraded as a battleground for parties. It must give direction to both Orthodox and Reform."[42] He was also concerned about the quality of textbooks for Jewish education and thought the

---

[40]Bentwich, 1964.

[41]Adler called this "next to the choosing of the new faculty, the most important achievement of Schechter's administration" (Adler, 1939). This change must have been greeted originally with some skepticism because in his 1904 commencement address he remarked that "our experiment to confine the teaching in the Seminary to post-graduates...did not prove such a failure as some prophesied." Schechter, "The Reconciliation of Israel," first graduation exercises, 6 May 1904, Seminary address, 1915. Solomon Schechter Papers.

[42]Bentwich, 1964. Letter from Solomon Schechter to Cyrus Adler, 1901, p. 171.

Teachers Institute should become involved in publishing them. He reorganized the faculty, adding to its ranks great scholars such as Louis Ginzberg, Alexander Marx, and Israel Friedlander, all of whom went on to become luminaries in their fields. Schechter required his faculty to do research and to publish. To facilitate their research, he worked together with Marx to build a first-rate library. By 1915, the library had grown to 46,000 from 5,250 volumes in 1902 and from just three to 1,782 manuscripts.[43] In addition, a new building including a library, classrooms, and offices was dedicated in 1903 in close proximity to what would be the Seminary's future home in Morningside Heights.

The dedication of this facility provided an opportunity to tell the community exactly what the mission of the Seminary was. Jacob H. Schiff, whose beneficence made the building possible, told the assembled that the purpose of most Seminaries is to train rabbis

> according to the particular religious views and tendencies of the founders. Entirely different are we situated. The organizers of the Jewish Theological Seminary of America have had only the one single purpose in view—to establish an institution which should appeal to all desiring to prepare for the Jewish Ministry, irrespective of the tendencies toward which they might be leaning.[44]

In his acceptance of the building from Schiff, Schechter reinforced Schiff's comments and noted that, by naming the Seminary the Jewish Theological Seminary *of America*,

> The Board of Directors...have distinctly shown their intention of avoiding sectarianism; for it is an especial American feature that no preference is given to any denomination or theological *Richtung*

[43]Adler, 1939, p. 89; *Students Annual*, 1915, unpaged.

[44]Jacob H. Schiff, speech, 1903. Solomon Schechter Papers, JTSA.

> [direction/tendency]...and [for] the Seminary to be really great [it] will have to be catholic, and [have a] direction or tendency of a uniting nature.[45]

The concept of catholicity was important to Schechter and his idea of catholic Israel became one of the key concepts for Conservative Judaism. According to Schechter, the center of Jewish authority laid not in the Bible nor was it "represented by any section of the nation, or any corporate priesthood, or Rabbihood, but by the collective conscience of Catholic Israel."[46] Catholic Israel is, then, the Jews of any given period who are "in touch with the ideal aspirations and religious needs of the age,"[47] that is, who are religiously observant and knowledgeable of the tradition. Schechter's vision was of a unified Jewry, one that would have no need for denominations or religious streams. "If only given proper leadership, granted the opportunity to study their tradition, and allowed to sink roots in this world, the Jews would create in America another Golden Age."[48] However, in looking back over his first ten years in office, he commented that one of the reasons that the Seminary's work had been so difficult was because of

> the great divisions among the people engendered by the extreme tendencies of the various parties, be they Reform or Orthodox, which could never understand a frame of mind that refused to be labeled by the names they wished to attach to it.[49]

When Schechter realized that his lay leadership was more interested in the Americanization of the immigrant

---

[45]Schechter, *Seminary Addresses*, pp. 50, 48.

[46]Schechter, *Studies*, 1970, p. 15.

[47]Ibid.

[48] Rosenblum, 1970.

[49]Solomon Schechter, "The Assistance of the Public," 8 June 1913, commencement address. Schechter, *Seminary Addresses*, pp. 229–37.

population than in building a center of Jewish learning that would reach out to all traditionally minded Jews, he reacted strongly:

> I must take it out of their minds that I came into this country for the purpose of converting the downtown [Lower East Side] Jews to a more refined species of religion.... [N]o consideration would ever have induced me [to assume the presidency of the Seminary] had I known that the Seminary was largely meant for a particular section of the community.[50]

In another instance, he commented:

> At present it seems that [members of] the Board are more interested in questions of civics than in rabbinical Jewish learning. Social work and sociological Judaism is what they expect from the rabbis. And this is not my province.[51]

Schechter felt that what was lacking was the "religious element."[52] He had come to America to mount a religious revival and therefore believed that the religious element had to be the Seminary's mission. His lay supporters

> had in mind an academic institution that would command the loyalty of the new immigrants and the admiration of the German Jews, and that could also be proudly held up as a model of intellectual and spiritual leadership in the Gentile as well as in the Jewish communities.[53]

The United Synagogue Is Created

Schechter lacked the funding to achieve all his goals. He wanted to continue to expand the Seminary's program;

---

[50]Bentwich, pp. 191–92; Sklare, 1955, p. 193.
[51]Bentwich, p. 190.
[52]Ibid.
[53]Davis, p. 46.

however, the endowment that had been established in order to bring him to America was not sufficient. Various competitive interests had emerged during the early part of his first decade, including the creation of Dropsie College for Hebrew and Cognate Learning in Philadelphia, which siphoned off support from the Seminary. The founding of Dropsie was a particular disappointment to Schechter because he had hoped to attract the college's funders to the Seminary.

By 1907, the Seminary was in financial trouble. Its expenditure budget was greater than the income from its endowment. Some 20 percent of its nonendowment income came from branches that the Seminary had set up in surrounding communities such as Philadelphia, Baltimore, Newark, and other parts of New York.[54]

Because of its desire to be "all things to all men," the Seminary did not have a clearly defined constituency on which it could depend for support. Although the Seminary was identified with Conservative Judaism by this time and there were synagogues and Seminary graduates who also identified themselves with Conservative Judaism, nothing bound them all together. The Seminary's rabbinical alumni association, which brought Conservative rabbis together, was a fledgling organization only founded in 1901. Although its members were desirous of any effort that would bring together all representatives of Conservative Judaism in a unified way, there was no organizational structure to do so.

Schechter realized that some action must be taken if the Seminary was to survive. He was cognizant of the lack of organization among Conservative forces and, moreover, was

---

[54]Board chairman Louis Marshall expressed disbelief over the lack of support for the Seminary. "It is strange that of the 850,000 Jews in this city, of whom 750,000 are in accord with the principles taught in the institution...so little support is provided us" (ibid., p. 136).

keenly aware of the inroads being made by the Reform movement and by other communal activities educationally, philanthropically, and religiously, and the success these efforts were having in attracting donors and leadership. In a letter to his benefactor, Judge Mayer Sulzberger, he admitted that if something was not done to bring together the "conservative forces," the synagogues would, in time, be lost to the Reform with the concomitant result that the Seminary would lose its entire support.[55] He thus set out to create a union of Conservative synagogues that would link the Seminary formally to those congregations and their rabbis and provide a firm base of support for the Seminary.

The idea was not popular with his board and certainly not with Cyrus Adler. Adler told Schechter that one of the reasons he was against the formation of a Conservative union was that "should it grow to be a strong body, the center of gravity would be removed from the Seminary."[56] Indeed, Adler also envisioned the United Synagogue as having the potential to become the overarching and unifying force for traditionalizing American Jewry.[57] If anything, Adler felt that the formation of such a group should emanate from within the rabbinical alumni rather than from the Seminary. In fact, it was the alumni more then anyone else at the Seminary "who felt the overwhelming need to build the new union as a vehicle for bringing the Seminary's message into the daily life of American Jewry."[58] Schechter was not insensitive to Adler's concern, for he also felt strongly that the Seminary must be the center of the community. He was relatively flexible about the makeup of the union "as long as [it] would be willing to publicly acknowledge that the Seminary must be

---

[55]Rosenblum, 1970.

[56]Arzt, 1949, pp. 10–20.

[57]Davis, p. 173.

[58]Rosenblum, p. 190.

the centre."[59] Schechter saw the idea of a Conservative union through to realization and, in 1913, the United Synagogue of America was created.

In a way, the creation of the United Synagogue was a contradiction of Schechter's concept. Staunchly opposed to the existence of denominational groups, he seemed to have created one with the establishment of the United Synagogue or at least to have given form and structure to an already existing ideology. As his biographer pointed out, "[his] aim was not to create a new, but to consolidate an old party."[60] Some observers, like Parzen, contend that with the formation of the United Synagogue, the Seminary was no longer able to be "all things to all people," and that with its creation, Schechter went from being the head of a school to being head of a religious group.[61] Indeed, Schechter served as the first president of the United Synagogue of America.

However, according to Finkelstein, the United Synagogue had no ideological base. It, like the Seminary, was to be above all parties. As chair of the committee to organize the United Synagogue and draft its platform, Schechter strove to perpetuate his ideal that the Seminary and those associated with it represented a normative traditional Judaism devoid of any descriptive term.

> I have always resisted any adjectives to my Judaism, believing that I belong to the mainstream of Judaism....I have been willing to let other people give themselves adjectives, orthodox, conservative, reform, radical or even Zionist. To that extent, therefore, I am a Jewish man and not a party man. Now as far as I have any voice, this will be the attitude of the new

---

[59]Ibid., p. 194.
[60]Bentwich, p. 210.
[61]Parzen, p. 68.

organization.[62]

In fact, the organization's constitutional platform reached out to all traditional elements within the Jewish community. The union was to be inclusive rather than exclusive "so as to come in touch with the work of the whole of Israel."[63]

To Schechter, the United Synagogue did not exist to promote Conservative Judaism or set itself apart from the larger community, but rather as a union to promote traditional Judaism, thereby affirming and supporting the mission and work of the Jewish Theological Seminary. Finkelstein described Schechter as being administratively and politically naive and thus unaware of the possible ramifications of such a Conservative union. According to Finkelstein, Schechter simply wanted a base of financial support and a way for the Seminary's rabbinical graduates to be connected with the institution. Schechter was not really interested in building a serious organization. Such an endeavor required a great deal of time and administrative acumen, neither of which Schechter had, according to Finkelstein. He had little idea of what administration entailed, preferring to teach a little and mostly do research and write.[64] In short, the United Synagogue was, for Schechter, little more than an idea.

Within two years of the creation of the United Synagogue Schechter died. Adler, who had become president of Dropsie College in Philadelphia while remaining active in the affairs of

---

[62]Bentwich, p. 11.

[63]Ibid., p. 210.

[64]Interview with Finkelstein, 14 February 1984. Finkelstein said that most of the faculty had little understanding of or regard for administration and related the story of Dr. Kaplan coming into his office at the end of an exhausting day. Kaplan said, "You look tired." Finkelstein replied, "I am tired," to which Kaplan replied, "How can a person get tired signing checks?"

the Seminary and the United Synagogue, was named acting president.[65]

[65]Adler was president of the United Synagogue from 1914 to 1917. He remained the president of Dropsie College during his tenure as president of the Seminary.

Chapter 3
Cyrus Adler (1915–40)[66]

Adler is named acting president and pursues Schechter's mission for the Seminary to be a center of higher Jewish learning. The Seminary's relationship with the Conservative Movement is not strengthened. Financial conditions worsen, and the Seminary turns to Conservative rabbis and their congregations for support as it celebrates its semicentennial. A new physical plant is built, and the collections of the library and the museum are increased.

Staying the Course

Although Adler was not a rabbi, he was a deeply influential community leader who was involved in the founding of a number of major Jewish communal organizations, many of which he served as president and often simultaneously.[67] "In truth, from 1890 to 1939 there was hardly a Jewish movement of any importance that did not bear the mark of his interest and participation."[68] As a result of his widespread communal involvement, he was well known to and respected by the great Jewish philanthropists of the day. As indicated previously, it was his influential relationship with Jacob Schiff that brought about the reorganization of the Seminary in 1902. This relationship with the broad spectrum of Jewish lay

---

[66]Adler was named acting president upon Schechter's death in 1915 and became permanent president in 1924.

[67]He was, *inter alia*, among the founders of the Jewish Publication Society, the American Jewish Historical Society, the American Jewish Committee. He edited a number of volumes of the *American Jewish Year Book*; he was a leader of the Joint Distribution Committee and was president of the Jewish Welfare Board.

[68] Robinson, 1985, p. xiii.

leaders made him an attractive choice to succeed Schechter who left a Seminary in need of financial support.

Adler was a committed observant Jew who was completely Americanized in culture and orientation. He earned his Ph.D. in Semitics from Johns Hopkins University, becoming the first American student to receive a doctorate in that field. He subsequently received an academic appointment at Johns Hopkins followed by a long stint at the Smithsonian Institution, first as librarian and then as assistant secretary.

Adler perpetuated Schechter's mission for the Seminary as a traditional Jewish school of higher learning that was to appeal to all Jews He did not, however, share Schechter's vision for a movement of laymen and congregations. By 1909, he came to realize that the Seminary "could not capture the entire community," and thus agreed to the formation of the United Synagogue as a "lay organization representative of traditional Judaism to mediate between the Seminary and the community."[69] Adler, however, would have preferred that the United Synagogue be an arm of the Seminary rather than a freestanding organization. Like Schechter before him and Finkelstein after him, he believed in the importance of Jewish studies for the preservation of Judaism and for the advancement of civilization.[70] Thus, for Adler, the Seminary was primarily a school, and as such was not the representative of any particular religious camp:

> Judaism is a very real religion, a long organic growth. Its mainstream has been Rabbinic Judaism. We are the representatives of that mainstream in America. We do not propose to be led into vagaries either to the right or left.[71]

---

[69]Naomi Cohen, in Robinson, 1985, 1:xxx.

[70]Finkelstein, "Necrology, Cyrus Adler," pp. x, 1–2.

[71]From a JTS pamphlet, "For the Perpetuation in America of Ancestral Judaism" (n.d., but believed to be from 1926–27).

The result of his adherence to this particular founding belief was that there was not much of a meaningful relationship between the Seminary and the nascent organizations of the Conservative Movement—the Rabbinical Alumni Association and the United Synagogue of America. The character of this relationship during Adler's administration is summed up in the Seminary's semicentennial volume, published in 1939. This comprehensive overview of the institution's first fifty years made no mention whatsoever of Conservative Judaism or the Conservative Movement. Moreover, it made no reference to the Rabbinical Assembly or the United Synagogue except to say that their offices were located at the Seminary. The institution portrayed itself only as an academic institution serving a constituency that Adler described as "the Jewish people of the United States."[72] In fact, there was a fairly common feeling that, under Adler, the Seminary's administration and faculty had narrowed Schechter's broad vision to that of only an academy.[73] For example, in 1937, the president of the Rabbinical Assembly expressed "some hopes for our Seminary that have not yet been fully realized."

> I should like to see the Seminary devote itself more consciously to a role of leadership in Jewish communal life...[and] show a greater measure of concern for the practical problems that confront us in the leadership of our congregations...by a more continuous close-knit co-operation with the Rabbinical Assembly and the United Synagogue.[74]

---

[72]Adler, 1939, p. 156.

[73]Parzen, p. 76.

[74]R.A, *Proceedings*, 1937, pp. 359–60. Testimony to the truth of the Seminary's narrowing of mission came from Finkelstein, who, in a letter to a Board member, remarked how another Board member had become "a leading spirit in this whole effort to widen the scope of the Seminary" (J. Solis Cohen to Louis Finkelstein, 28 December 1937). Toward the end of the 1930s, greater efforts were made to reach out to the community.

This same rabbi bemoaned the fact that there still was no descriptive statement that articulated clearly what Conservative Judaism stood for.

Members of both the United Synagogue of America and the Rabbinical Alumni Association, as well as the Seminary's faculty, were unhappy about this reality and thought that there was a need to recognize and endorse the existence of a Conservative movement. As early as 1919, an effort was mounted by a few members of the Seminary's faculty, among others, to help bring this about. This group wrote to the Seminary's leading scholar, Professor Louis Ginzberg, and invited him to a planning meeting whose purpose was

> to formulate in terms of beliefs and practice, the type of Judaism that we believe you profess in common with us. We have failed as a group to exert an influence on Jewish life in any way commensurate with the truth and strength of our position, and that, primarily, because we have never made our position clear to the rest of the world....[W]e maintain that the time has come for us to state frankly and emphatically what we believe in and what we regard as authoritative in Jewish

---

For example, a conference of rabbis and Jewish leaders in New Jersey was called to discuss various fundamental questions of Jewish life and religion. "For the first time," said Board chairman Sol M. Stroock, "the Jewish Theological Seminary, *which is primarily an institution of higher learning* [italics mine], will step beyond *its purely academic interests* [italics mine] and try to focus in public manner, the learning and experiences of the ages on specific modern problems" (interview with Sol Stroock, with material dated 1935–38). Yet Adler's view of the Seminary's mission was a narrow one, for even at the end of the decade, he argued that the Institute for Interdenominational Studies, which was to become a major outreach vehicle for Finkelstein, should be "purely academic." Moreover, Adler reaffirmed to Finkelstein his view that in the area of improving Jewish-Christian relations, an area that would also be a major one for Finkelstein, the Seminary "ought to do its part but I do not think it can play the major role." Adler to Louis Finkelstein, 21 July 1939, "Response to Louis Finkelstein's letter of 12 July."

> practice....We feel that no good can come to Judaism either from petrified traditionalism or from individualistic liberalism, and that it is our duty to point the way to a Judaism that shall be both historic and progressive.[75]

Ginzberg refused to attend the meeting and, together with Adler and most other members of the faculty, remained steadfast in his belief that Conservative Judaism was not a "distinct movement or separate party but...the mainstream of Jewish religious life and therefore required no label or qualifying term."[76]

During Adler's term, the program of the Seminary's Teachers Institute, which Schechter had established in 1909, was expanded through the creation of an extension center in order to meet "the growing interest in Jewish studies on the part of Jewish youth and of the increasing demand for trained workers in the field of Jewish service."[77] This new department offered special courses designed to train Sunday school teachers and club leaders. It proved to be quite popular among young people who had a strong feeling about the Jewish people and Jewish culture, if not the Jewish religion.[78] During Adler's twenty-five-year tenure, the Teachers Institute expanded its curriculum to four years, receiving authority to grant degrees at the bachelor, master's, and doctoral level. It

---

[75]Friedlander, Kaplan, Margolis, et al. to Louis Ginzberg, 9 June 1919. Included in the group were Seminary professors Mordecai Kaplan and Israel Friedlander. Rubenowitz, p. 69. Two years earlier, in 1917, Friedlander gave a series of five lectures entitled "Aspects of Historical Judaism," in which he articulated a philosophy of the Conservative Movement. Shargel, 1985, p. 104.

[76]Friedlander, Kaplan, Margolis, et al. to Louis Ginzberg, 9 June 1919; and Ginzberg, 1966, p. 148.

[77]Jewish Theological Seminary of America, *Register*, 1902–70, pp. 21–22.

[78]Glazer, 1972, p. 93.

also established a joint program with nearby Columbia University that enabled students of the Teachers Institute to pursue a Seminary degree and a secular degree simultaneously.[79]

While Adler was able to acquire significant new collections for the Seminary's library and its museum, as well as to build a considerable physical plant, much of his tenure was plagued by the lack of sufficient financial resources.

Seminary Finances and the Conservative Movement

In the first two decades after the Seminary's reorganization in 1902, it depended for its support largely on the endowment that had been created to bring Schechter to America. However, it was not long before the income from that endowment was insufficient to meet the operating expenses, and the Seminary found itself yet again searching for financial support much as it did in the pre-Schechter era. To the extent that it was successful in Americanizing the Eastern European immigrants, many of its old and substantive donors abandoned the Seminary for other emerging causes such as hospitals and social agencies. As one observer noted, "political, cultural, and philanthropic [activities] were so rich and variegated and vigorous compared with the floundering religious life of the twenties."[80] Many of these donors did not identify with the Seminary ideologically and thus had no interest in funding the institution once it achieved, at least in their minds, the goal they had set for it.[81]

---

[79]This arrangement, begun in 1929, was with Teachers College of Columbia University. In 1954, a similar arrangement was struck between the Seminary and Columbia's School of General Studies. Adler, 1939, p. 137; R.A, *Proceedings*, 1954, p. 49.

[80]Glazer, 1972, p. 88.

[81]Sklare, 1955, pp. 316–17.

No sooner had Adler assumed the presidency of the Seminary in 1915 than fiscal conditions compelled him to write to his good friend and Seminary librarian, Professor Alexander Marx, denying Marx's request for an assistant librarian and a raise for a member of the library staff, noting that "the present resources of the Seminary do not permit thereof." Adler went on to say, "If the present resources of the Seminary can be strengthened, I am sure that the Board will be glad to endeavor to carry these recommendations into effect."[82] These words would be heard many times during the next twenty-five years.

By 1921, the institution was facing bankruptcy. To deal with the crisis, "An Outline of a Plan Which Might Be Helpful in the Work of Placing the Seminary on a Sound Financial Basis" was drafted. The author of that document was in disbelief that what he termed so great an institution could be in such poor financial health and traced the problem in part back to the original $500,000 endowment. "People don't know enough about the Seminary. They think it is supported by millionaires"[83] (the primary source of the original endowment). But the Seminary's financial difficulties were due to more than just inadequate publicity. President Harding had signed the Immigration Restriction Act in 1921, which effectively brought an end to the mass immigration of Eastern European Jews to the United States. This act was further strengthened by additional acts restricting immigration between 1924 and 1927, and by President

---

[82]Cyrus Adler to Alexander Marx, 4 May 1916.

[83]Jewish Theological Seminary of America, *Register*, 1902–70. According to the campaign feasibility report, this perception was still active in 1943. John Price Jones to Jewish Theological Seminary Board of Trustees, 7 June 1943.

Hoover's Executive Order of 1930, which capped the number of Jews permitted to immigrate to the U.S.[84]

Second, in keeping with the tenor of the times, second- and third-generation Jews in ever increasing numbers were fleeing their Judaism to become "fully American," for that was the emphasis of the day. Indeed, "popular writers criticized Jews for maintaining a seclusive solidarity instead of becoming 'Americans first.' "[85] An obvious result of this trend was the downward spiral in denominational vitality, a decline in church and synagogue attendance, all notwithstanding national prosperity. The problem in the 1920s was not the availability of money as much as it was a lack of commitment among the people to support institutions such as the Seminary.[86] As Reinhold Niebuhr wrote: "A psychology of defeat of which both fundamentalism and modernism are symptoms has gripped the forces of religion."[87] Religion was often viewed with a hostile eye and so as the decade of the 1920s wore on, scientism, behaviorism, and humanism became more conspicuous in the thought of the time.

The plan to deal with the Seminary's financial problems proposed that the Seminary organize groups of supporters in every Conservative congregation. These groups, it was suggested, might be known as "Seminary branches" and the individual contributors might be called "annual subscribers." A National Advisory Board of Seminary representatives from the local branches would then be formed, providing a connecting link between the Seminary and the community.

---

[84]Between 1870 and World War I, two million Jews entered the United States while only 250,000 got in right after the war.

[85]John Higham, 1957; also in Karp, 1969, 5:367.

[86]1923 to October 1929 were "seven fat years for American industry and business." Allen, 1972, p. 138.

[87]Handy, 1960.

This plan was launched at a major fund-raising dinner in New York in May 1922, which was held "to keep the Seminary from closing."[88] At this dinner, the Rabbinical Assembly undertook to raise $100,000 in annual contributions, donor pledges were made, and a laymen's committee was named. The campaign was fairly successful and by 1924, the Seminary had a balanced budget. However, just one year later, it closed the fiscal year with an operating deficit of $29,000, with little hope for additional revenues in the year ahead. Once again, Adler informed Marx that the Board had turned down his request for increases in the library, and in his letter pointed out that the "upkeep of the library [for the past fiscal year and exclusive of Marx's salary] cost $25,296.50"—virtually the deficit for that year! The situation for the library, which was separately incorporated in 1923–24, was to grow only worse as the Seminary's financial condition worsened.[89]

In the face of this financial crisis, Dr. Adler and Dr. Marx maintained a correspondence about whether it was more advisable to remodel existing facilities for the library or to build a new building that would be "especially planned" as a library. This correspondence was but one of numerous examples of the Seminary expanding or of giving consideration to expansion at a time of financial distress. In

---

[88]Louis Marshall, Cyrus Adler, Sol Stroock, and Max Drob spoke at the dinner. Included in a report describing a fund-raising event in New York that was held as part of the effort to keep the Seminary from closing, 12 May 1922.

[89]Parzen, p. 96; Waxman, 1964, p. 175; Sklare, 1955, pp. 316–17. There are those who suggest that the incorporation was done as a direct response to the financial crisis, for it would facilitate donations from individuals who might otherwise not give to the Seminary because of divergent religious beliefs. Others vehemently denied this assertion. R.A., *Proceedings*, 1960, p. 122. Cyrus Adler to Alexander Marx, 3 November 1926.

fact, in 1929–30, the Seminary did manage to erect three new buildings at its Morningside Heights site. Spearheaded by a substantial bequest from Louis Brush to erect and maintain a dormitory building, the Seminary successfully raised sufficient funds to also build new library and classroom buildings.[90]

Although a new campus was erected, the financial woes of the Seminary continued unabated, and its financial condition continued to deteriorate. By 1930, the Library was no longer able to purchase new books and the Seminary's extension centers had to be dropped.[91] Even the telephone service, among other expenditures, had to be reduced "in the interest of economy."[92] Once again, Dr. Marx was the recipient of a letter informing him that the library would lose five telephone extensions. Two months later, in February 1932, Marx received another letter urging him to conserve and save as much as possible:

> [T]he continued existence of the Seminary will depend in a large measure upon our ability at this critical time to conserve our resources in every possible direction. We now find ourselves compelled to resort to saving in even minor matters.[93]

---

[90]Brush left $1.4 million, 25 percent of which was to be used to build a dormitory, 25 percent to maintain it, and 50 percent for scholarships and endowment. Louis Finkelstein, report to Board of Directors, 16 January 1941.

[91]Adler, 1939, pp. 120, 133–34.

[92]Joseph B. Abrahams to Alexander Marx, 10 December 1931.

[93]Joseph B. Abrahams to Alexander Marx, 10 February 1932. Just how minor is seen from the Seminary's handling of a request from the president of the New York branch of the National Women's League, the organization of sisterhoods affiliated with the Conservative Movement. The request was for permission to use an extension from the Seminary's telephone switchboard to her desk located within the Seminary. She expressed a willingness to refund all necessary charges and the cost of outgoing calls. The request was denied. Memoranda between Joseph Abrahams and Cyrus Adler, 21, 25, and 26 March 1935.

One gets a fuller picture of the state of affairs from a letter that Dr. Adler wrote in March to the president of the Women's League, who had written to ask Adler how the Women's League could better cooperate with the Seminary. Adler told her that through shrinkage of income (because of the Depression, the endowment was not earning what it once did), the Seminary was in a very serious situation. "We had to close the old building [on 123rd Street], we have been obligated to reduce all our salaries and even with all of this we can only see our way ahead to the first of July of this year."[94] He said that the Seminary did not need scholarships or prizes, but rather a steady income to cover its operating expenses.

A short time later, Dr. Finkelstein, who at the time was the assistant to President Adler, was invited to address a Women's League convention. He was asked to help the sisterhoods take a more active interest in the raising of funds for the Seminary. Finkelstein turned to Adler for advice and commented: "I do not like to get too much identified with that [financial] aspect of our work."[95]

Adler instructed him to ask Rabbi Drob to speak about the finances of the Seminary, since he represented the rabbinic alumni on the Seminary's Board. Adler further instructed Finkelstein to make certain that Drob did not go into detail with the women. Adler wrote:

> It would seem quite sufficient to point out the two major items which concern our present situation; the one is the increase of cost of operation due to the new buildings and the other, the loss of income due to the fall-off of [synagogue] memberships. But again, I say, I do not want them to be given our budget details.[96]

---

[94]Cyrus Adler to Mrs. Minkin of the Women's League, 14 March 1932.

[95]Cyrus Adler to Louis Finkelstein, 29 April 1932.

[96]Ibid.

Despite these pressing financial difficulties, Sol M. Stroock, chairman of the Seminary Board, wrote in September 1932 to suggest that the Seminary begin a series of public lectures on the problems of Jewish cultural, economic, religious, and general interest. He proposed that it would be a separate department of the institute and therefore would in no way be connected with the Seminary's fiscal problems. He saw this project as purely educational and of singular importance to the community, believing that separate funds could be raised for it from private donors.

The loss of income from declining memberships mentioned above was an ongoing source of concern for Adler. He and Stroock discussed filling some seven vacancies that existed on the Board of Directors with lay people who were the presidents of the Seminary branches because "that is the way in which...our membership [will] develop."[97]

The Seminary's semicentennial was also approaching, and Adler reflected on capitalizing on this opportunity for fund-raising purposes. He requested of Stroock that the Board appropriate funds for the celebration of the semicentennial at its January 1934 meeting and asked that the Board consider "whether or not this fiftieth anniversary could not be made the occasion for securing some funds for the Seminary. Nearly every institution does this sort of thing and we certainly have no superfluity of funds."[98]

The Board decided to utilize this opportunity, in part for fund-raising purposes, and the Seminary brought in Joseph Willen, a professional fund-raiser, to guide them. Willen was head of the New York Federation, which raised funds to support local Jewish institutions. Although they were hopeful that Willen's work would bring into the Seminary's orbit a large group of wealthier Jews whom they had been unable to

---

[97]Cyrus Adler to Sol M. Stroock, 18 April 1934.

[98]Ibid., 23 December 1935.

attract, they also remained committed to the continuation of a campaign to obtain a broader base of support for the Seminary by increasing the number of small contributions.

During this period, Stroock commented that the semicentennial was doing a great deal to promote a better understanding of Judaism among Jews and Gentiles and that

> to launch a so-called drive would seriously impair what we are trying to do. Instead we intend to confine ourselves to two activities. The first will be a quiet effort to obtain outstanding gifts, such as endowed professorships, a memorial auditorium, memorial gifts to fund Library collections, etc. The second will be through our alumni, who will help us to get memberships and special contributions from their congregations.[99]

It was at this point that this particular connection between the Rabbinical Assembly and the Seminary began in earnest. The Rabbinical Assembly agreed that, during the semicentennial year, it would raise $50,000 for the Seminary. The Seminary's ambivalence about fund-raising was reflected further in a June 1937 report of the Semi-Centennial Committee to the Board of Directors. The report indicated that the semicentennial program had been a "most effective instrument for public education with regard to Judaism, as well as *incidentally* [emphasis mine] with regard to the Seminary." As regards fund-raising, it reported that it was "not our purpose to raise any considerable sums this year." Indeed, the institution had hired, presumably at Willen's suggestion, the firm of John Price Jones, a major public-relations and fund-raising firm, to help with the semicentennial, only to abandon them in favor of adding to the staff someone who could help in this area. The idea proposed to the Board called for the hiring of a person,

---

[99]Greenberg newsletter, 13 May 1949.

preferably an alumnus of the Seminary, to assist Dr. Finkelstein and the Development Committee in the membership and general fund-raising campaigns.

> We do not want to departmentalize the fund-raising effort and to separate it from public relations and general public extension education. To do that would involve us again in what we have always been trying to avoid, namely, a public campaign for funds. In undertaking our present mode of presenting its needs to the public, the Seminary has chosen a dignified path which will lead to permanent results.[100]

Discomfort with fund-raising also was expressed in the results of the semicentennial celebration, which the Board viewed very positively. Henry Hendricks, an influential member of the Board and chairman of the semicentennial wrote to a fellow Board member in June 1937: "the semicentennial raised $150,000 from six hundred donors plus $75,000 legacy." He described this as "a good start...for the second half century."[101]

They achieved these results despite the death of Felix M. Warburg in 1937. Plans had been made to hold a conference called by Warburg around which the Seminary would conduct a membership campaign. The Seminary had few supporters of the substance of Warburg, and his death represented a substantial loss. Finkelstein wrote Adler that the development committee of the Board "seem[ed] to have a sense of heavy responsibility devolving on all of them because of [his] death."[102] Their satisfaction with this campaign was evidenced by Adler's comment:

---

[100]Report of the Semi-Centennial Committee to the Seminary's Board of Directors, June 1937.

[101]Henry S. Hendricks to Sol M. Stroock, 11 June 1937.

[102]Louis Finkelstein to Cyrus Adler, 28 October 1937.

> I do not know that there has been a single year since the reorganization of the Seminary in 1902, when we have gained so many new adherents....[A] year ago...there was no one outside of the Board who showed an interest in the institution, and there were a number of men on the Board who showed no interest at all.[103]

Among the beneficiaries of this "campaign" was the faculty of the Rabbinical Department, who had their salaries restored, after they had been reduced in 1932.[104]

However, the celebration was short-lived because the additional revenue generated by the semicentennial clearly proved insufficient to rescue the Seminary from its fiscal difficulties. So in a very short time, the institution was back to "crying poverty" and haranguing its alumni to do more. In fact, the rabbinical alumni had not met the goal of $50,000 mentioned earlier, and the Seminary was quite upset by this lack of support. To register its unhappiness, Finkelstein drafted a tough letter that he proposed be sent to himself by two leading members of the Seminary's Board. In the letter, Finkelstein had those Board members say, "It's incredible to us that the alumni of the Seminary should be so unresponsive to [the Seminary's] needs....[A]t the end of the year we will have to recommend to the Board a curtailment of the Seminary budget.[105]

Notwithstanding this failure of the Rabbinical Assembly,

---

[103]Report of the Semi-Centennial Committee to the Seminary's Board of Directors, June 1937.

[104]Cyrus Adler to Louis Ginzberg, 24 June 1937.

[105]Louis Finkelstein to Arthur Oppenheimer, 17 March 1938; Arthur Oppenheimer and Lewis Strauss to Louis Finkelstein, 17 March 1938; Sol M. Stroock to Cyrus Adler, copy to Louis Finkelstein, 8 July 1938. Stroock acknowledged to Adler that "the other causes for which appeals are made to our alumni and their congregations do seem more pressing to them than simply the expansion of the Seminary."

it and the Seminary forged ahead in the fall of 1938 with a new plan to mount a systematic, nationwide campaign among the R.A.'s membership. Rabbi Simon Greenberg, who would join the Seminary administration some years later, was then the president of the Rabbinical Assembly and a staunch supporter of the Seminary and of this campaign effort. In a letter to his colleagues, he wrote:

> The Jewish Theological Seminary is the fountainhead of our inspiration and the most impressive symbol of our Movement....Not only will [this campaign] strengthen our Seminary, not only will it strengthen our position of leadership in the American Jewish community, but above all, it will be the greatest concerted effort we have ever made to bring the message of our Movement to American Jewry from coast to coast.[106]

Adler was, at best, ambivalent about this campaign, which entailed a more public stance vis-à-vis fund-raising than the Seminary had heretofore taken. Board chairman Stroock wrote Adler and indicated that the time had come to be more public about the Seminary's financial condition and the results that would derive from inadequate funding:

> [U]nless [the Seminary Development Committee] can definitely say that the Seminary is in great danger of having its work interfered with, even our own alumni won't raise money for us.[107]

Greenberg believed that this new Rabbinical Assembly campaign would need some professional leadership, specifically a campaign director; but here, too, Adler was ambivalent about the commitment of additional funds.

---

[106]Simon Greenberg (as president of the Rabbinical Assembly) to "Colleague and Friend," 20 September 1938.

[107]Sol M. Stroock to Cyrus Adler, copy to Louis Finkelstein, 8 July 1938.

The Assembly appointed a campaign chairman and a campaign committee to work in cooperation with the Seminary. A detailed campaign plan was sent by Dr. Greenberg to all members of the Assembly.[108] Notwithstanding all the planning that went into the campaign, its meager results forced Dr. Greenberg to express publicly his surprise at and regret of the resistance that the campaign encountered from members of the Assembly:

> It was disheartening therefore to meet with members...who responded to the Seminary's call with indifference or indolence.... [T]he very fact that laymen have as yet not taken up the burden voluntarily is in itself a reflection of our leadership."[109]

By June 1939, the campaign had raised $43,030.70, exclusive of expenses, and Finkelstein predicted it would not raise more than $70,000 in total.[110] Nonetheless, the additional funds enabled the institution to bring that academic year to a close without incurring any debt, something that had not occurred for fifteen years.[111] It was clear from this first year that an ongoing Rabbinical Assembly fund-raising effort on behalf of the Seminary was one solution to the Seminary's ongoing fiscal problems. Finkelstein was particularly optimistic because the monies raised in the first year came mostly from congregations outside the large cities, which meant that even more money could be raised once they were able to fund-raise within these larger congregations such as those in New York, Boston, and

---

[108]Simon Greenberg (as president of the Rabbinical Assembly) to "Colleague and Friend," 20 August 1938.

[109]Simon Greenberg, Bulletin of the Rabbinical Assembly, March 1939.

[110]Louis Finkelstein to J. Solis-Cohen, 29 June 1939.

[111]Ibid.

Chicago.[112] In fact, these larger communities were to be the focus of Dr. Max Arzt's attention in the coming year in his capacity as director of Field Services and Activities.[113]

Adler never lived to see whether those large cities did produce funds for the Seminary. He died in April 1940, at the age of seventy-six. He left a Jewish community that had been expanded and developed by his efforts, and a Seminary that had acquired an excellent physical plant, a significant library, and a substantial collection of Jewish ceremonial objects, but that lacked funding, a young faculty, and a vision for the next half-century.

---

[112]Louis Finkelstein to Sol M. Stroock, 3 August 1939.

[113]Louis Finkelstein to Cyrus Adler, 3 August 1939.

Chapter 4
Louis Finkelstein and the Seminary's Mission[114]

To foster an environment in which Jews and Judaism could thrive, Finkelstein believed that the Seminary had to concern itself with the role of religion and its ability to affect the quality of life in America. The Seminary had to expand outward to include programs that would promote group understanding and an understanding of Judaism so that Jews and Judaism would be accepted in the non-Jewish world.

Finkelstein's Vision

While Louis Finkelstein's mission for the Seminary was built on the foundations created by his predecessors, Dr. Solomon Schechter and Dr. Cyrus Adler, he took the Seminary in directions that they could only have dreamed about. The Seminary had been established in 1886 as a nondenominational rabbinical school. Schechter had expanded the mission, making the Seminary a center of Jewish learning, training teachers and engaging in serious Jewish research and scholarship. Adler expanded the Seminary's communal outreach, developing its museum and its classes for the general Jewish community. While each administration remained committed to that which it inherited, they saw fit to expand the Seminary's outreach into the community in keeping with the needs of their era. Finkelstein was to be no different.

---

[114]Finkelstein served as the head of the Seminary from 1940 to 1972. This study, however, only covers the period until 1955 because, in the words of Dr. Simon Greenberg, Seminary professor and Vice Chancellor in the Finkelstein administration, Finkelstein accomplished virtually all that was of importance by that date. Interview, 18 April 1985.

Finkelstein had been associated with the Seminary for twenty years by the time that he assumed the presidency in 1940. He had been ordained as a rabbi by the Seminary in 1919, and while a Seminary student had earned a Ph.D. from Columbia University Following his ordination, he served a congregation in the Bronx for twelve years, during which time he ascended the academic ladder at the Seminary, becoming a full professor in 1931. During the years between ordination and the presidency of the Seminary, he published several important research works, earning a reputation as a noted scholar. It was during the latter part of this period that he joined the Seminary's administration. From 1934 to 1937, he served as assistant to President Adler, and from 1937 until 1940 he was the Seminary's provost. Adler was not well in the last years of his presidency, and for all intents and purposes, ran the Seminary from his home in Philadelphia. Accordingly, he depended greatly on his assistant, Louis Finkelstein. During this period, Finkelstein exercised considerable influence on the operation and direction of the institution. By 1938, Finkelstein had already formed the essence of his vision for the Seminary he was to lead.[115]

> I have little doubt that it can only be through the strengthening of religious work in all denominations, and the creation of better understanding and increased cooperation among them, that we can find our way out of the slough of despond [*sic*] of the twentieth century.[116]

Finkelstein believed that Judaism could survive in America only if the environment was one that was characterized by peace, brotherhood, and a deep belief in what was then

---

[115]His difficulty in convincing Seminary constituents of the appropriateness of this broadened mission is the subject of the next chapter.

[116]Louis Finkelstein to Henry S. Hendricks, 13 May 1938.

referred to as "the democratic way." Moreover, Finkelstein was convinced that, in order for Jews to feel comfortable and secure in America, the larger non-Jewish community needed to understand the meaning of Judaism and the significant value of religion in society.

> The real difficulty we must face...is the...heathenization or paganization of such a large part of the population both Jewish and Christian. For as Jews, the problem happens to be more urgent and vital than for others; because the destruction of religion in America will involve the destruction also of the religious tradition of freedom, and with that our civil liberties....From the long range point of view, I do not know of anything we can do more important than to make some contribution to the preservation of religion as a vital force in America. So far as Jews are concerned...there is no safety for them unless they manage to establish higher ethical standards in their own life. To do this means to revitalize Jewish religion and prevent the growth of secularist tendencies which are undermining it. To achieve this end, it is necessary to make the Jews, and particularly Jewish youth, understand that Jewish religion is not something singular and queer. It has its place in the modern world order. It therefore becomes essential for the future of Judaism itself that its advancement should be correlated with a similar effort to advance the cause of religion generally.[117]

The depth of this feeling was conveyed in a letter from Finkelstein to philanthropist and Seminary supporter Max Warburg:

> I feel very strongly that it is vital for us to constantly keep in mind the fact that the Jewish problem is but a phase of the world problem. In taking action we must remember that the things which are happening to the Jews today are but a part of the general disintegration

[117]Louis Finkelstein to Cyrus Adler, 26 July 1939.

> anticipated by philosophers and historians of different schools for almost half a century.[118]

Finkelstein understood that for his vision to succeed, he would need to make the Seminary the vehicle for the creation of an intellectual environment in America that would recognize the importance of and be sympathetic to religious thought. He knew well the loss of standing in society that religion experienced in the 1920s and 1930s.

> During [these] inter-war decades there was a distinct decline in the relative moral force of the Churches [and synagogues]. They simply were not as important a factor in the molding of public attitude as they had been….The pulpit...had lost [its] preeminence.[119]

Accordingly, he wrote:

> We need not a book [that summarizes the knowledge of the times and gives it a religious and ethical interpretation] but a school which shall continually present to the religious world the facts of science and interpret them at once in terms of religious and ethical values.[120]

He saw Judaism as a pivotal force in the establishment of a world order and saw the Seminary as the single greatest Jewish institution in the world and as such, saw it as the vehicle for bringing the message of Judaism to the world.

> It is the function of religious institutions to consider not alone the immediate problems of their time, but to anticipate future developments....[Religion] tries to view every accident in the perspective of history, and against the background of the cosmos....This has been the approach of this Seminary to every problem which has arisen in American Jewish Life under the presidency of

---

[118]Letter from Louis Finkelstein to Max Warburg, 14 June 1940, JTS Archives.

[119]Ahlstrom, 1972, p. 950.

[120]Louis Finkelstein to Cyrus Adler, 26 July 1939.

> Schechter and Adler. Others must undertake to deal with the day to day affairs of our faith and the nation.
>
> The Seminary must always call attention to the long-range view....It is a grave matter to enter a war, without adequate military preparation; it may prove fatal to come into peace, without moral and religious preparation. It is with these thoughts in mind...that this Seminary has undertaken various talks looking toward the increase of understanding among various faiths, and also among the various intellectual disciplines, with a view to strengthening the moral and spiritual fiber of the American people. We realize that Judaism as a faith can survive only in an atmosphere of general faith.[121]

Thus, his broad vision of the Seminary's mission was clear. It had to be, in addition to a training institution for rabbis and teachers, and the center of intellectual inquiry (all of which it was under Schechter and Adler), an institution that was concerned with nothing less then the quality of American life and with the impact religion could have on it. He was convinced that "in the long run nothing [the Seminary] can do either for Judaism or religion can be more important."[122] "The Task of restoring Jews to Judaism and strengthening religious faith generally, is either the most important thing to be done or it is the most shocking waste of effort."[123] Finkelstein's vision called for the institution to grow from what he called "a school of Jewish history" to "a school of religion and ethics not only for ourselves, but...for the world at large."[124] For him, this vision was little else but the realization of the Seminary's ultimate purpose and potential. That he was prepared to devote his life to the

---

[121]Report to Board of Directors, 6 April 1941.
[122]Simon Greenberg to Louis Finkelstein, 12 July 1939.
[123]Report to Board of Directors, 6 April 1941.
[124]Louis Finkelstein to Cyrus Adler, 26 July 1939.

realization of this vision is evidenced in the following statement:

> I hope to devote all of my spare time, which ordinarily would go to research, my summers, and every ounce of strength I can muster, to further the project....Whether this is a major or a minor contribution to the solution of the problem of religion and Judaism in this country only time can tell. Believing as I do in the power of Ideas, and having strong faith that it is God's will that even when we do not wish it we should be made the instruments of spreading His knowledge in the world, I feel that the proposal is important; and so far as I am concerned, more important than any other particular task to which I could set myself.[125]

It is here that we get more than a glimpse not only of the vision but of the single-mindedness and determination that were to shape the Seminary for the next thirty years and that came to characterize Finkelstein's leadership of both the Seminary and the Conservative Movement.[126]

---

[125]Ibid.

[126]His unwavering commitment to the realization of his vision was again evidenced in his decision in 1942 to turn down an appointment to the American Jewish Committee, giving as his reason that his plans "have finally crystallized...and I am encouraged to believe that given wise direction, we can win for Judaism once more what it had in antiquity—universal respect as a way of life. Such an objective seems to me to transcend in importance any other to which I can make a contribution in the world" (Louis Finkelstein to Lewis Strauss, 2 January 1942). Another such example was seen in his letter to Arthur Hays Sulzberger of the *New York Times*, with whom he had a close relationship: "On reflection it seems to me that I can best save the cause in which we are all most interested—the preservation of our democratic traditions—by avoiding issues which involve practical decisions and arouse so much heat. It may be advisable from many points of view for me to stick to my own work which deals with general ideas and principles" (Louis Finkelstein to Arthur Hays Sulzberger, 6 September 1942).

He maintained that once Judaism would become what Schechter called "fashionable" to the non-Jewish world, Jews would themselves embrace it and return to the fold. In an interview (14 February 1989) with this writer, Finkelstein characterized this approach of first winning the acceptance of non-Jews toward Judaism as a "flanking movement," explaining that "you can't win Jews by just willing it—or just proclaiming them Jews."

Jews were, by and large, still rebelling against the old-world ways of their parents and grandparents. They did not want their lives complicated by behavior patterns that would set them apart from mainstream America. Thus, his strategy was first to make non-Jews knowledgeable about and comfortable with Judaism, in the belief that Jews would follow closely behind. He believed that it made little sense to improve the condition of society as regards the "brotherhood of man" and "fatherhood of God" only to fail at persuading Jews to embrace their Judaism.

Accordingly, even before he assumed the presidency of the Seminary, he devoted a great deal of time to a program whose purpose was to bring knowledge of Judaism to leaders of the non-Jewish world, while simultaneously bringing together religionists of all faiths. At that time, his program to accomplish that goal was called the Institute for Interdenominational Studies. In time, its name was changed to the Institute for Religious and Social Studies, reflecting Finkelstein's broader vision. He was convinced that

> great harm has already come to Judaism and the whole of modern civilization through the tendency of those who feel that they disagree, to avoid meeting each other even for mutual discussion and enlightenment. As a result of this refusal to meet, differences of opinion

> become exacerbated and theological disagreements develop into personal animosities.[127]

Finkelstein believed that the Institute was critical to changing these conditions and his conviction was strengthened each time he saw how he was able to counter resistance from non-Jews toward Judaism into support for Judaism simply by explaining and clarifying one or another misconception: "I now feel more convinced than ever that we can do an indispensable and vital piece of work through this Institute of Interdenominational Studies, especially if we organize it in connection with a Council for Better Understanding."[128]

So strong was his conviction to this work that by the time of his appointment as president, he had already developed a reputation for what later became known as interfaith work.

> The choice of Rabbi Finkelstein has given the Seminary a learned and a spiritual leader, who has won the friendship and respect of many persons of other faiths. I am sure that his indefatigable endeavors to break down the wall between the theological, philosophical and scholastic worlds will now bear fruit. His deep understanding of the American scene will do much to remove the religious antagonisms in this country.[129]

Even within the Conservative Movement, there were those who recognized the impact that he had on the institution before he assumed the presidency. In spring 1939, the *Bulletin of the Rabbinical Assembly*, the organization of Conservative rabbis, noted:

> The alumni and friends of the Seminary view with pleasure and approbation the greater field of activity into which our school has emerged. This enlarged

---

[127]Louis Finkelstein to Milton Steinberg, 28 September 1940.

[128]Louis Finkelstein to Lewis Strauss, 15 February 1939. (There is no record of this council ever being formed.)

[129]Aaron Benjamin, *The Jewish American*, 24 May 1940, p. 243.

> program comes as a welcome answer to the desire, inarticulate to a large extent but universally felt, that the Seminary was not wielding the influence which it had the right and duty to exercise in American Jewish life....The Seminary has emerged from the cloister, and lovers of traditional Judaism can only applaud....We have really witnessed a complete revolution of the status of our school in the public mind.[130]

With Finkelstein's succession to the presidency, the Seminary and the Conservative Movement gained a young, energetic leader who gave the institution a dynamic and forward-looking vision that was absent under Adler. The Seminary was now emerging from the lethargic decade of the 1930s, and was beginning to confront the difficult and challenging pre– and post–World War II era.

From Vision to Program

Finkelstein wasted little time in translating his vision into program, a program that was to evolve continually and expand over the course of his first four to five years in office. In early 1941, following through on his belief that one of the Seminary's primary duties was to create opportunities for the free interchange of opinion and knowledge, he proposed the formation of conclaves where "men who differed widely among themselves, [could] me[e]t to exchange ideas, information and above all to learn from one another."[131]

By fall 1941, he was engaged in meetings about the formation of a conference or institute in which the pressing problems of Judaism might be analyzed and solutions proposed. Such an institute on the future of Judaism was held at the Seminary in July 1942, with some ninety rabbis in

---

[130]Bulletin of the Rabbinical Assembly, March 1939.

[131]Report of Board of Directors, 6 June 1941.

attendance.[132] It was followed by one for lay leaders in November 1942. The latter conference, entitled "Strengthening of the Jewish Future and the Democratic Tradition," was chaired by then-Governor Herbert H. Lehman. Each conference was used by Finkelstein as a vehicle to evolve the Seminary's mission, to win adherents for this mission, and to bring attention to the institution, in this case simply by having the governor of the state as conference chair. In a letter from the governor to conference participants, he wrote: "[I]t's the deterioration of the moral and spiritual standards in America which poses a threat to civilization. The failure to stress the relationship between democracy and religious traditions is yet another such threat."[133]

The letter also called upon the conference participants and the Seminary to cease dealing with the problems incrementally and to put together a "well-integrated program utilizing all the intellectual and spiritual resources at the Seminary's command...[for] the preservation of Judaism...is an essential element in the defense of civilization."[134] Finkelstein astutely had the governor call for the very mission in which Finkelstein believed so deeply.[135] It is not a coincidence that at this very same conference, Finkelstein submitted a program for the Seminary that, by his own description, covered a wide scope:

> Virtually every important aspect of Jewish life is represented. This is because the Seminary, originating purely as a theological school for the training of rabbis,

---

[132]First Institute of Commission on the Future of Judaism at the Jewish Theological Seminary of America, 6–14 July 1942.

[133]Draft letter from Governor Herbert H. Lehman to guest list.

[134]Ibid.

[135]The files clearly demonstrate that the letter sent out over Governor Lehman's signature was written by Dr. Finkelstein.

> has been compelled by the logic of events to undertake many new responsibilities, such as the Library, the Museum, the National Academy for Adult Jewish Studies, and the Institute for Religious Studies.[136]

There was yet a third such conference in spring 1943, where Finkelstein again spoke of his all-encompassing worldview.

> We cannot solve the Jewish problem until there is justice for all. In a world of injustice Jews will always suffer. For the past twenty-five years we carried on our work as a little nation with imperialistic strivings. We have been isolationists. We must be [*sic*] of all isolationists. We must turn attention to theological problems bringing cure to [*sic*] entire world.[137]

When Finkelstein spoke of the need to be concerned with the "entire world," as he did above, it was not merely presidential rhetoric. For example, in 1943, Finkelstein corresponded with A. A. Berle of the U.S. Department of State regarding matters concerning Jews in Latin America. Finkelstein proposed the establishment of an Institute for Latin American Judaism to raise money to bring students to the United States to study for the rabbinate and teaching, and to send professionals to Latin America. Finkelstein believed that there would be no problem raising money, getting students, or forming a board for this institute.[138] In fact, in fall 1944, the Seminary inaugurated the Inter-American Commission on Judaism, which was to visit South American countries "in order to develop programs of religious training, civil protective work, etc. Nine students from South American countries entered the Seminary that year."[139] Finkelstein was determined to save

---

[136]Conference report on the Seminary program and its problems, 8 November 1942.

[137]Institute on the Future of Judaism, 1943.

[138]Louis Finkelstein to A. A. Berle, Department of State, 5 February 1943.

[139]Draft report on all aspects of the Seminary, 3 August 1944, p. 3.

Jews and Judaism and to do what he felt he had to do to "cure [the] entire world."

At yet another conference, in which Finkelstein hoped to galvanize support for his far-ranging vision for the Seminary, a resolution was passed that gave formal acknowledgment to this expansive vision. The 400–500 congregational delegates attending this conference, whose theme was "The Task of the Seminary in the War and Postwar Eras," were convinced of the need for a Seminary that would follow Finkelstein's vision and acknowledged this need in their resolution:

> The wider scope of the Seminary necessitates a greater measure of support from our people and calls for the voluntary efforts of lay leaders throughout the land. This conference, therefore, calls upon the Board of Directors and the Executive Committee of the Conference to create a joint committee for the purpose of planning a nationwide appeal, which will provide the Seminary with the means to carry out its historic role and increased responsibilities.[140]

After almost three years of conceptualizing the Seminary's expanded mission and cultivating support for it, the Seminary Board's Executive Committee gave its approval to this expansion effort by authorizing that steps be taken toward a major fund-raising campaign. Without the addition of significant sums of money, the programs that Finkelstein envisaged as the vehicles through which to achieve the larger mission would not have been possible. These programs and activities, and their relationship to the Seminary's mission, were eventually compiled into a forty-nine-page document entitled "American Judaism Faces the Future: Its Opportunity, Its Problems, and a Program for Leadership." Actually, the plan was one that had evolved over time, with

---

[140]"Program of the Conference on the Seminary and Judaism in the War and Postwar Era," 17 November 1943.

various parts of it having been begun along the way. For example, in 1944, the *Eternal Light* radio program, which brought Jewish values and life through drama to Jews and non-Jews across America, was inaugurated. A new field office was opened in Chicago and a Seminary rabbinical graduate was added to the Seminary's staff for community education and fund-raising. Frieda Schiff Warburg, a Board member and Seminary donor, donated her home on Fifth Avenue, the Warburg mansion, to the Seminary. The plan also included a revision of the Rabbinical School curriculum.

In speaking to the Rabbinical Assembly, the rabbinical arm of the Conservative Movement, about the Seminary's expanded mission, Finkelstein conveyed his desire to increase the enrollment of the Rabbinical School for the first time in fourteen years. This was of particular interest to the Rabbinical Assembly. He told the assembled that he hoped to be able to graduate forty rabbis per year for the next twenty-five years to meet the need of congregations. To graduate that many rabbis, he proposed opening a number of preparatory schools across the country that would enroll students who were not yet qualified to enter the Rabbinical School. He knew that the members of the Rabbinical Assembly would look favorably upon such activities because such efforts would strengthen their ranks and increase the number of Conservative congregations.

In this talk to the Rabbinical Assembly, he also spoke of his dream of a new museum, the need to catalog the Seminary library, and his desire to institute summer sessions for alumni. He reported that the Institute for Religious and Social Studies had expanded to Chicago and expressed hope to open extensions of the Institute in other major cities. He also acknowledged a number of other challenges to be met. He spoke of the need for textbooks for Jewish schools and the need to retrain scholars from abroad. He said that he would like to be able to give special training to rabbis and teachers from Latin America.

Being comprehensive, Finkelstein's plan also included a ten-year plan to reclaim Jewish youth to religious and ethical life. The plan called for the creation of religious centers for young people in selected areas of the country where the Seminary would supply the manpower and essentially underwrite the cost.[141]

Finkelstein attempted to capitalize on every opportunity available to put forth this expanded program for the Seminary, because he knew that it would need a broad base of support to succeed. For example, the rabbis of Conservative synagogues were provided with a sermon for Passover 1944 in which the Seminary was again portrayed as the salvation of American Jewry and of Judaism in America.

> Now we must...[build] a vital life in America, which will take the place of the devastated European Jewries....The Seminary has the spiritual resources and the program to guide us through the present crisis....The Seminary is engaged in a battle for the *survival of Judaism in the Western Hemisphere* [italics his].[142]

As evidenced in the above quotation, Finkelstein and his colleagues were sensitive to the implications of the destruction of the great European centers of Jewish learning and thought that the weight of responsibility had now fallen upon the Jewish Theological Seminary of America to carry on in America what those centers of learning and piety had done for the Jewish communities of both Europe and America. He used this very theme to close a presentation to the Seminary's Board in which he was once again promoting his expanded

---

[141]"Seminary's Ten-Year Plan to Reclaim Jewish Youth to Religious and Ethical Life," 9 June 1944.

[142]Letter from Max Arzt to members of the Rabbinical Assembly, 21 March 1944.

program. In a quotation from the Prophet Elijah, he revealed the burden and sense of responsibility he felt.

> They have thrown down my altars, They have slain thy prophets with the sword; and I, even I only, am left; and they seek my life to take it away.[143]

Marsha L. Rozenblit observes that Seminary leadership "responded to the Holocaust in ways that reflected their fundamental convictions and commitments at that time. Their behavior reflected that of American Jewry they so eagerly sought to lead."[144]

By 1945, Finkelstein was describing[145] the work of the Seminary as falling into four categories: a research institution; a center of teaching; a center of mass education; and a center of education on the broadest possible scale for democracy.

When speaking about the first category, he referred to the young people who had been added to the faculty and who had published notable volumes in their fields. About the second category, he pointed to the increased registration in all the Seminary schools, except the Rabbinical School, where registration had been down because of the war. When speaking about the Seminary as a center of mass education, he referred to the Jewish Museum and the *Eternal Light* radio program. In speaking about the last category, he referred to the Institute for Religious and Social Studies and the Conference on Science, Philosophy, and Religion.

---

[143]1 Kings 19:10.

[144]Rozenblit, 1997, 2:298. Rozenblit explains that between 1930 and 1945 the Seminary sought to save Jewish scholars, "labored tirelessly on projects that…would fight the forces of totalitarianism," p. 273.

[145]At a specially called meeting of the Seminary's Board of Directors held on 17 April 1945 for the purpose of confronting critics of the Seminary's mission.

Five years into his administration, Finkelstein had succeeded in breathing new life into the Seminary. He had succeeded in broadening the institution's mission and in reaching out to communities beyond the Seminary to increase the spread and understanding of Judaism. His accomplishments were noted by President Franklin Roosevelt on the occasion of the Seminary's fifty-fifth anniversary with a personal message to Finkelstein and in an editorial in the *New York Times*:

> The Seminary...has earned an enviable place in the educational and religious life of our community and nation....For more than half a century it has espoused the cause of religious and spiritual tolerance and by its courageous and farsighted vision has played no small role in upholding our American culture....As long as the doors of the Jewish Theological Seminary of America and like institutions speaking for the brotherhood of man remain open, our democratic traditions and ideals cannot be destroyed.[146]

Similarly, Judge Simon Rifkind, a key member of the Seminary Board and an ally of Finkelstein, wrote:

> There is no doubt in my mind that you are creating a new kind of educational institution, richer in purpose than our popular institutions, and vastly better articulated with modern life than our religious academies. When you shall have achieved your aims, Jewish life in America will have attained maturity. Very directly, I believe you are shaping the course of Jewish life for the next century—and toward an exalted objective.[147]

With such support, Finkelstein set forth a most ambitious "Five-Year Program of Religious Rehabilitation," which called for doubling the enrollment in the Rabbinical School,

---

[146] *Seminary Progress* (January 1943).

[147] Judge Rifkind to Louis Finkelstein, 26 June 1945.

increasing fivefold the number of congregations affiliated with the synagogal arm of the Conservative Movement, the United Synagogue of America, and more than tripling the number of individual contributors to the Seminary. The Seminary's own publicity was now proclaiming it a "beacon light, illuminating *all* [italics mine] phases of Jewish life and thought and guiding the spiritual progress of a people whose tradition is vital to the world today."[148]

The Seminary produced a handsome brochure entitled "Vision and Action," which set forth in detail this five-year plan.[149] The brochure described how the Seminary sought to appeal to both the religious and nonreligious members of the Jewish community, noting that those affiliated with the Conservative Movement could identify with the Seminary's Rabbinical School, Teachers Institute, and the United Synagogue, while others would identify with the Seminary's *Eternal Light* radio program, its library, museum, and Institute for Religious and Social Studies. In other words, the Seminary had established a rich and diversified program that could appeal to a cross-section of the entire Jewish community.

In keeping with his basic commitment to link the work of the Seminary to the needs of both Jewish and Gentile communities at large, Finkelstein sought every opportunity to bring the Seminary to the larger community. In a newspaper interview, Finkelstein spoke of the Seminary's duties as extending beyond the training of rabbis, explaining that the

---

[148]*Seminary Corner* 12, public-relations material, 1945–48.

[149]This five-year campaign brochure did identify the institution with the Conservative Movement and did mention the United Synagogue and the Rabbinical Assembly in contrast to the earlier version, "American Judaism Faces the Future: Its Opportunity, Its Problems, and a Program for Leadership," which made no mention whatsoever of the Movement or the affiliated organizations. This seemingly ambivalent relationship between the Seminary and the Movement will be discussed fully in the following chapters.

Seminary "must have a civilizing influence on the modern world....Jews have a job to do in this world—and the job is to act as bridgers and conciliators."[150]

At the end of World War II, Finkelstein saw the dawning of a new era, in Judaism as well as in civilization. He believed that the community at large still did not have a full appreciation of the spiritual aspects of Judaism and that the Seminary had thus far failed to use its enormous prestige, and the scholars connected with it, with sufficient effectiveness to build respect for Judaism and for Jewish scholarship. To move this agenda forward, Finkelstein wrote to his senior colleague and leading member of the faculty, Professor Louis Ginzberg, suggesting that the faculty meet with him to consider "the question of where we as the faculty and the Seminary...go from here."[151] Of course, Finkelstein knew where he wanted to go, but he wanted to keep the faculty involved so that they would feel comfortable with the plan and his agenda would have their support. Finkelstein was always careful that he had the support of the senior faculty. Quite often, he would take two or three of them with him to a meeting when he knew that he might be attacked. In this instance, Finkelstein wanted the faculty to draw up a statement that would be directed to "the Jewish people and the world calling for the spiritual rehabilitation of the Jews."[152]

Out of this meeting came an eight-page statement from the faculty that put them on record as supporting a wide array of programs and initiatives that Finkelstein wanted the Seminary to take. The document acknowledged a world in which Jews and Judaism have been under attack and a world that was poorer because of the destruction of European

---

[150]Cincinnati Enquirer, 24 June 1945.

[151]Louis Finkelstein to Professor Louis Ginzberg, 23 August 1945.

[152]Ibid.

Jewry, thereby "plac[ing] a unique responsibility upon American Israel."[153] With great humility, the faculty issued a call to all Jews to join with the Seminary to, for all intents and purposes, save Judaism in America.

Typical of a Finkelstein vision statement, this document was far-ranging. It called for a commission of faculty and alumni to visit Europe "to bring what healing we can,...to offer them the opportunity to participate in our enterprise, and to labor with them for a better future."[154] Similarly, the statement proposed a faculty commission to visit "the Holy Land" in order to secure the cooperation of scholars in both places and to lay the groundwork for advanced study in Israel by the faculty. In keeping with this goal, the faculty articulated the need to set up research projects in various fields of Judaica on a collaborative basis with scholars from other academic institutions. The faculty spoke of the need to expand the Seminary's educational activities among the masses and to create a research department of applied studies, specifically in Jewish religious education and Jewish social service. The statement reaffirmed the value of a Jewish education for every child and proposed that the Seminary establish preparatory schools around the country to enable young men and women to prepare for advanced study at the Seminary.

Finally, no pronouncement by Dr. Finkelstein would ever be complete without reference to the need for inter- and intra-group cooperation and the implied role of the Seminary's Institute for Religious and Social Studies. The faculty statement reiterated the essence of Finkelstein's mission calling for a kind of "one-for-all, all-for-one" pattern of thought and behavior, for only then would civilization

---

[153]Statement by the faculty of the Jewish Theological Seminary of America, 1946.

[154]Ibid.

flourish within Jews and Judaism. Finkelstein's own words eloquently convey the depths of his commitment to these programs:

> The era of isolationism is at an end, whether it applies to the isolation of nations, of peoples, or of cultural spheres. We must learn at last that just as there is no security for anyone against disease, except in measures which bring security to all, there can be no isolated solution limited to any single aspect of human life. Moreover, we came to realize that the political, the economical, the cultural and even the moral and spiritual realms are interdependent. There can be no religious piety without social justice, no lasting economic prosperity without the sense for the spiritual; no political stability without compliance with moral principles. There is one God, one mankind, one law. The spirit of life is indivisible. It is the same in feeling and in thought, in speech and in action, in private and in social life, in national and international affairs. It is only the modern expression of paganism to set God up as a departmental Deity—even were this department the whole province of Ethics.
>
> Let us never forget that the sense for the sacred is as vital to us as the light to the sun. There can be no nature without the Torah, no brotherhood without a father, no humanity without God. The individual man and group must learn to overcome their tendencies toward selfishness and antagonism, and reorient their minds to see life not as a hunt for pleasure, but as an engagement for service; not as a race involving victories and defeat, but as a pursuit of goals that transcend the interests of single nations and generations.
>
> This reorientation is long overdue. The effort to effect it began with the birth of Judaism and it is of profound significance that the overwhelming insight into the need of such reorientation should come with a war which has brought the Jewish people unparalleled sorrow.

> We hope that the goals we are setting forth may become the aspiration of men of many institutions, groups, and even nations; that each will seek to contribute what it can, to the establishment of a civilization which will be at once dynamic and pacific; which will have all the creative energy of our own western society without the hunger for power which inevitably makes our very progress a threat of undoing.
>
> The problems of the ethical and social life transcend any group. Cooperation among scholars of all faiths concerning such problems is part of the Jewish tradition. We deem it appropriate to seek the clarification of the philosophical and moral problems of our time, insofar as they affect all men and require skills to be found in all groups, through cooperation across all differences and boundaries. We shall seek to further this cooperation because we believe that it can only lead to the deepening of our faith in Judaism, to the deepening of devotion to the true spirit of the Prophets among our neighbors.[155]

Implicit in this statement was a message to his critics indicating that the faculty supported him and that denominationalism should not be the only principle around which the Seminary structured its activities.

Finkelstein's mission for the Seminary came to full bloom in an article he bylined in the *Jewish Exponent* entitled "A Jewish University in America: Its Aims and Functions." In this article, he discussed proposals to further reorganize the Seminary as a Jewish university, by which he meant one that would embrace the study of contemporary Judaism in addition to the study of the Jewish past. In his words, "the whole realm of Judaism will be provided for,"[156] and that is what would make it a university. For Finkelstein, this vision

---

[155]Ibid.

[156]Louis Finkelstein, "A Jewish University in America: Its Aims and Functions," *Jewish Exponent*, 14 September 1945.

"implie[d] no basic alteration in [the Seminary's] outlook or function,"[157] although some others thought it did. The Seminary's mission and its fulfillment, as Finkelstein saw it, were now clear.

His efforts on its behalf now took the form of making use of every opportunity that came by him to accomplish his goal; to wit, he turned to his good friend and sometime confidant, General David Sarnoff, for advice on his plan to approach the wealthy and famous industrialist Bernard Baruch for permission to establish a foundation bearing his name, which would support the Institute for Religious and Social Studies, the Conference on Science, Philosophy, and Religion, and Finkelstein's latest idea, which called for the awarding of fellowships "to people who might not otherwise reach their potential."[158] Specifically, Finkelstein wanted to offer fellowships in the fields of art, music, letters, philosophy, and some of the social sciences:

> The effort would serve to develop in the course of years a number of men and women excelling in different skills, who would also bring their specific fields a spiritual outlook derived from Judaism, and a knowledge of their faith which they might translate into those techniques.[159]

Finkelstein sought no less than $5 million from Baruch in addition to the use of his name. Ultimately, the solicitation of Bernard Baruch was not successful, but the proposal underscored again Finkelstein's commitment to seek funding for his vision, as well as his unwavering belief in the need to work together to focus on what groups and individuals have in common—to work for the common good rather than individual or organizational aggrandizement.

---

[157]Ibid.

[158]Louis Finkelstein to David Sarnoff, 27 October 1946.

[159]Ibid.

> Professor Liston Pope of Yale and I have been working on the problem of getting groups and institutions to overcome the tendencies toward regarding themselves as ends, instead of means. By this we mean that each group and institution of major importance in American life has a program for America as well as for its own advancement. Curiously enough...the program for America is usually forgotten while that for the institution is overstressed. Religious institutions are of course the ones which should be the first to overcome this tendency....Unless the various component institutions are trained by their leaders to think of the whole, each group becomes a pressure group, self-seeking and dividing the nation against itself.[160]

In a letter to a Seminary Board member, just after returning from a fund-raising trip, Finkelstein wrote: "While I was out west I tried to do everything I could to stimulate interest *not only in the Seminary but in all Jewish educational activities* [italics mine]."[161] This was but one of many examples demonstrating that Finkelstein practiced what he preached. In keeping with this philosophy, the Seminary launched the World Brotherhood Committee which was to emphasize in dramatic form the central role of world brotherhood in the Jewish tradition.[162] A year later, in 1952, the Seminary founded the Israel Institute "in the hopes that it will be an effective instrument for the interpretation of the spiritual values we think are inherent in the State of Israel and, through stressing these values, also help foster them."[163] This effort was in keeping with his plan to rehabilitate Jews

---

[160]Louis Finkelstein to Arthur Sulzberger, 19 March 1948.

[161]Louis Finkelstein to J. Solis-Cohen, 29 June 1939.

[162]This effort had an annual dinner at the Waldorf Astoria at which awards were given. Bernard Mandelbaum was appointed director of the World Brotherhood movement.

[163]Jewish Theological Seminary of America, *Register*, 1953–54.

spiritually and through that effort to serve as a catalyst for the respiritualization of the larger community.

During his administration, and certainly for the period under study here, Finkelstein's basic vision and institutional mission never wavered. The projects and activities changed to fit the times or the donor. Sometimes the labels changed—for example, from spirituality and democratic values in the 1940s to a concern with the moral and ethical ideals by which people lived in the 1950s.[164] But the core values underlying his vision/mission remained virtually the same. Finkelstein never lost his concern for all Jews—indeed for all humanity—nor for the quality of life. Twelve years into his presidency, he was still writing to his constituency about the

> new insights into the contributions which scholars and men of letters can make to peace and freedom in our time. Any program which seeks to achieve security and stability for the free world should include an effort to clarify ourselves, in America, to other men, the meaning of the ideas of freedom, democracy and the good life....The Jewish Theological Seminary of America has a specific contribution to make to the problem of better understanding across differences of background.[165]

Finkelstein had indeed transformed the Seminary into something greater than a school for the training of rabbis. In the words of two of the Seminary's key lay leaders, Alan M.

---

[164]In fall 1953, the Seminary sponsored a conference dealing with moral and ethical problems not only in education, but in all aspects of society, including business, labor, family, and private behavior as well as creative expression in the arts and the sciences.

[165]Louis Finkelstein, statement from Israel and England, 4 August 1952. Finkelstein would often spend the better part of each summer in England, and after the establishment of the State of Israel, in England and Israel, where he would do research, meet with the "men of affairs," as he liked to refer to politicians and academics, and reflect on the problems of the day. This letter was written from England.

Stroock and Judge Rifkind, the Seminary was "no longer merely one more academy among many";[166] "it is the greatest institution of Jewish learning in the world today [and has] the awesome responsibility to disseminate the religious ideas which alone have the power to unite mankind."[167]

This mission to which Finkelstein was so steadfastly committed was evident in all that the institution undertook. New programs were created to foster this mission, such as the *Eternal Light* radio and, later, television program. Regular school activities were packaged to fit into it. For example, a group of good students studying Talmud became the Institute on Talmudic Ethics.[168]

Finkelstein had what every successful leader needs—a clear vision about which he was passionate. He articulated that vision with forcefulness and eloquence, establishing himself as a charismatic leader of American Jewry.

Public Relations

The Seminary under Finkelstein's leadership worked hard to position itself in the community at large as *the* institution of higher Jewish learning in the United States and as the representative and spokesperson for all of American Jewry. It spoke of its Judaism as quintessential classical Judaism rather than as the Judaism of a particular party, sect, or denomination within American Judaism, which in actuality, it was. That the institution was ultimately successful in achieving some of these goals is evidenced by the appearance of Dr. Finkelstein on the cover of *Time* magazine in October 1951. In the article, Finkelstein is referred to as the "leader of

---

[166] Judge Rifkind to Louis Finkelstein, November 1954.

[167] Alan M. Stroock speaking at the Seminary convocation, 14 September 1952.

[168] Although this institute was not formally established until 1956, planning for it began earlier.

perhaps the most influential school of Jewish theology in the United States today."[169] Similarly, Finkelstein was invited to the White House to give the invocation at the presidential inauguration of Dwight D. Eisenhower.

The Seminary's self-promotion took every opportunity to trumpet its broad mission. The aforementioned campaign brochure, "Vision and Action: A Five-Year Program," addressed itself to the "Jews of America." Throughout that document, the institution was portrayed as the saving grace of Judaism, of Jewish spirituality, and the quality of civilized life.

> We need to assume responsibility for the direction of Jewish spiritual life.
>
> We need to restore Judaism as a living force in civilization.
>
> Unless we act now, the Jews of America will have failed in their historic duty to preserve the light of Judaism in the world.

Another publicity brochure included the statement that all the Seminary's work was aimed at "helping the Jews of America to achieve a full security of the spirit and to find guidance and strength in their ancient faith."[170] Similarly, a plan was drafted in 1944 for the establishment of an American Jewish Hall of Fame at the Seminary in the belief that such a program would give "tacit recognition of the Seminary as the agency most qualified to select and honor designees."[171]

More significant, he indicated in a letter sent to potential lay leadership that the Seminary and its leaders, past and present, are responsible for the reemergence of the Jewish faith as an effective voice in the spiritual and moral councils

---

169*Time*, 15 October 1951.

170"A Tower of Strength," publicity brochure, 1947.

171Plan for American Jewish Hall of Fame, 23 July 1944.

of the world! The letter concludes with the bold assertion that "the Seminary today is our mouthpiece, voicing the teachings of the prophets and Sages of Israel to the Jewish community of America, and to the world."[172]

Finkelstein himself contributed to the development of the notion that the Seminary, and that he as its leader, were playing on a world stage. In a Seminary newsletter, he wrote:

> The board and my colleagues [faculty] have generously offered to permit me to visit Israel and Europe in the spring....World peace will ultimately depend upon mutual good will among people and their leaders. We know how much has been achieved throughout our Institute for Religious and Social Studies and Conference on Science, Philosophy, and Religion. We are convinced more can be done. Therefore, I am eager to discuss with leaders of the State of Israel and with other scholars and religious leaders in Europe, the general outlook on cooperation across differences of background and interest.[173]

A fairly routine trip is thus given a larger meaning, and Finkelstein is portrayed as a key player on the world scene.

Clearly, if one did not know differently, one would have concluded that the Jewish Theological Seminary of America was the only Jewish institution of higher Jewish learning in America at the time and that it represented all of American Judaism. The fact was, however, that it was not, for there was the Hebrew Union College (Reform), Yeshiva University with its Rabbi Isaac Elchanan Theological Seminary (Orthodox), as well as the Jewish Institute of Religion (Reform), all of which were disseminating their brand of Judaism, training rabbis and teachers, and engaged in communal work of one form or another.

---

[172]Louis Finkelstein to Alan M. Stroock, 17 August 1953.

[173]Newsletter, 31 October 1950.

Programmatically, the Seminary devoted much time and attention to the creation and cultivation of those activities that best served this larger mission, i.e., the Institute for Religious and Social Studies; the *Eternal Light* radio program; the Conference on Science, Philosophy, and Religion; and the Museum.

Finkelstein's vision was not only articulated well by him, but it was also captured effectively in all the institution's communications with the public, be they press releases, brochures, or letters to constituent groups. Through its public-relations efforts, the Seminary strove to make itself and its leader highly visible in the broader community.

Eternal Light

In early 1944, Dr. Finkelstein was in touch with the director of religious programming for the National Broadcasting Company, inquiring whether they would be interested in a radio program devoted to the interpretation of Judaism. Finkelstein maintained that most existing radio shows were too specific in their theology and thus did not emphasize sufficiently religion's universal values. As a result, these shows reached only a small audience. "Our thought," he wrote, "is that the program which would be established under the auspices of the Seminary would be dedicated to a popular presentation of Jewish tradition and its ideals."[174] Finkelstein proposed that the program could be under the supervision of a committee made up of representatives of different Jewish groups.[175] In explaining his intention behind the program, he said that it

[174]Louis Finkelstein to Max Jordan (director of religious programming for NBC), 31 January 1944.

[175]Finkelstein originally proposed a committee consisting of 11 laymen, 2 Reform rabbis, 2 Orthodox rabbis, and 2 Conservative rabbis,

> should attempt to interpret the Jewish religion in terms that will reach as wide a group as possible, both within and without Jewish groups. Further, the program should do much to promote the general spiritual aims common to all religions.[176]

Specifically, Finkelstein saw this as "an almost necessary outgrowth of our regular educational work."[177] In a lengthy letter to Frieda Schiff Warburg, he wrote:[178]

> We have two tasks. The first is to provide a Jewish radio program, appealing not simply to the religious people who ordinarily listen to a rabbi, but also to the large number of Jews (now probably the vast majority) who do not attend synagogue or tune in sermons. You will doubtless agree that essentially most of these Jews are religious at heart. In some respects some of them are among the most religious persons I know, but they have been separated from Jewish observance and the rabbinate, and we cannot expect them to return suddenly of their own accord. The translation of Jewish religious principles into a program to interest such people, and particularly their children who do not attend religious school requires much thought. It will not be undertaken except by an educational institution like our own. This aspect of our work appealed greatly to the National Broadcasting Company. When I discussed it with Dr. Jonah B. Wise, he agreed that it was an important task and joined me in urging the National Broadcasting Company to give us radio time.

---

one of which was himself. Louis Finkelstein to Niles Trammell (NBC), 11 February 1944.

[176]Louis Finkelstein to Frieda Schiff Warburg, 22 February 1944.

[177]Ibid., 2 March 1944.

[178]Frieda Schiff Warburg subsequently became a sponsor of this proposed series of broadcasts, but not before she expressed her "mental reservations whether you [Finkelstein] are not in danger of having too many irons in the fire in your eagerness for spreading the influence of the Seminary into new fields and channels." Mrs. Warburg to Louis Finkelstein, 27 February 1944.

> The second task of the program will be more general. If we can translate religious ideas into language clear to the ordinary American unaffiliated with church or synagogue, we will be paving the way for other religious programs. You may know that religious programs are extremely unpopular. Broadcasting companies give time to churches as the newspapers give space to reports of sermons—unwillingly. This is because no group has learned to express the ideas of religion simply enough, although religious teachers of earlier ages were able to do so for their contemporaries. Many popular preachers suppose that this consists in talking of transient issues, but that is not the case. In addition it actually takes auditors away from basic religious matters. The difficult but vital need is to keep to the principles of the faith and its complex teachings but to have them so clearly in mind that they may be explained readily to the uninitiated. An example will perhaps clarify this point better than extended abstract discussion. The first Chapter of Genesis is written in terms that a child can understand. Nevertheless, its ideas are among the most civilized ever conceived, including the dictum of the equality of all men, of the equality of the sexes and of world progress. Especially in biblical times, these concepts must have appeared extremely difficult, yet their explanation was perfectly simple. Obviously we cannot expect to approach the success of such interpretation and translation. However, I think we can improve on the work now being done, moreover, it is our duty to try.[179]

In short, this one program succeeded in accomplishing several of his goals: to raise the spiritual level of the community; to promote Judaism;, to bring people of all religions together; and, not least, to bring attention to the Seminary.[180]

---

[179]Louis Finkelstein to Frieda Schiff Warburg, 2 March 1944.

[180]Evidence of Finkelstein's success in this particular goal is a letter received from a prominent Reform rabbi, Solomon Freehof of Pittsburgh,

Indeed, no sooner had the program been launched than a feature story in the *New York Times* regarding the program concluded with the statement, "In the meantime [Catholics and Protestants] and the Jewish people owe a singular debt to the Jewish Theological Seminary for providing a genuine contribution to drama, radio, and religion."[181] Other accolades were heaped upon the program, including a mention in Eleanor Roosevelt's syndicated newspaper column. Following the lead of the first *Eternal Light* broadcast, which was devoted to Rhode Island's Touro Synagogue, the oldest synagogue in America, and the idea of religious freedom, Gimbel Brothers created a window display in its New York store displaying an enlargement of George Washington's letter to the Jews of that synagogue against a backdrop of Jewish ceremonial objects borrowed from the Seminary's museum. Religious schools, clubs, and discussion groups signed up to receive program scripts on a regular basis. Public libraries sought to include the scripts in their collections, and the Armed Forces Radio made extensive use of the program. Within a short time, the Hooper Rating Company reported that *Eternal Light* was reaching some six million listeners. In the Seminary's five-year plan, a new goal of eighteen million listeners was set.

The Seminary took particular pride in the praise accorded the radio program by the radio editor of the *New York Times* in his column of December 17, 1944:

> [I]t provides rich stimulation of the spirit of brotherhood among all men and an opportunity for

---

acknowledging that the *Eternal Light* was a magnificent program but bemoaning the fact that it was used "as means of constant propaganda for the Jewish Theological Seminary." Solomon Freehof to Louis Finkelstein, 7 December 1944.

[181]"Latest Developments in Seminary Activity," public-relations publication, 1946.

> renewal of the individual's faith, be it Jewish, Protestant or Catholic....This blend of dramatic and religious aims is believed unprecedented in a religious group's use of radio but patently has not been unwanted. The Jewish Theological Seminary apparently has pointed the way for a wider utilization of the air that, if fully realized, presents untold possibilities for churches and synagogues in every community.[182]

By 1948, the Seminary had expanded to television, first with CBS and then in 1951 with NBC, under the *Eternal Light* name. Both the radio and television work continued to captivate the American religious scene for decades, winning numerous awards. The broadcasts were eagerly anticipated in homes around the country. For many people, but for many Jews in particular, the *Eternal Light* program was their link to the Seminary and their sourcebook of Jewish values. For many in the non-Jewish community, *Eternal Light* was able to demystify the Jewish tradition, enabling the non-Jew to be more accepting of his Jewish neighbor.

The Jewish Museum

The Jewish Museum[183] was another activity through which the Seminary fulfilled its expansive mission. Begun in 1904 with the presentation to the Seminary of a few religious objects by Judge Mayer Sulzberger, it was given a semipermanent home at the Seminary when the campus at 122nd Street was erected in 1930. Between 1930 and 1947, it was operated as an extension of the Seminary library. Until the early 1940s, the Museum was of little importance to the

---

[182]G. Gould to Louis Finkelstein, 30 August 1945.

[183]Frieda Schiff Warburg had proposed "Judaica Museum" as the name. Finkelstein reported to her that the Executive Committee of the Seminary Board and the faculty wanted it to be called "The American Jewish Museum." The Jewish Museum was the compromise. Louis Finkelstein to Frieda Schiff Warburg, 8 April 1946.

institution. Evidence of its relative unimportance is seen in correspondence between President Cyrus Adler and the then-director of the Museum, Dr. Paul Romanoff, and similar correspondence of a few years later between Finkelstein and Romanoff. During the summer of 1938, Adler had written to Romanoff: "[There is] no real place at the Seminary for you.... [T]he little museum is more or less a fixed thing. I have no desire to build up a great Museum nor have we the means."[184] Three years later, responding to a plea from Romanoff for encouragement in the form of a salary increase, Finkelstein reiterated Adler's blunt words and added, "This is of course true today, as it was in 1938." Finkelstein echoes Adler's earlier sentiments urging Romanoff to find another job because this post as Museum director is "purely temporary."[185]

In just three short years, the situation changed considerably. In one of the earlier (1942) expositions of the Seminary's expansive program, Finkelstein spoke of the Museum as possibly "becom[ing] one of its most important educational departments."[186] Only a year and a half later, Dr. Finkelstein was engaged in correspondence with Frieda Schiff Warburg regarding the possibility of her giving her 92nd Street mansion to the Seminary for the museum and other Seminary activities. In a seven-page letter to Warburg, he made the case for why her home would be a fitting gift and why it would serve the Seminary's needs so well. Finkelstein envisaged it holding not only the museum, but also the Seminary's other two major outreach projects of that time, the Institute for Religious and Social Studies and the

---

[184]Louis Finkelstein to Dr. Romanoff, 3 June 1941.

[185]Louis Finkelstein to Dr. Romanoff, 3 June 1941.

[186]"The Seminary Program and Its Problems," conference report, 8 November 1942.

Conference on Science, Philosophy, and Religion.[187] Finkelstein told Warburg that having the mansion will "enable the Seminary to embark on a much more effective program of education for the entire community."[188] More to the point,

> I regard the establishment of this museum as one of the most important steps ever taken to educate the American community, both Jewish and Christian, in the permanent significance of Judaism as a force in civilization.[189]

There is absolutely no reason to believe that the Seminary was interested in expanding the Museum beyond attracting a group of volunteers to help spread its message within the community. However, the Warburg gift opened up "new possibilities of vast service to the whole American Jewish community, and indeed to the Nation at large."[190] It also was a stimulus to the institution. In Finkelstein's words:

> [I]t has stimulated us to a new vision of the meaning of the Museum and the Institute for Religious Studies. It has led to our rethinking of the whole Seminary situation and is largely responsible for the fact that Professor Kaplan, for example, has arrived at his new conception of the Seminary as a university of Judaism.[191]

Finkelstein was now committed to both "a" and "the" museum. In another of his frequent letters to Warburg, he wrote that this museum "must be regarded not simply as another museum, but...*the* museum in the city of New

---

[187]Louis Finkelstein to Frieda Schiff Warburg, 6 January 1944.

[188]Ibid., 14 January 1944.

[189]Ibid., 10 September 1944.

[190]Louis Finkelstein to Hillel Bavli (presumably a form letter to all faculty), 24 January 1944.

[191]Louis Finkelstein to Frieda Schiff Warburg, 10 April 1945.

York."[192] Subsequently, the Seminary invested $100,000 in the renovation of the building so that it could function properly as a museum.

One look at the attendance figures following the museum's relocation to the Warburg mansion was indication enough that the acquisition and refurbishment of the mansion had been the right thing to do. For the five-year period from 1932 to 1937, the total museum attendance was approximately 78,000.[193] However, for the first five years of its existence in the Warburg mansion, total attendance exceeded 400,000![194] The Seminary may not initially have intended to "build up a great Museum," but that is certainly what it did do.

The road to reach this point, however, was not a smooth one. Fifteen months after Frieda Schiff Warburg had officially[195] offered her home to the Seminary, Finkelstein had to report to her that the Seminary did not have the money to move ahead with the intended renovations.[196] This fact is of interest at this point in the study because of the way in which Dr. Finkelstein proposed to deal with the difficulty. His approach was but another example of his ability not to lose sight of his vision and of his ingenuity in directing potential funding to those programs that he favored most.

In this particular instance, when Frieda Schiff Warburg learned that the Seminary was unable to move forward, she decided to sell the building and set the proceeds aside for a special fund. Dr. Finkelstein proposed that the fund be for

---

[192]Ibid., 10 September 1944.

[193]Paul Romanoff, annual report on Jewish Museum, 23 May 1939.

[194]*Register*, 1953–54, p. 111.

[195]Letter from Frieda Schiff Warburg to Louis Finkelstein, 13 January 1945.

[196]Louis Finkelstein to Frieda Schiff Warburg, 10 April 1945. Seminary Board authorizes work to begin again on museum renovation. Louis Finkelstein to Frieda Schiff Warburg, 28 November 1945.

"Improving Human Relations" since, he argued, that was to have been one of the primary uses for the house.

> By using such a broad expression...it would be possible to use the fund ultimately, together with other free funds...to establish another building on our campus dedicated to the very subject of better understanding among all peoples. On the other hand, if we should not be able to put up such a building, we could use the income from these funds for the Conference [on Science, Philosophy, and Religion]...and the Institute for Religious Studies and for Studies in the Jewish religion [*sic*].[197]

In other words, with or without the Warburg mansion, the Conference and the Institute for Religious Studies were to be supported as long as Finkelstein was in charge. Ultimately, however, the Seminary was able to raise the renovation money.

While the programs that were to be housed in the mansion were dedicated to the reduction of group tensions, Finkelstein hoped to make the new museum itself a living example of group cooperation by having the Reform movement's seminary be a partner. For a period of several months, meetings took place and correspondence was exchanged between representatives of the Jewish Theological Seminary and the Reform Movement's Hebrew Union College (HUC) in Cincinnati. The Seminary was, at one point, prepared to entertain a museum governance structure in which the Museum would be directed by a board of overseers to include five representatives of HUC. The Museum would acknowledge that it included HUC's collection, and HUC would have its own room in the building. The Seminary's offer was deemed insufficient by the HUC board, which insisted on joint operation. The committees representing

---

[197]Louis Finkelstein to Frieda Schiff Warburg, 28 September 1945.

both institutions, which had been negotiating this possible partnership, had already concluded that a joint operation of the Museum was not feasible. The collaborative arrangement never materialized.[198] Notwithstanding these difficulties and challenges, the Seminary by 1949 was most pleased with its new entity:

> Alan M. Stroock [chairman of the board] particularly felt that the Museum ha[d] more than justified itself financially as one of the main talking points in the Seminary fund raising effort, and that its existence, quite apart from its educational importance, [was] a fine Seminary investment.[199]

That year (1949), attendance at the Museum was breaking all records and all predictions with the average Sunday attendance surpassing fifteen hundred, excluding organized groups.[200] The Museum, more than being just a "talk point," had become a significant vehicle for the Seminary outreach in keeping with the institution's mission to bring the Jewish tradition to the masses and to decrease group tensions through better understanding.

> Since it was conceived with the conviction that people of all faiths are concerned with the well-springs of the Jewish spirit, the Museum represents a significant stride toward the brotherhood of all men. Emphasizing as it does the common interest which all faiths share in Judaism, the sense of oneness which the Museum

---

[198]Louis Finkelstein to the president of Hebrew Union College, Julian Morgenstern, draft of letter, 28 April 1944; Julian Morgenstern to Alan Stroock, 11 May 1944; Alan Stroock to Julian Morgenstern, 12 January 1945; Louis Finkelstein to Arthur Sulzberger, 15 May 1945.

[199]Louis Finkelstein to Frieda Schiff Warburg, 11 May 1949.

[200]Greenberg newsletter, 1 March 1949. This newsletter was one means by which Simon Greenberg communicated with Seminary constituencies during the period of Finkelstein's sabbatical.

> evokes among all people is a strong weapon against prejudice and misunderstanding.[201]

Through the Museum, the Seminary was able to preserve the Jewish past using the collection's artifacts and ceremonial objects didactically to bring Jews and non-Jews in touch with the Jewish tradition. The Museum, although a part of the Seminary, was not perceived by most people as a denominational institution and thus was able to serve as a gathering place for all Jews. Its prestigious location and unique mission among New York museums gave the Seminary a visibility that it might otherwise not have had.

Institute for Religious and Social Studies

As is manifestly clear from the foregoing description of the Seminary's broadened mission, no program or activity reflected this mission or captivated Finkelstein's attention more than did the Institute for Religious and Social Studies and the Conference on Science, Philosophy, and Religion, which came soon afterward.[202] These two programs served as Finkelstein's primary vehicles to reach into the broader community and confront intergroup tensions. Unlike the *Eternal Light* programs, whose impact was diffuse, these two programs fostered direct contact between the Seminary's leaders and academic and religious leaders of various disciplines and denominations.

The seeds of these programs were sown in the late 1930s by the personal experiences that Adler and Finkelstein had in dealing with non-Jews. Both had encountered unbelievable

---

[201]Possible draft of a public-relations piece or section of the *Register* describing Seminary programs, 1950.

[202]Were it not for these programs and his commitment to them, Finkelstein might well have carried out his thought of resigning as president of the Seminary, Louis Finkelstein to Arthur Sulzberger, 12 February 1945, p. 4. See pp 115,116.

ignorance in the community as regards Jewish beliefs and practices. For example, someone asked Finkelstein whether Jews still offered sacrifices in their synagogues, and one Christian clergyman told Adler that the love of man came into the world only with the New Testament.[203] It was in no small measure because of experiences like these that the Seminary sought to establish what was at first called an institute of interdenominational studies to reach out to non-Jewish clergy and theological students so that they might have a better understanding of Judaism.[204] This institute was established informally in 1938 with a series of lectures. In the fall of 1939, Finkelstein invited Governor Herbert H. Lehman of New York to speak at the institute's formal opening. In his letter to the governor, Finkelstein explained that "for some time I have been working on plans for the expansion of the institute, which would increase its value to the community as a whole."[205] Indeed, Finkelstein had great hopes for the institute, imagining that one day it would "become a permanent part of the American system of religious education."[206]

Similarly, Finkelstein believed that one of the ways to bring people of all faiths back to religion was through the assembling of a conference of scientists, philosophers, and theologians. His case was articulated in a letter to Dr. Mortimer Adler of the University of Chicago:

---

[203]Louis Finkelstein to Frieda Schiff Warburg, 24 January 1938.

[204]Finkelstein wrote to Board member Hendricks and referred to a *Life* magazine article that showed how Catholics approached the problem of better understanding, namely, to make themselves understood. Finkelstein brought the article as an example of what the Seminary wanted to do.

[205]Louis Finkelstein to Governor H. Lehman, 27 October 1939.

[206]Ibid.

> I am convinced that there is no hope for civilization, unless we can get people who are living in democratic countries to bring to their civilization the same religious passion which motivated the subjects of totalitarian, pagan communities. And I am also convinced that this cannot be done without a vivid, philosophical, and profound faith in God, which must permeate our field of thought....My thought in arranging this Conference...is that bringing together these men who have, each of them, a fragment of knowledge about the reasons for the decay of our civilization, we shall be able for the first time to present the complete case to the public....If it turns out that we cannot work out a common platform of educative action, my hope for democracy and civilization in our time will be turned to despair; for no armies can protect us against the disintegration of our own thought.[207]

This conference, whose founding meeting took place at the Seminary in the fall of 1939,[208] was launched in September 1940. One of the founding members of the conference, Professor Van Wyck Brooks of Columbia University, described the significance of this first meeting:

> No one who was able to be present at all the meetings...could have been otherwise than deeply impressed by the significance of the meeting as a whole. It is believed that on no previous occasion in recent times has so representative a group discussed so freely, frankly and competently controversial questions in philosophy and religion, and certainly for the first

---

[207]Louis Finkelstein to Mortimer Adler, 20 July 1940.

[208]Those present were: Henry Sloane Coffin of Union Theological Seminary, Arthur H. Compton of the University of Chicago, Hughell E. W. Fosbroke of General Theological Seminary, Frederick C. Grant of Union Theological Seminary, Harold D. Lasswell of Washington School of Psychiatry, John A. Mackay of Princeton Theological Seminary, Alexander Marx of the Jewish Theological Seminary of America, Anton C. Pegis of Fordham University, Harlow Shapley of Harvard Observatory, and Louis Finkelstein of the Jewish Theological Seminary.

> time in the history of American culture, eminent scholars of widely differing interests, convictions and faiths found themselves united in the friendliest of fellowships, striking to build bridges of communication from one mind to another, seeking for some identity of meaning behind diversity of expression...desirous, above all, for some clear definition of fundamental accord.[209]

Translating the noble ideas that gave shape to these two programs into a viable reality was an arduous task. It was particularly difficult to raise the necessary funds needed to operate them.[210]

Finkelstein was personally pulled between the tasks of raising money for the programs and actually planning the first meeting of the conference. Determined that the conference meeting would be a success, he gave up his vacation and devoted his summer to preparations. While these efforts did produce a good beginning, it was only a beginning, and much work was to be done before the conference could be judged worthwhile.[211]

---

[209]Van Wyck Brooks, Conference on Science, Philosophy, and Religion, 1940.

[210]In a letter to a friend and donor from whom Finkelstein hoped to receive significantly more money than he was giving at the time, Finkelstein confided: "Two of my chief worries during the past winter have been the problem of obtaining funds for both the Conference on Science, Philosophy, and Religion and the expansion of the Institute of Interdenominational Studies" (Louis Finkelstein to L. Littauer, 5 April 1940).

[211]The *New York Times* devoted two columns to the conference, under the heading "79 Leaders Unite to Aid Democracy, Men of Science, Philosophy and Religion Issue Call to Safeguard Freedom" (Van Wyck Brooks, Conference on Science, Philosophy, and Religion, 1940). In a report that was compiled following the conference to evaluate the proceedings, it was noted: "Undoubtedly it was a Herculean effort on the part of Rabbi Finkelstein, almost single-handed, to bring the Conference into being. But since it is intended that the Conference will transcend the

In the early days of these programs, Finkelstein held out the hope that he would be able to create an entire school around the Institute for Interdenominational Studies and the Conference on Science, Philosophy, and Religion. Such a school would include a lecture series, a department that would communicate with radio and motion-picture leaders, and another department granting M.A. and Ph.D. degrees. Finkelstein and his colleagues who were involved in planning the conference believed that such a school had the potential to be "an effective bulwark against the insidious spread of Nazi and Communist doctrines in our country."[212] He returned to the idea a couple of years later and proposed a significant expansion of what was then called the Institute for Religious Studies.[213]

Finkelstein was not interested in merely creating goodwill among people of difference; he wanted to educate people and develop their minds. Accordingly, he found groups such as the Conference of Christians and Jews to be superficial.[214] Believing that the more than five hundred ministers of religion who had already participated in the Institute had had an effect on the community, and noting that "religious educators of other institutions of learning...[have] urg[ed] that

---

limitations of the usual academic convocation, judging from the material at hand, it must now go to work." Conference on Science, Philosophy, and Religion, report on Files 9–11, September 1940.

212Louis Finkelstein to Lucius Littauer, 3 November 1939. Finkelstein had the idea to create a School of Religions, which would be affiliated with JTSA, but not be an integral part of it (plan for Proposed School of Religions, 1939).

213In a letter to Littauer, Finkelstein noted that this new name was chosen after long deliberation with a number of eminent Catholic and Protestant scholars. Louis Finkelstein to Lucius Littauer, 5 November 1940.

214Interview 6 January 1992 with Jessica Feingold, who was director of the Institute for Religious and Social Studies and who began to work with Finkelstein in 1938.

the Institute expand its activities, by making provision for research and studies in the oriental religions,"[215] he proposed enlarging the Institute. Just as with the original idea for the Institute, the expansion concept was significant and included the establishment of a graduate school, a system of fellowships patterned after the Guggenheim fellowships, the establishment of branches around the country, a summer school, and more. Yet another time he proposed establishing correspondence courses "to enhance the scope of [the Institute's] influence."[216] He also considered publishing a journal of religions.

Such enthusiastic planning existed side by side with the lack of adequate funding and repeated failed attempts to raise the needed level of support for these programs.

> I had hoped to be able to report at this [Board] meeting that we had obtained the funds [to expand the Institute]. That hope has not, however, been realized. The organization set up for fund-raising for the Institute proved inadequate; the Welfare Funds resist any new requests; in this city we have not found any large measure of support outside of our congregations.[217]

Finkelstein was deeply committed to the Institute for Religious and Social Studies and the Conference on Science, Philosophy, and Religion, not only because he saw their potential for bringing recognition to the Seminary, but because he believed that they were the very embodiment of traditional Jewish values. By fostering these programs, the Seminary would not only be promoting itself, but through the balancing of scholarship and piety with good deeds and love

---

[215]Louis Finkelstein, "A Proposal for the Expansion of the Institute for Religious Studies," 1941(?).

[216]Louis Finkelstein to Board of Directors, report, 6 April 1941.

[217]Report to Board of Directors, 6 June 1941.

of man, it would be acknowledging "the imminence of a peril to our country, and civilization."[218] Accordingly, these activities could not be allowed to falter and deserved to receive the institution's complete support.

Those two programs were critical to the fulfillment of Finkelstein's vision because of their investment in the future. Finkelstein acknowledged to his brother-in-law Norman Bentwich that he was concerned about what was to happen when World War II came to an end.[219] He reasoned that "if this war is to lead to a world society of people, an international educative effort looking toward more complete mutual understanding by the various people of the world is an indispensable prerequisite."[220] The Institute and the Conference represented that "international effort." Only a few years later, he wrote:

> I have been assured [doesn't say by whom] that if this conference [Science, Philosophy, and Religion] continued, we would be able to obtain the cooperation of all governments, both the great powers and the governments in exile, in working out plans for an enduring peace.[221]

In fact, in 1945 Finkelstein wrote to Board member Lewis Strauss,[222] noting that the Conference was no longer a part-time project. He told Strauss that two key members of the Conference, Professor Lyman Bryson of Teachers College, Columbia University, and Professor Robert MacIver, also of Columbia University, wanted him to lead the Conference on a full-time basis. For a time, Finkelstein actually considered

---

[218]Report to Board of Directors, 6 April 1941.

[219]Louis Finkelstein to Norman Bentwich, 1940.

[220]Louis Finkelstein to José Bentwich, 1941.

[221]Louis Finkelstein to Frieda Schiff Warburg, 4 August 1943.

[222]Strauss was a member of the Seminary's Board and chairman of the Atomic Energy Commission.

changing the Seminary administration either by replacing himself or by bringing in another individual at the top in order to free him of this task. After all, he thought, "in view of the fact that I have given so much thought and time to the very problem of integration among people different from one another," the change would seem logical.[223] Although Finkelstein did not devote himself full time to the Conference, he continued to give the Conference and the Institute a great deal of attention.[224]

While the lack of adequate funding continued to frustrate him, extensions of the Institute were opened in Chicago in 1944 and a year later in Boston.[225] Over the course of the next decade, both programs grew and flourished. According to *New York Post* columnist Francis E. McMahon:

> The Nation owes a great debt to Doctor Louis Finkelstein, President of the Jewish Theological Seminary of America. For the past five years he and Professor Lyman Bryson of Teachers College (who deserves equal credit) have been bringing together some of the country's most eminent scholars to discuss vital questions at the Conference on Science, Philosophy, and Religion in Their Relation to the Democratic Way of Life.[226]

---

[223]Louis Finkelstein to Lewis Strauss, 7 September 1945.

[224]After discussion with some Board members, Finkelstein was persuaded to remain as president of the Seminary. Louis Finkelstein to Lewis Strauss, 7 September 1945; Lewis Strauss to Louis Finkelstein, 11 September 1945.

[225]The Boston branch was opened under joint auspices with the Academy of Arts and Sciences ("Latest Developments in Seminary Activity," a public-relations piece, 1946). Finkelstein hoped to establish branches in Atlanta, Baltimore, Los Angeles, and Texas in 1945. Louis Finkelstein to David Heyman of New York Foundation, 27 December 1944.

[226]"Latest Developments in Seminary Activity," 1946.

In an attempt to persuade Bernard Baruch to meet with Dr. Finkelstein, regarding the solicitation referred to earlier, the well-known American Jewish leader Judge Joseph M. Proskauer wrote to General David Sarnoff and made reference to the Institute for Religious and Social Studies: "[Finkelstein's] Institute...has, in my opinion, been a most potent factor in a clearance of understanding between Catholic, Protestant and Jewish scholars. It is one of those rare projects which meets anti-Semitism affirmatively and not negatively."[227]

Notwithstanding the recognition that it received, both activities continued to want for money. At one point, the New York Foundation, which had given $20,000 annually for several years, informed the Seminary that it did not want to continue to fund the program because the Institute should look to raise its own funds.[228] Some thought was given to separately incorporating the Institute and establishing an independent board of directors in order to assist it in establishing a more secure foundation, but for reasons that are not clear, this idea was never carried out. Even with funding problems, the Institute was able to publish numerous volumes of its work, which were used widely as texts in colleges and which influenced theological thought in many denominations in the country.

By the late 1940s, the Conference on Science, Philosophy, and Religion, which was maintained by the Institute, gave birth to the Mohonk Conference.[229] This was an annual gathering that took place over a week with a number of

---

[227]Louis Finkelstein to Proskauer; Proskauer to Sarnoff; Sarnoff to Baruch, November 1946, regarding establishment of Bernard Baruch Foundation.

[228]Louis Finkelstein to Governor Lehman and Governor Lehman to Louis Finkelstein, 30 March 1948.

[229]So-called after the location of the meeting in Mohonk, New York.

academics, most of whom were active in the Conference on Science, Philosophy, and Religion. The entire week was devoted to "spend[ing] all our time in an effort to clarify upon our different points of view the spiritual and moral problems of the day."[230] Finkelstein was quite proud of this gathering, for he did "not suppose that there is anywhere else the kind of team which this diverse group of Catholic, Protestant, Jew and agnostic repress [*sic*], working and thinking for the common good of the Republic."[231]

Evolving from this conference came the idea that by way of marking the fiftieth anniversary of its reorganization under Solomon Schechter, the Seminary should conduct an academy that would be based on the then new concept of "team thinking." The idea was to provide an opportunity that would enable teams of scholars and men of affairs, perhaps no more than fifteen in total, to deal more effectively with some basic issues of that time.[232] The group, it was envisaged, would include a cross-section of the world's geographical and religious population. The Seminary would supplement the program dealing with universal problems with its own seminars dealing primarily with religion and Judaism. This thinking laid the foundation for what was the Conference on Moral Standards, which subsequently took place in September 1953.

The programs and activities described above served as the centerpieces of the Seminary's expanded mission and certainly were the ones that received the greatest public

---

230 Louis Finkelstein to Arthur Sulzberger, 19 March 1948.

231 Ibid.

232 The proposed list of possible topics ranged from "The More Effective Organization of the United Nations" to "A Program for the Study of Madern [*sic*] Man: Development of methods to bring within focus of effective sudy [*sic*] the complexity of modern societies and cultures." Louis Finkelstein to Greenberg, 13 June 1950, thought piece for Mohonk Conference.

attention. They reveal Finkelstein's creative imagination, his insight into understanding the needs of the times in which he was leading, and the depth of his commitment to the Seminary's expanded mission. In addition, the goals of this mission were reflected in other institutional activities as well as in the academic curriculum of the Rabbinical School.

The University of Judaism

The original thought had been to turn the Seminary itself into a university of Judaism. The idea for this was put forward in a speech given by Seminary professor Mordecai M. Kaplan in spring 1945.[233] Kaplan was one of the Conservative Movement's most original thinkers and a seminal figure in American Jewish life. He had come to study at the Seminary from an Orthodox background. Ordained by the Seminary in 1902, he became the rabbi of an Orthodox synagogue in New York City, leaving it in 1909 to accept an invitation from Schechter to assume the post of dean of the Seminary's Teachers Institute. He also served as professor of homiletics on the Seminary's faculty. "Kaplan's willingness to take a chance on new definitions of Jewishness—to follow where critical, pragmatic reasoning led—resulted in his compulsion to address in the most serious, painstaking fashion an exceptionally wide range of topics and issues."[234] He is probably best known as the father of Reconstructionist Judaism, a philosophy of Judaism that branches off from Conservative Judaism. This philosophy, laid out in his study *Judaism as a Civilization*, sees Judaism as an "evolving religious civilization." He believed that Judaism needed to be

---

[233]A year earlier, at the 1944 Rabbinical Assembly Convention, Kaplan remarked, "It is Dr. Finkelstein's thought that the Seminary ought to be a Jewish University of the Diaspora" (R.A., *Proceedings*, 1944, pp. 318–19).

[234]Seltzer, 1990, p. 7.

"reconstructed" from supernaturalism to naturalism, and thus he rejected the traditional notion of a supernatural God. He maintained that Judaism is more than a religion; it is also Jewish art, music, dance, literature, land, and language. Hence, Judaism must be seen as a "civilization" to be fully appreciated. From this concept came his idea for the creation of a University of Judaism.

Kaplan observed that the Seminary was already a "veritable Niagara of the spirit that could be made to turn the wheels of Jewish life." "What it needed," he contended, "was a University of Judaism to convert all that knowledge into living energy."[235] Kaplan believed:

> Such a University of Judaism is the new instrument which American Jewish life must evolve in order to cope with the disintegrative influences to which the modern environment with its naturalism and its nationalism is subjecting our people. This is the new way in which we can approve our ability to adapt ourselves to maladaptation and our fitness once again to survive on this planet as a people.[236]

For technical reasons having to do with restrictions placed by the New York State Department of Higher Education on the use of the word "university," as well as the strong feeling among Seminary leadership that the Seminary's current name was too well established and that the Seminary would be hurt as a result of a name change, the decision was made in 1946 to establish the University of Judaism in Los Angeles as a West Coast branch of the Seminary.[237] The Los Angeles community had grown significantly in the 1920s and again in the early 1940s. What was happening in Los Angeles

---

[235]Kaplan, 1946, p. 18.

[236]Ibid., p. 19.

[237]Hoffnung, 1991, p. 7.

was "different from anything which had been taking place in any other region of the United States."[238]

Finkelstein acknowledged that such an undertaking "may mean financial sacrifice for the Seminary [but] we are convinced it is important for the entire American Jewish community and indeed for the entire American community."[239] As has already been illustrated above, lack of funds was not an impediment to Finkelstein's forward motion. To Finkelstein, conditions of Jewish life in Los Angeles were deplorable and the only way to correct them was "to establish a center to radiate positive understanding of Jewish ideals and Judaism—thus the role of the University of Judaism."[240] During one of his many trips to the West Coast to establish the school, he wrote to Professor Saul Lieberman:

> The more I see of this city the more I wonder how long Judaism can survive here unless something vigorous is done to stimulate it....The most remarkable thing about it is that the great mass of Jews here are quite unaffected with the whole business since they never go to synagogue at all.[241]

Notwithstanding such feelings, Finkelstein was ever the optimist, believing that "there is a good deal of Jewish spirit latent here which could be made effective."[242] Finkelstein, together with Seminary provost Simon Greenberg, who initially headed the University of Judaism, pressed on, working closely with the Los Angeles community and a coterie of lay leaders to establish the branch. The task was formidable because of the irreligiosity of the community and

---

[238]Ibid., p. xiii.

[239]Louis Finkelstein to Governor Lehman, 10 December 1946.

[240]Ibid.

[241]Louis Finkelstein to Saul Lieberman, Los Angeles, 19 August 1947.

[242]Ibid.

because of the strong sense of independence manifested by West Coast residents relative to East Coast institutions. Finkelstein, in a letter to Greenberg, worried that the university was already consuming much staff time; should they encounter community opposition, it would require even more, which would be "at the expense of the development of Judaism in the east."[243] A few months later, he wrote to Seminary librarian Alexander Marx:

> Our project [in L.A.] is moving a little more slowly than I had anticipated. The building up of faculty, gaining the good will of the population, and working out an effective organization of our own, all present overwhelming problems.[244]

Even a year later, in summer 1948, the university was cause for much concern, as Dr. Greenberg commented in a letter from Los Angeles to Dr. Finkelstein:

> What still remains in doubt about our local situation is the question of whether this activity will continue to be the great drain on our financial resources that it has been until the present or whether in the next year it will begin to carry itself more adequately.[245]

Finkelstein's intent was to establish on the West Coast an institution of higher Jewish learning similar to the Seminary, with the single exception that it would not have a rabbinical school. Thus, a group of schools including a school of education, a graduate school, an extension department, and an annual program of public lectures were all started in the fall of 1947. In addition to the establishment of the schools, which necessitated the acquisition of a building and the erection of a university library, the Seminary also opened an extension of its Jewish Museum. Carrying out the Seminary's

---

[243]Louis Finkelstein to Simon Greenberg, 11 March 1947.

[244]Louis Finkelstein to Alexander Marx, 15 July 1947.

[245]Simon Greenberg to Louis Finkelstein, Los Angeles, 20 July 1948.

broad mission, the university was "expected to serve all groups of Jews alike, and endeavor so far as possible to transcend differences among them,"[246] yet another example of the Seminary's commitment to bringing together the various spheres of Jewish life: "the aesthetic, the intellectual, the religious and the social."[247]

That the Seminary's expansive mission also touched the academic core of the institution has been demonstrated in the references above, first to the idea of changing the Seminary itself into a University of Judaism, and later to the actual establishment of such an institution as a branch of the Seminary in Los Angeles. The University of Judaism was one such example of the impact that this mission had on the academic program. There were others, perhaps most notably the curriculum of the Rabbinical School.

Curriculum of the Rabbinical School

While a comprehensive review of the Seminary's academic programs in general or that of the Rabbinical School in particular is neither intended nor required here, it is important to note that the mission laid out in the preceding pages did have a direct impact on the Seminary's central academic program—the Rabbinical School.

Since the early leaders of the Seminary could not know what the long-term needs of the American Jewish community would be, they had great difficulty in knowing what kind of a rabbi to train.[248] Adler spelled out what the Seminary's rabbinical education was to look like:

---

[246]Seminary *Register*, 1953–54.

[247]Simon Greenberg, "A Force for Reconciliation and Unity," convocation address at his inauguration as provost of JTSA, 30 March 1947, pp. 10–11.

[248]R.A., *Proceedings*, 1960, p. 123.

> [The Seminary] aims to carry the student back to the sources of Jewish law, history, liturgy, philosophy, theology and practice, believing that men so grounded in the knowledge and essentials of the great historic structure which we call Judaism, will preach it and practice it.[249]

Such a description was fitting for an institution whose goal was to train men[250] to be scholars, teachers, and preachers, and whose task it was to then "preach it and practice it." Its graduates were to study "Judaism," not a particular branch of Judaism, and go out into the community and teach this normative traditional Judaism.[251]

> The Seminary...did not seek to indoctrinate [its students] with any single outlook on Jewish life and left them the responsibility for formulating their own philosophy of Judaism on the basis of their own thought and experience.[252]

The foundation of such a curriculum was laid by Schechter in the very early days of the reorganized Seminary. In one of his addresses, Schechter stated, "The ultimate goal at which we are aiming is union and peace in American Israel."[253] To accomplish such a goal, Schechter, as well as Adler and Finkelstein after him, believed that the Seminary and its rabbinical graduates had to be "all things to all people"[254] and that it had to maintain a religious position that would be acceptable, at least in some ways, to the different

---

[249]Adler, 1933, pp. 262–63.

[250]Women were not admitted to the Rabbinical School until 1983.

[251]Schechter maintained, "There is no other Jewish religion but that taught by the Torah and confirmed by history and tradition and sunk into the conscience of Catholic Israel." *Seminary Addresses*, p. 23.

[252]Sklare, p. 181. This was in contradistinction to the Reform Movement's Hebrew Union College. See Karff, 1976, pp. 52, 58.

[253]Schechter, *Seminary Addresses*, p. xiii.

[254]Ibid.

groups within the American Jewish community. Again, it was Schechter who said:

> You must not think that our intention is to convert this school of learning into a certain groove of thinking or rather, not thinking....I would consider my work...a complete failure if this institution would not in the future produce some extremes as on the one side a raving mystic who would denounce me as a sober Philistine; on the other side an advanced critic who would rail at me as a narrow minded fanatic, while a third devotee of strict orthodoxy would raise protest against any critical views I may entertain.[255]

Such thinking also characterized the academic planning in the Finkelstein administration. He was proud of the fact that his faculty represented a wide latitude of theological opinion, and that the institution was strong enough and large enough to contain such widely divergent views as represented by Saul Lieberman on the right and Mordecai Kaplan on the left.

Schechter did not want the Seminary's first graduates "to constitute [them]selves into a sort of *Synagoga Militans*, and to widen the gap which is already deep enough to divide Israel into regular sects."[256] On the contrary, he wanted them to be agents for "the reconciliation of Israel." So Finkelstein wanted no less for graduates during his presidency. If his broad and outward-looking mission was to be fulfilled, it would require representatives within the community who espoused the values that had been the bedrock of the Seminary's curriculum under Schechter and Adler and that were now the core values for the Seminary's mission under Finkelstein. Therefore, the curriculum was one that consciously did not indoctrinate its students with a clearly defined view of Judaism. Instead, it taught a form of Judaism

---

[255]Ibid., pp. 23–24.
[256]Ibid., p. 76.

to which it felt all people could come "so far as fundamental values [were] concerned."[257]

Conclusion

While Finkelstein did not accomplish every one of his goals, after fifteen years as president, he did successfully establish the Jewish Theological Seminary of America as a significant force on the religious landscape of America. His success at that juncture was captured succinctly by Board Vice Chairman and Chairman of the Executive Committee Judge Rifkind:

> Whether by accident or design the Seminary has developed into an institution unique not only in our time but in all Jewish history. [Circumstances] have combined to give the Seminary unprecedented advantages in three distinct fields:(a) that of scholarly profundity; (b) that of religious influence over American Jewry; and (c) that of spiritual moral influence over American education as a whole....Today, the Seminary is a mature institution.[258]

---

[257]Adler, 1933, p. 183.
[258]Judge Rifkind to Louis Finkelstein, November 1954.

Chapter 5
The Seminary's Critics

The Seminary's expanded mission in the Finkelstein administration was severely criticized by rabbis, among others, for not being sufficiently concerned about the development of Conservative Judaism and the needs of the Conservative Movement. The Seminary's Board of Directors supported Dr. Finkelstein.

Almost from the beginning of the Finkelstein presidency, the broad and worldly mission that was described in the preceding chapter met with strong criticism. Many within the Conservative Movement had hoped that with a change in leadership, the Seminary would become an institution more committed to the promotion of Conservative Judaism. When Finkelstein did not take steps to lead the Seminary in that direction and, on the contrary, championed an expansion of the Seminary's mission, which to a large extent focused on the broader American community, followers were deeply disappointed. The bulk of criticism was voiced within the first five years of Finkelstein's presidency (1940–45) and reached its denouement in 1945, at a meeting of the Seminary's Board, which was almost tantamount to a vote of confidence or no-confidence in Finkelstein's leadership.

The Critics and Their Criticism

The criticism emanated from any number of quarters. The Seminary faculty, while not vocal in their opposition to the Seminary's expanded mission, were, for the most part, indifferent to it. The laity of the Conservative Movement, that is, those Jews who were members of Conservative synagogues, shared in much of the criticism being voiced by their rabbis.[259] Indeed, it was from the members of the Rabbinical Assembly that the strongest and most vocal criticism came. Most of the critics were unhappy with the new direction in which Finkelstein was leading the Seminary for the very reason Finkelstein valued it, namely, its breadth. Rabbi Milton Steinberg, a member of the Rabbinical Assembly and rabbi of a leading Conservative congregation in New York, maintained that the Seminary had been "distracted" from its main mission. "[T]he Seminary has allowed itself to be so terribly distracted, to undertake a variety of odd jobs, all sorts of enterprises indeed except that most necessary for the survival of Jewish life."[260] The "variety of odd jobs" that Steinberg was referring to was none other than the Institute of Religious and Social Studies, the *Eternal Light* radio program, and the Conference on Science, Philosophy, and Religion—the very programs that were the core of the Seminary's look outward.

> I very naturally approve of all efforts to establish good will among religious denominations. I am not sure, however, that such efforts fall in the province of Conservative Judaism...and if they do pertain to Conservative Judaism, the United Synagogue, not the Seminary, ought logically be the sponsoring body.[261]

Professor Louis Ginzberg, the senior member of the Seminary's faculty, also was not enamored of the idea of the creation of an institute for interdenominational studies. At

---

[259]Finkelstein, however, believed that laity were more interested in dealing with the problems of the world than were the rabbis of their congregations. He also believed that since the members of the Seminary's Board were also Movement laity, and since they supported the direction in which the Seminary was going, *q.e.d.* laity did support the Seminary's mission. Interview with Louis Finkelstein, 4 January 1989.

[260]Milton Steinberg, "Crises in Conservative Judaism," sermon, 1943–44.

[261]Ibid.

the very inception of this institute, he told Finkelstein that he would not attend a planning meeting on the Institute, to which he had been invited. Ginzberg wrote:

> Whatever results one might expect from a school for the study of interdenominational studies, one must not deceive oneself in believing that it would serve as a bulwark against Communism or Nazism. Moreover, the establishment of such a school by the Jews will be doomed to failure from its very beginning. We Jews are poverty stricken, spiritually more so than economically. We have a large number of intellectuals but very few among them distinguished by their spirituality.[262]

Similarly, on more than one occasion, Board member Jack Solis-Cohen Jr. also challenged Finkelstein on the Institute. In one instance, he wanted to be certain that the program was not using Seminary funds—that is, that special funds were being raised to support it.[263] In a later challenge, he told Finkelstein that he had heard that the senior faculty opposed the Institute and suggested that the Board should meet with the faculty to discuss it.[264] Solis-Cohen believed that Finkelstein was exceeding his authority and leading the Seminary in the wrong direction.

> The Seminary was founded for certain purposes....[Schechter and Adler] believed in a simple, dignified institution...as opposed to the present policy of rapid expansion, convocations, institutes, citations and other activities that bring publicity to the Seminary. I see no reason for changing the traditional teachings of the Seminary.[265]

262Louis Ginzberg to Louis Finkelstein, 1 November 1939.

263Louis Finkelstein to J. Solis-Cohen, 4 March 1943.

264Ibid., 6 July 1944.

265D. Hays Solis-Cohen, Esq., to Henry Hendricks; J. Solis-Cohen Jr. to entire Special Committee, 25 September 1945.

The severest and most persistent criticism, however, emanated from the rabbis. Joining Rabbi Steinberg of New York in his attack on the Seminary and its president was Rabbi Solomon Goldman of Chicago. Goldman, whose critique, like Steinberg's, was vitriolic and unceasing, engaged in lengthy correspondence with Finkelstein over their differences.[266] In addition to his criticism of the Institute, Goldman was also most critical of the Conference on Science, Philosophy, and Religion. After all, he argued, given his understanding of Catholicism and its dogmatism, the possibility that it would alter its views toward Protestantism or Judaism seemed nil. In one letter, he implored Finkelstein not to waste his time and energies "by following a will o' the wisp....These artificial conferences and good will and better understanding meetings are contemporary. Leave them to men who live in the contemporary world."[267]

Criticism of these two Seminary programs, the Conference and the Institute, came from outside the Seminary community as well. For example, one of the leaders of the orthodox rabbinate, Dr. Samuel Belkin, who at the time was dean of Yeshiva College in New York and subsequently went on to a distinguished career as the president of Yeshiva University, was also very much opposed to the kind of activities in which these two programs were engaged. He saw them as being a part of what was referred to as the "goodwill" movement and believed that "the religious part of good will is the most dangerous Movement in America. He...consider[ed] it as serious a danger for the perpetuation of...Judaism as missionary work."[268]

The American Jewish Committee was also critical. Their delay in taking positive action regarding the Conference

266This correspondence is dealt with extensively in Weinstein, 1973.
267Solomon Goldman to Louis Finkelstein, 31 October 1940.
268Samuel Belkin to Henry S. Hendricks, 1942.

motivated Finkelstein to write to his board chairman, Sol Stroock, and express his concern that Stroock, who was a member of the Committee, was not speaking up on behalf of the Seminary Conference on Science, Philosophy, and Religion. Finkelstein felt that such reticence was unjustified and argued:

> It is true that our motives may be misrepresented, but that is after all the penalty of participation in public affairs. We should not permit misrepresentation by a few who fail to appreciate values, to stand in the way of an effort which would benefit the general public...if the effort is doomed, I must be sure that it is through no reticence on my part.[269]

Most of the critics, certainly the ones within the Conservative Movement, wanted Finkelstein to bring the Seminary and the Movement closer together. They wanted the Seminary to identify itself more publicly with the Movement. Moreover, they wanted the Seminary to limit the scope of its mission to providing for the academic and spiritual needs of the membership of the Conservative Movement. These critics saw no connection between their goal and the Seminary's mission. Finkelstein himself acknowledged the pressure that was being exerted on him to alter his plans and thus the Seminary's mission:

> [L]ast year the Institute for Religious Studies was under severe attack....In the meantime, some of our friends are again raising an issue as to whether the Institute...would not do more harm than good to Judaism.[270]

Finkelstein reported to another colleague the fact that at a gathering of rabbis, "the men indicated that they regarded the

---

[269]Louis Finkelstein to Sol M. Stroock, 15 February 1940.

[270]Louis Finkelstein to Arthur Sulzberger, 18 November 1942.

Seminary as purely an academic institution which should avoid taking an active part in organized Jewish life."[271]

So strongly did Steinberg feel about what Finkelstein was doing that he took the unusual step of criticizing him publicly from the pulpit. Acknowledging that "no sermon in [his] rabbinic career ha[d] been so difficult to preach as this [one]," he launched into an attack against Finkelstein, accusing him and the Seminary of nothing less than abetting what he believed to be the horrible state of affairs of the Conservative Movement. Among his criticisms was the membership of the Board of Directors of the Seminary, which he said was "made up of persons who neither practice Conservative Judaism, nor profess it, nor sympathize with it." On another occasion, Steinberg actually introduced a formal resolution into the Rabbinical Assembly regarding what he believed to be the unrepresentative makeup of the Seminary Board.[272] Another leader of the Rabbinical Assembly wrote Finkelstein that because the Board consisted of people who were not Conservative Jews, it would not be right for the Seminary to publish a Passover Haggadah. The Rabbinical Assembly should do it instead.[273]

Moreover, he preached that the Seminary was unduly controlled by "one man" (Finkelstein). Steinberg wanted the Seminary to focus its efforts and resources on strengthening American Judaism, or more specifically, on strengthening the Conservative Movement. Steinberg asked rhetorically, "Why, when an adolescent youngster faces religious doubts, do I have no book to put in his hands?"[274]—the point being that

---

[271]Louis Finkelstein to Rabbi Mordecai Brill, 4 January 1943.

[272]Milton Steinberg, "Crises in Conservative Judaism," sermon, 1943–44. Goldman also leveled the same criticism (Weinstein, p. 42). Also, Rabbi Solomon Goldman to Louis Finkelstein, 12 September 1944.

[273]Israel Goldstein to Louis Finkelstein, 10 June 1941.

[274]Steinberg, op. cit.

the Seminary should be busy making certain that the Conservative Movement had the tools needed to raise up a loyal and committed membership. So displeased was Steinberg that he took the even more unusual step of withholding economic support for the Seminary by refusing to conduct a Seminary appeal on the holiest day in the Jewish Year—Yom Kippur. Finkelstein was furious when he learned of this and wrote a strong letter to Steinberg, admonishing him for this decision without at least first having given Finkelstein the courtesy of a discussion. Finkelstein was less bothered by the criticism than he was by the threat to withhold support for what was so dear to him.

> To take the position at this time, when the lights of so many institutions of Jewish learning have been extinguished, that until we can achieve unanimity with regard to detailed issues of Jewish observance and theology, so that the Seminary will be able to have a consistent policy without finding itself at odds with any of its alumni, the Seminary should not receive support is...unworthy of your place in Jewish life.[275]

His counterattack was of no avail. To the contrary, Steinberg was only further antagonized by the tone of the letter and more steadfast in his refusal to conduct the appeal. The situation had deteriorated to the point where Steinberg bluntly informed Finkelstein that insofar as his refusal to conduct the appeal was concerned, "one and only one issue is involved—and that is whether it is morally possible for me to subscribe to what the Seminary has come to represent under your leadership."[276]

Rabbi Goldman was no less biting in his criticism. He, like his colleague Steinberg, saw the Seminary under Finkelstein as "veering away...from the conception of the

---

[275]Louis Finkelstein to Milton Steinberg, 25 September 1944.

[276]Milton Steinberg to Louis Finkelstein, 25 September 1944.

Seminary as the Academy of Conservative Judaism and the institution of Conservative Judaism to a position of neutrality."[277] It had been Goldman's hope that with the transition from Cyrus Adler to Louis Finkelstein, the Seminary would have set forth a Conservative position that would have been of help to the rabbi in mediating the Jewish tradition with the challenges of modernity. Instead, Goldman was now convinced that Finkelstein remained distant from an identification with Conservative Judaism and was leading the Seminary in an entirely different direction.[278]

> Let the Seminary attend to its own ideological problems, build its own great library, give its own graduates the proper tools and techniques of the modern rabbinate, educate its own laymen to leadership.[279]

As Goldman analyzed the activities of the Seminary under Finkelstein's leadership, he divided them into two categories: those befitting an educational and spiritual center of the Conservative Movement and those not befitting "an overall institution that...seek[s] the integration of the separatist bodies in American Israel, the harmonization of Judaism with science and philosophy, and a closer understanding with Christianity."[280] It was his strong conviction that the Seminary should be engaged only with programs and activities that related to the Seminary as the educational and spiritual center of the Conservative Movement. Moreover, he believed that the vast majority of Jews who "look upon the Seminary as their institution...expect it to be zealously dedicated to and concentrating on Conservative Judaism."[281]

---

[277]Solomon Goldman to Louis Finkelstein, 12 September 1944.
[278]Rosenblum, 1970, p. 244.
[279]Weinstein, 1973, p. 43.
[280]Solomon Goldman to Louis Finkelstein, 26 September 1944.
[281]Ibid., p. 2.

Goldman argued that Conservative Jews were fearful that in an attempt to be all things to all men, Conservative Judaism in general, and the Seminary in particular, were "adulterat[ing] and compromis[ing] [their] own ideology and program."[282] These Conservative Jews, according to Goldman, believed that "a dispersive force is inferior to a collective and that the squandering of energy over a multiplicity of efforts does not result in the replenishment of vitality but in its evisceration."[283] These individuals "do not want to travel under false colors and to disguise their missionary aim....If the Seminary wants to 'de-denominationize' American Israel, they insist that it be the common enterprise of all the 'denominations' concerned."[284]

Perhaps most poignantly, Goldman pointed out that these Seminary supporters "do not possess the means of shouldering support of [both] a Conservative Seminary, and in addition, an overall institution."[285] Goldman, like his colleague Steinberg, also surprised Finkelstein by his public criticism of these programs. In 1944, the Seminary invited Goldman to participate in an academic convocation at the Seminary in memory of Dr. Solomon Schechter. At that convocation, Goldman attacked these new programs and the whole tendency of the Seminary to engage in what he referred to as "world problems."[286] Even when the Seminary chose to honor him, Goldman did not miss the opportunity to level his criticism. Two years to the month following this convocation, the Seminary held a luncheon honoring, in addition to Goldman, David Sarnoff of NBC and Julian Morgenstern, president of the Hebrew Union College. In his

---

282Ibid.

283Ibid., p. 2.

284Ibid., p. 3.

285Ibid.

286Louis Finkelstein to Frieda Schiff Warburg, 8 April 1946.

remarks, Goldman observed that "the Jew, to our sorrow and shame, has become foremost among the conformists. His greater desire has been to cease to be distinctive."[287] Was this, wondered Goldman aloud, the price to be paid for the Seminary's long-standing commitment to the Americanization of the Jew? In sum, Goldman believed that the Conference on Science, Philosophy, and Religion, the Institute for Religious Studies, and the *Eternal Light* radio program together with the wide public thrust of the institution had

> in the minds of many educators, Rabbis, laymen and some of the most creative Jews in the country (a) cast the shadow of suspicion over the institution and hurt the cause of Conservative Judaism, (b) redounded to the humiliation of the Conservative laity, and (c) further estranged from it the Jewish masses.[288]

For Goldman, the Seminary was approaching the "juncture where it will have to ponder the old question—whether it is possible to remain true to one's self and at the same time to be all things to all men."[289]

Other members of the Rabbinical Assembly shared with Goldman their unhappiness about the Seminary, and Goldman suggested that they "draw up a list of particulars" to be presented to Finkelstein. This group included Rabbis Israel Levinthal, David Aronson, Ira Eisenstein, and Judah Goldin.[290] Like Steinberg and Goldman, they wanted a Seminary whose role was limited to serving as the academic center of the Conservative Movement, whose business would be the issues and concerns of the Movement, and whose

---

[287]"On The Convocation and Luncheon Meeting at the Jewish Theological Seminary," *New York Times*, 7 April 1946.

[288]Solomon Goldman to Louis Finkelstein, 26 September 1944, p. 3.

[289]Ibid., 12 September 1944.

[290]Weinstein, p. 43.

leadership would be Jews who identified with the Conservative Movement. In Rabbi Steinberg's words:

> I want [Finkelstein] to begin to move toward the transfer of lay authority in the affairs of the Seminary to Conservative Jews and Conservative congregations….I want the Seminary to take the lead in making Judaism really historical Judaism….I want the Seminary to do something practical about the Jewish law of divorce, about shabbos observance, Kashruth, about vitalizing Jewish worship. What else are the Seminary and Conservative Judaism for?[291]

These critics within the Conservative Movement all believed that without the Seminary's leadership, the Movement would flounder because no other organization had the ability to be the leader. While Steinberg and Goldman spoke as individual rabbis, the leadership of the Rabbinical Assembly leveled similar criticism.

But the rabbis were not alone in their unhappiness with the Seminary. For example, an important Seminary donor from Cleveland refused to join the Seminary's Board of Overseers because, after visiting the Seminary, "he failed to carry away with him the feeling that [the Seminary] had a definite plan and a sense of direction in [its] work."[292] Goldman told Finkelstein he could not even recommend people for this Board of Overseers because he did not understand what it was all about. Another layman remarked, bemoaning the Seminary's insistence on having the widest appeal possible, that "the Seminary which regards us as its children, when it comes to the question of helping the Seminary...very often refuses to permit us to recognize it as our mother."[293] All these critics saw the Seminary as the

[291]Ibid., pp. 43–44.
[292]Joel Geffen to Simon Greenberg, 24 January 1947.
[293]Sklare, p. 221.

fountainhead of the Movement and yet believed that it was giving scant attention to the Movement's needs. Many of these critics also felt the need for greater definition and clarity of Conservative Judaism, for a philosophy of Conservative Judaism. Seminary official Rabbi Max Arzt acknowledged this desire, noting that "the demand for concise definition [of Conservative Judaism] has of late become more vocal than ever before."[294] But this was something the Seminary was very much against because, according to Finkelstein, "to define is to exclude"[295] and the Seminary's intent was to keep Jews within Judaism and supportive of the Seminary, regardless of their affiliation or nonaffiliation.

Even Finkelstein's desire for a University of Judaism, be it at the Seminary proper or a new branch in Los Angeles, met with criticism. One source of this criticism came from Finkelstein's close friend and supporter Arthur Hays Sulzberger, publisher of the *New York Times*. He wrote to Finkelstein:

> [A] school for Jewish communal service seems to me to be a step backward....And a center of Jewish music, arts and letters seems to me at least to open the way to trea [*sic*] on a sectarian line that which should have a broader more general approach.[296]

Fellow Board member Frieda Schiff Warburg also disapproved of a new school in California, although for reasons quite different from Sulzberger's. She felt it was a time for consolidation, not expansion.[297]

Indeed, there never seemed to be a moment when someone or some group was not attacking Finkelstein

---

[294]Arzt, 1949, p. 10.

[295]Interview, 14 February 1984.

[296]Arthur Sulzberger to Louis Finkelstein, 11 November 1946.

[297]Louis Finkelstein to Frieda Schiff Warburg, 19 September 1947.

because he was never far from a crisis.[298] At the height of the controversy with Goldman and Steinberg, Finkelstein received a letter signed by fifteen alumni who castigated him for his "erratic and destructive leadership against [his] association with Mordecai Kaplan and his devastating and ruinous Reconstructionist philosophy—against [his] timidity in leading a dynamic path of creative and effective Conservatism."[299]

Response to Critics

Throughout these first few years (1940–45) of his administration, Finkelstein made one effort after another to justify the Seminary's mission to its critics. Whether through public speeches such as to the membership of the Rabbinical Assembly, or through correspondence such as that conducted with Rabbi Solomon Goldman of Chicago and referred to above, he went to great lengths to respond to their criticism, to give them reason to feel proud of the Seminary, and to encourage their full support. At all times, he was steadfast in maintaining that the Seminary "is the hope of American Judaism....[N]owhere outside it...is there so much being planned and done for preservation and advancement of Judaism in this hemisphere."[300]

Finkelstein also tried to explain to his critics again and again that "the religious problem of the Jew in America at that time [could] not be treated independently of the religious problem of the world."[301] He deeply believed that the difficulties that the forces of European totalitarianism were

---

[298]Interview with Chancellor Emeritus Gerson D. Cohen, 29 July 1985.

[299]Fifteen alumni to Louis Finkelstein, 30 July 1945.

[300]Louis Finkelstein to Milton Steinberg, 25 September 1944.

[301]Louis Finkelstein to Louis Ginzberg, 3 November 1939, response to letter of 1 November 1939.

causing in certain parts of the world could easily exist in America unless the tendencies that underlie this totalitarianism and that exist in America were overcome.

But his attempts to appease his critics were less than successful. By 1943, the middle of this period, he was feeling the frustration of a leader unable to satisfy those on whom he depended for economic support. In a personal letter to Judge Joseph M. Proskauer, who had just been elected president of the American Jewish Committee, Finkelstein shared his uncharacteristically candid thoughts about the American Jewish scene and his frustration with his detractors:[302]

> Holding these rather unpopular and old fashioned views, I find myself at odds with almost all my fellow Jews at this time. I do not know how I would be able to carry on at all, if I did not find comfort in the great Jewish classics, and reassurance in the fact that I am simply the disciple of virtually every great Jewish teacher in the past, in taking this position.[303]

The "position" and "unpopular views" he was referring to were his strongly held belief that neither the Seminary nor the United Synagogue and the Rabbinical Assembly should be "getting involved in any of the more immediate issues [of the day]," but rather that they should devote their efforts "to deal with long-range, spiritual problems of the Jewish people and the world."[304] Finkelstein continued:

> I believe, most earnestly, that the basic problems of our time are not those which are most vivid and immediate, but those, which are, at the moment, less vivid, but are

---

[302]Louis Finkelstein to Judge Joseph Proskauer, 1 February 1943, unsent. This letter was marked "not sent" in Finkelstein's own handwriting.

[303]Ibid.

[304]Ibid.

> sure to become quite important within fifteen or twenty years.[305]

He noted that he was "much more concerned by the question of the spiritual and moral attitudes of the Jews who lived south of the Rio Grande, than most any other question in Jewish life, today."[306] Another example of how discomfited he was by these critics is revealed in a letter from Finkelstein to a prominent rabbi:

> I think that you can understand...how deeply I feel about this whole business which has arisen between [Rabbi] Sol Goldman and myself, and how much I suffer because of what is going on. It is no small matter to be told that Sol, who has been my friend for thirty-five years, instead of waiting to come and talk out with me whatever issues are troubling him, virtually summons me to a din-Torah [court of Jewish law] before my colleagues on accusations of heresy and apostasy. The fact that I cannot say anything about it, for fear that I might say too much, doesn't help me.
>
> I want you to believe me when I say that I am trying very hard to be as frank and candid with everyone about the Seminary as I possibly can be. I have no reservations, no secret plans, and (I don't know whether you will believe me when I say this) no personal ambitions. I accepted the responsibilities of being president of the Seminary, knowing well what that implied with regard to my life-long aspirations in the field of rabbinic studies, because I think I can render a service here; and, naturally, I am trying to do so to the best of my ability.[307]

By spring 1945, the dueling between Finkelstein and his colleagues, among others, had reached its peak. Finkelstein

---

[305]Ibid.

[306]Ibid.

[307]Louis Finkelstein to Rabbi Louis Epstein, 13 December 1944, in response to his letter of 30 November 1944.

once again turned to Arthur Hays Sulzberger and in a five-page letter, posted air mail special delivery, poured out his heart and talked of resigning as president of the Seminary. He appealed to Sulzberger's long-time commitment to the Conference on Science, Philosophy, and Religion and the Institute for Religious Studies, as well as to his support for the general direction in which the Seminary was going. Finkelstein was able to report to Sulzberger significant success in both these programs, which only served to deepen the frustration that Finkelstein felt:

> Just when our "outside" activities seem to be reaping fruit...I am faced with perhaps the most difficult decision that I have been forced to make. It is for that reason that I have wanted to see you and that I am going to Washington on Wednesday to see Lewis Strauss. This is a time when I must have the counsel of my real friends.[308]

In this letter, Finkelstein talked about the "Seminary alumni who did not fully appreciate the Institute for Religious Studies and [the other] allied activities"[309] and mentioned Rabbis Goldman and Steinberg by name. In providing Sulzberger with an overview of the tensions, he wrote that "the whole situation is rapidly assuming, on the part of the two rabbis, the nature of a crusade."[310] He conceded that he held out little hope of stopping these two men and, in point of fact, told Sulzberger that although "both Doctor Goldman and Rabbi Steinberg [were] having luncheon with the senior members of the faculty and [him]self,...[he] h[ad] no hope

---

[308]Louis Finkelstein to Arthur Sulzberger, 12 February 1945, p. 2. Were it not for these programs and his commitment to them, Finkelstein might well have carried out his thought of resigning as president of the Seminary, p. 4.

[309]Ibid.

[310]Ibid., p. 3.

that anything...will result."[311] Given the situation, Finkelstein told Sulzberger that he was considering tendering his resignation:

> As you and Lewis [Strauss] well know, personally I would be delighted to be relieved of the burdens attendant upon the Seminary president. I find the work of administration continually more difficult as the institution grows, and, as a result, my own plans for study have virtually been wrecked. I feel quite earnestly that I could do very effective work apart from the Seminary, and would welcome an opportunity to leave it.[312]

Finally, Finkelstein pleaded for speedy counsel, noting that "the crusaders will not grow less active and the task will become increasingly more difficult with the creation of new opponents."[313] Indeed, it was only two weeks later that Finkelstein again wrote to Sulzberger:

> [T]he problem grows continually more complex....The difficulties are spreading, as I feared they might. Just last night...I was warned by a friend that there is going to be a concerted attack on the Seminary. This will take the form of accusing the institution of neglecting Jewish scholarship for other activities, notably the Institute.[314]

Both Sulzberger and Strauss were most supportive of Finkelstein, and Strauss observed: "Students in future generations, assuming these documents are preserved for them, will surely hold it to be as pointless and myopic as the shallowest sectarian schism of the Middle Ages."[315]

---

[311] Ibid.

[312] Ibid., p. 4.

[313] Ibid., p. 5.

[314] Louis Finkelstein to Arthur Sulzberger, 26 February 1945.

[315] Louis Finkelstein to Lewis L. Strauss, 3 December 1945.

By March 1945, Finkelstein had consulted with his key lay leadership and had decided that he had the necessary support to win a vote of confidence for the Seminary's mission and his leadership from the Seminary's Board of Directors. On March 17, 1945, the members of the Board were called to a special meeting to be held on April 17, 1945. The notice indicated that the Board meeting was called for the purpose of reviewing the position of the Seminary regarding:

> a) the attitude it has taken, as an academic institution, to organizational issues and differences in the Jewish and the general community;
>
> b) its program to make Judaism, as a spiritual force, significant for the unsynagogued, as well as those to whom our graduates minister;
>
> c) its program for increased collective thinking among religious and intellectual leaders of all types to strengthen democracy as a spiritual and cultural force in the United States.[316]

The notice acknowledged that "these subjects have caused animated discussion among the alumni and other friends of the Seminary [and] it is felt that the time has come for the leaders of the faculty and Board as a whole to review the policies of the institution."[317] Professors Louis Ginzberg, Alexander Marx, and Mordecai Kaplan, members of the senior faculty, received a special invitation to the meeting for, as Weinstein has noted, Finkelstein "knew the effect that would be gained from having Kaplan [theologically left] and Ginzberg [theologically right] present."[318] Also in attendance were Rabbis David Aronson, Louis M. Epstein, and Leon Lang as representatives of the Rabbinical Assembly, all of

[316]Jacob Gutman to Board of Directors, 27 March 1945.
[317]Ibid.
[318]Weinstein, pp. 44–45.

whom were familiar with the views that Goldman and Steinberg represented.

The meeting, called for 5:30 P.M. and expected to run until 9:00 P.M., did not adjourn until 10:00 P.M. The lengthy session did, however, produce a victory for Finkelstein. Five planks were put forward, each formulated around an aspect of the Seminary's current mission as put forth by Finkelstein, and all were accepted. Four of the five passed unanimously. Plank number one affirmed:

> [The] Seminary [will] continue its historic[al] attitude as an academic institution and not become involved in organizational issues and differences which may arise in the Jewish or general community; it being understood that the administration officers of the Seminary and the officers as well as other members of the Board of Directors, have complete freedom of action and expression, analogous to that provided in the concept of academic freedom of the faculty.[319]

Plank number two stated:

> [T]he Seminary [will] continue its program designed to make Judaism a spiritual force, significant for all Jews, both those to whom its graduates minister and those outside those congregations.[320]

Plank number three said:

> [T]he Board of Directors regard a Jewish school for social work and a cantorial school [both of which were being considered at the time] as within the purview of the Seminary.[321]

The fourth plank was in many ways the most significant of the five for Finkelstein, because it was the work to which it referred that the Institute for Religious Studies and the

---

[319]Board of Directors, minutes, 17 April 1945.

[320]Ibid.

[321]Ibid.

Conference on Science, Philosophy, and Religion were committed. This plank read:

> [T]he Seminary [will] continue its program for increased cooperation among religious and intellectual leaders of all types, with the aim of strengthening democracy as a spiritual and cultural force in the United States.[322]

This plank was also adopted with one of the three Rabbinical Assembly votes casting a negative ballot.[323] Not only had Finkelstein won, but he had succeeded in dividing the Rabbinical Assembly. The fifth and final plank asserted:

> [T]he Board of Directors reaffirms the traditional association of the Seminary, the Rabbinical Assembly and the United Synagogue in the common effort to preserve and further the cause of historical Judaism.[324]

This plank contained language that offered some consolation to the critics who favored a more denominationally oriented Seminary in that it formally acknowledged the place of the Seminary in the constellation of the three major organizational segments of the Conservative Movement. It also supported "historical Judaism," which was understood to mean Conservative Judaism.

While Finkelstein had succeeded in frustrating his critics' efforts to undermine his leadership and alter the Seminary's course, he was not able to bring a halt to their constant complaining. Indeed, much of this criticism continued through the period of this study, with new voices replacing the old but essentially arguing about the same issues. Even when the Seminary did draw somewhat closer to the Movement in the mid-1940s, as will be discussed in the

---

[322]Ibid.

[323]Rabbi Louis M. Epstein subsequently resigned from the Board.

[324]Board of Directors, minutes, 17 April 1945.

following pages, these criticisms continued unabated. An entire plenary session at the 1946 convention of the Rabbinical Assembly was devoted to a reevaluation of the Seminary's expansion program. The session was characterized by sharp exchanges and challenges to the Seminary leadership. Finkelstein was present and thanked the assembled "for this frank...discussion"[325] and appealed to them to give him and the Seminary's faculty the benefit of the doubt:

> [I]f that Faculty [whom you believe to be good Jews] voted on a matter and agreed to a man, and it seemed to you that it is a mistake, then you have to say to yourself, "But there must have been some reason for it." After all, the whole Faculty didn't go crazy. Maybe there is a particular reason for it.[326]

But the critics never did quite give Finkelstein or the Seminary the benefit of the doubt and continued to critique the mission and the Seminary's role within the Movement.

---

[325]R.A., *Proceedings*, 1946, p. 227.
[326]Ibid., p. 231.

Chapter 6
The Seminary's Relationship to the Conservative Movement

The relationship of the Seminary to the Movement and to the organizations within the Movement was beset with tension and ambiguity, as can be seen by the Seminary's relationship with the United Synagogue of America, the Rabbinical Assembly, the National Women's League, and the Federation of Jewish Men's Clubs. Its relationship to the Movement is also evident in two of its own programs: the Ramah Camps and the Leadership Training Fellowship.

Finkelstein's vision for the Seminary called for it to be a national institution rather than a parochial one—one that would concern itself with the welfare of mankind and not just those Jews and the synagogues that constituted the Conservative Movement. Many in the Movement were critical of such a role for the Seminary, believing instead that the Seminary's time and energy should be focused on building Conservative Judaism in America.

Notwithstanding the show of support that Finkelstein received from the Seminary's Board of Directors for his vision, the critics were not altogether wrong in their description of the Seminary's relationship to the Conservative Movement at that time. Nor were they wrong in their belief that the Conservative rabbinate and laity wanted a closer and more focused relationship with the Seminary. For example, in 1943, the Seminary had hired a fund-raising firm to explore the possibility of its undertaking a large campaign. Among the findings of that study was the feeling on the part of constituents that "Much can be done—in fact is crying out to be done—to bring the Seminary closer to its own groups: alumni, congregations and special friends."[327]

What was the relationship of the Jewish Theological Seminary of America to the Conservative Movement? The question is best answered by looking at the relationship that the Seminary had with the constituent organizations of the Movement: the United Synagogue of America, the National Women's League, the Federation of Jewish Men's Clubs, the Rabbinical Assembly of America, and the programs and activities that the Seminary itself conducted, such as the Ramah Camps and the Leadership Training Fellowship, both of which reached into the grass roots of the Conservative Movement.

The United Synagogue of America

The Seminary, together with the Rabbinical Assembly (R.A.) and the United Synagogue of America, constituted the national organizational structure of the Conservative Movement. Although the Seminary promoted itself as an umbrella institution open to all Jews, it was nonetheless identified by the public as a Conservative institution. Because the Rabbinical Assembly and the United Synagogue evolved from the Seminary and were, in one way or another, dependent upon the Seminary, the national structure was an unbalanced one; that is, the Seminary was larger, stronger, more stable, and thus more powerful.

The United Synagogue was expected by the Seminary and the Rabbinical Assembly to be a force that would rally synagogues around the banner of Conservative Judaism. It was also expected by them to service the synagogues and their diverse populations with program materials, leadership training, educational textbooks, and guidance for their

---

[327]John Price Jones to JTS Board of Trustees, 7 June 1943.

afternoon schools. In addition, the United Synagogue was the public voice of the Movement on issues of social welfare. In the opinion of many within the Movement, these responsibilities were not being lived up to or at least not well, either because of inadequate funding or weak leadership or both. Furthermore, as Finkelstein pointed out in a critique of the United Synagogue, its conduct of affairs was causing significant problems for the Seminary, then trying to establish itself in the community at large. In that critique, he noted that the Rabbinical Assembly was most unhappy with the United Synagogue for admitting congregations with "free-lance" rabbis, thereby not obligating those synagogues to select a Rabbinical Assembly rabbi; that some former leaders of the United Synagogue had been alienated by its bad finances and that this, in turn, soured them on the entire Movement;[328] that the Seminary was often blamed for things that the United Synagogue did, but over which the Seminary had no control. For example, when the United Synagogue held a convention in a nonkosher hotel or when it arranged a program that required participants to ride in violation of the ban against riding on the Sabbath, it proved embarrassing to the Seminary.[329]

While the United Synagogue had been created by Schechter "to nurture the spirit of Conservative Judaism as well as to provide the Seminary with a firm and fixed base of support," it was at this point not doing either very well. The lack of sufficient financial resources and the absence of strong leadership resulted in its never quite achieving the level of effectiveness expected by the Seminary, the Rabbinical Assembly or, for that matter, many of its own members.

---

[328]By 1936, the United Synagogue had current assets of $16,746.95 and liabilities of $45,158.56; from "United Synagogue: 1934– ," Finkelstein file.

[329]Memorandum, Louis Finkelstein to Cyrus Adler, 26 October 1936.

Indeed, there was widespread dissatisfaction with the organization throughout the Movement, and a deep feeling that something needed to be done about the United Synagogue. As Adler put it:

> I firmly believe that the United Synagogue ought to be...made a more useful organization....The United Synagogue has been going on in the same way for quite a number of years. Nearly every organization requires a certain amount of self-study and investigation.[330]

The Rabbinical Assembly had become so upset with the organization and so concerned about its financial status that its Executive Council approved a resolution that proposed that there be an examination of the organization.[331] Indeed, the chasm that had developed between the United Synagogue and the Rabbinical Assembly was a cause of concern for Seminary officials. Board member Arthur Oppenheimer wrote:

> [The] conflict between the United Synagogue organization and the Rabbinical Assembly organization interferes very seriously with the work of the Seminary, and with the development of the Conservative Movement generally.[332]

In response to both the criticism and its own fiscal realities, the United Synagogue began, in the spring of 1936, to address many of these complaints. Among the steps it took to strengthen itself was the effort to organize a Committee to Overcome Religious Indifference,

> through which it intended to muster a number of important laymen for the purpose of studying the

[330]Cyrus Adler to Louis Finkelstein, 11 June 1935.

[331]Ibid., 29 April 1932; this request was reiterated in the Rabbinical Assembly *Proceedings*, 1938, pp. 416–17.

[332]Undated memo from "United Synagogue: 1934– ," Finkelstein file.

> activities of the United Synagogue, the ways in which they could be improved and advanced and to raise the necessary funds for the conducting of the United Synagogue program.[333]

A reorganization of the United Synagogue did subsequently occur in 1939 after an earlier attempt to improve its financial picture ran into difficulties. This earlier attempt failed because, in 1937, the Seminary marked the semicentennial of its founding and had planned to conduct a fund-raising campaign within its congregations, that is to say, within the congregations of the United Synagogue of America. However, the United Synagogue had planned to raise funds from among these very same congregations. Caught in the middle were the rabbis of the congregations, who wanted to be helpful to both the United Synagogue and the Seminary, but felt that they could not go to their donors twice for what was essentially the same cause, namely, Conservative Judaism.

In order to deal with this situation, a committee, the first of many, was established to deal with the interrelationship of the Seminary, the Rabbinical Assembly, and the United Synagogue.[334] All three were represented. While an accommodation was reached that allowed the Seminary to

---

[333]"The United Synagogue as a Functioning Institution," 1937.

[334]Dr. Greenberg, who at the time was president of the Rabbinical Assembly, observed that "for many years there was the widespread conviction among us that the work of those three national bodies should be more closely coordinated and more effectively integrated....[However,] as long as the Seminary did not find it necessary to appeal to the large numbers in order to broaden its base for its maintenance, we could manage to overlook the lack of coordination. But with the celebration of the Seminary's semi-centennial...the Seminary embarked upon a vigorous effort to win support for itself among the members of our congregations...that at once led to a conflict with the money raising efforts of United Synagogue" (R.A., *Proceedings*, 1938, pp. 426–27).

press forward with *its* semicentennial fund-raising efforts, the tensions and lack of coordination that had existed among the three organizations continued.[335] In a letter between Seminary Board members, the United Synagogue is referred to as "the perennial subject."[336] Similarly, the president of the Rabbinical Assembly acknowledged in his presidential address in 1939 that "matters affecting the relationship between us and...the Jewish Theological Seminary and the United Synagogue…appropriated…a very large portion of our time, energy and thought."[337] Neither the Seminary nor the Rabbinical Assembly had much regard for the work that the organization was doing. In fact, at one point, the Rabbinical Assembly considered forming a new federation of synagogues that would have been a direct challenge to the United Synagogue and a public embarrassment to the Conservative Movement. Notwithstanding these tensions and the feelings that underlined them, both the Seminary and the Rabbinical Assembly knew it was in their organizational self-interest, and the interest of the entire Movement, for there to be good relationships between the three organizations.[338] Simon Greenberg, president of the Rabbinical Assembly, wrote to Finkelstein:

> I think it would be helpful all around if we could still work out some manner of satisfactory relationship

---

335The United Synagogue's fund-raising initiative was launched at a major New York dinner attended by four hundred congregational representatives. Because of the Seminary's semicentennial fund-raising, these efforts by the United Synagogue had to be "considerably curtailed and limited" ("The United Synagogue as a Functioning Institution," 1937).

336Henry S. Hendricks to Lewis L. Strauss, 29 February 1940.

337Rabbi Simon Greenberg in R.A., *Proceedings*, 1938, p. 422.

338"In the eyes of the public, particularly our congregants, the Seminary and Rabbinical Assembly are one" (minutes of Executive Council of Rabbinical Assembly, 13 January 1943).

> between us and the United Synagogue if only on a temporary basis because it certainly would not do our Movement any good to have an open clash.[339]

Even with these widely shared sentiments, the overall relationship among the three organizations did not improve significantly. In 1941, the Seminary undertook to convene a conference of United Synagogue congregations, which the Seminary described as "the congregations to which our graduates are ministering."[340] This conference's purpose was "to bring some of [the Seminary's] new activities to the attention of our congregants, and also [to] try to get the congregations of both the synagogues and the schools to adopt measures necessary in view of the present world emerging."[341] To its dismay, the United Synagogue was neither consulted about this conference nor invited to be a cosponsor, something one would rightly have expected if the relationship between the organizations were better.[342] To Finkelstein, this conference was designed to bring the Seminary's message to the constituency on whom he relied

---

[339]Simon Greenberg to Louis Finkelstein, 12 September 1938.

[340]Louis Finkelstein to Frieda Schiff Warburg, 20 August 1941. In this letter, he refers to congregational sisterhoods and men's clubs as "ours" also, even though they were not a formal part of the Seminary organization.

[341]Louis Finkelstein to Frieda Schiff Warburg, 20 August 1941; Louis Finkelstein to Salo Baron, 25 August 1943; "Program for the Conference on the Seminary and Judaism in the War and Postwar Era," 17 November 1943; Executive Committee Board meeting, 17 November 1943; Louis Levitsky to Louis Finkelstein, 5 September 1941; first report of the president of JTSA for the academic year 1941–42, June(?) 1942; report of Board of Directors, 6 June 1941.

[342]Letter from United Synagogue executive director Rabbi Samuel Cohen to Louis Finkelstein: "In the 30 years of its existence, the United Synagogue has acquired valuable information...and I am therefore surprised that its facilities and knowledge are not being availed of" (Rabbi Samuel Cohen to Louis Finkelstein, 19 May 1942).

for the Seminary's support, and to place the Seminary in direct communication with them. While Finkelstein did use the opportunity to put forth the mission of the Seminary as described in the chapter on "mission," Finkelstein was simultaneously, and not so subtly, making a play for the loyalty of the laity. His message included any number of efforts to bring the lay person into the Seminary's orbit. For example, he offered to train laity as club leaders and youth leaders; he offered adult education both at the Seminary and in the congregations; he offered the creation of popular literature programs so that traditional Hebrew texts would become accessible to lay people through interpretative and creative guides; he spoke of the need for direct contact between the Seminary and lay leaders, which included the establishment of annual lay institutes at the Seminary and the creation of a newsletter to bring Seminary news to the laity; his plan also reached out to Jewish women through the Seminary's own Women's Institute of Jewish Studies and by claiming the Women's League of the United Synagogue as a helpmate.

While all the above could be described as educational ventures totally befitting an academic center, they nonetheless represented an extensive outreach effort by the Seminary to Jewish laity that, given the weakness of the United Synagogue, could only be seen as a threat to its future success.

The United Synagogue thought that until its role in the Movement was properly recognized, it would not be able to do what was expected of it and Conservative Jewry would not mature.

> [T]he United Synagogue of American[*sic*] must be something more than a service agency. It must do even more than is usually associated with the workings of a service agency. The United Synagogue must...become the voice of the laity....It requires something more than

> the finest rabbis, to activate American Jewry. That can only come about when laymen are given their proper places and if their voice is heard in the councils of Conservative Judaism.[343]

The Seminary's position regarding competition with the United Synagogue was cogently stated by a member of the Seminary's staff, Dr. Max Arzt, at a meeting of the Executive Council of the United Synagogue. In his opinion:

> [T]he difficulty in the past existed because of a lack of confidence in the ability of the United Synagogue to do the work which needs to be done. If the United Synagogue undertakes a project and the Seminary and the Rabbinical Assembly feel that the United Synagogue will be able to carry out the project, there will be no effort to duplicate it. If, however, that confidence does not exist, and there is a definite need for these activities, other organizations will perform them....[W]hen the United Synagogue is properly strengthened, we will find that the Seminary and the Rabbinical Assembly will cooperate with it.[344]

At that time, the United Synagogue was seen by the Seminary and the Rabbinical Assembly as, at best, an unnecessary irritant. The Seminary repeated this same slight a year later, when it held another major conference of scholars and laymen around the theme "Strengthening of the Jewish Faith and the Democratic Tradition" and did not include the United Synagogue. In each instance, Finkelstein did not use the occasion for Movement building or the strengthening of organizational ties, but rather to establish the Seminary's agenda and gain the loyalty of those in attendance. In 1944, the Seminary established an annual National Laymen's Institute that consisted of three to five days of study at the Seminary, in which laymen from around the country were

---

[343]Karp, 1964, p. 82.

[344]Minutes of United Synagogue Executive Council, 8 June 1944.

exposed to Seminary faculty. These institutes were sponsored by the Seminary's National Academy for Adult Jewish Studies and the Federation of Jewish Men's Clubs, but not the United Synagogue of America.

The United Synagogue continued to struggle even as the Seminary continued expanding its program. By 1944, the United Synagogue had an indebtedness of $45,000.[345] In 1945, United Synagogue president Sam Rothstein acknowledged to Finkelstein that the organization had failed to accomplish the program that it had set for itself in 1939 when it attempted to reorganize, and he indicated that the failure was due to a lack of leadership in the past.[346] Especially negative was an in-depth analysis of the United Synagogue that had been prepared by its own field director and that revealed an organization fraught with problems. The report spoke of the continuing "lack of harmony between the constituent groups of the Conservative Movement."[347] This was compounded for the United Synagogue by infighting and disorganization. The United Synagogue had a number of affiliates, which, although autonomous, had a connection with it, among them the National Federation of Jewish Men's Clubs, the National Women's League, and the Young People's League.

The National Women's League

The oldest of these affiliated organizations was the National Women's League, the central body of sisterhoods in Conservative synagogues, which had been established in 1918

---

[345]Minutes of Administrative Committee of the United Synagogue, 23 October 1944.

[346]When Rabbi Albert Gordon assumed the position of executive director of the United Synagogue in 1945, he said, "We need a sense of direction and discipline as well." Karp, 1964, p. 75.

[347]Preliminary report on direction of field activities of the United Synagogue, Stanley Rabinowitz, 4 October 1945.

by Mathilde Schechter, the widow of Seminary president Solomon Schechter. It was founded for the purpose of perpetuating traditional Judaism in the home, synagogue, and communities. It focused on youth and adult education, the blind, and the welfare of students at the Seminary.

From its inception, the Women's League had been a strong supporter of the Seminary, raising significant funds for many of its projects over the years. But the United Synagogue had its difficulties with it, as stated above. An example of these difficulties and of the tensions among all the organizations of the Movement was a request made by the president of the United Synagogue to the president of the Women's League. He requested that she appoint five women to meet with United Synagogue, Men's Clubs, and Young People's League representatives to study the relationship of those organizations to the United Synagogue.[348] Mrs. Samuel Spiegel, president of the Women's League (1928–44), said that she would participate in such a meeting only if the Seminary and the Rabbinical Assembly were participants, "since the idea for calling such a meeting is to evolve a program that would strengthen Judaism in America."[349] The response from the United Synagogue president was that such an expanded meeting would be counterproductive![350] Some five years later (1947), a committee made up of professionals representing the Seminary, the Rabbinical Assembly, and the United Synagogue agreed that a meeting be set up "to work out the relationship of the Women's League to the United Synagogue"[351] (and, by implication, to the Seminary). In the

---

[348]Mrs. Samuel Spiegel (president of Women's League) to Louis Moss (president of United Synagogue), 15 June 1942.

[349]Ibid.

[350]Ibid.

[351]Minutes of Inner Committee, 27 November 1947.

meantime, the relationship of the National Women's League to the Seminary continued to grow.

In 1941, when the Seminary was faced with a shortfall in scholarship money, it called together Women's League leadership and got them to agree to raise $10,000 annually for this purpose.[352] In 1942, the Seminary again turned to the sisterhoods and tried to interest them in raising money for a synagogue building. In his appeal to them, Dr. Finkelstein acknowledged that the "Women's League has been so generous to the Seminary and so understanding of our needs."[353]

In 1945, the Women's League launched the Torah Scholarship Fund to raise $100,000 by June 30, 1946, to provide for Rabbinical School scholarships. Only three years later, the Seminary and the 250-sisterhood-strong Women's League were involved in discussions regarding the Women's League's launching a dormitory fund. In 1952, their fund-raising successes led them to formulate plans that ultimately led to a $500,000 pledge for the creation of a residence hall. By 1950, Dr. Finkelstein was moved to write that "the Women's League...is now a bulwark in our fund raising for the whole Seminary."[354] Indeed, between 1942 and 1948, the amount raised by them increased almost twentyfold, from $8,000 to $150,000, exclusive of any special projects.[355]

---

[352]Louis Finkelstein report to Board of Directors, 16 January 1941.

[353]Louis Finkelstein to Mrs. Samuel Spiegel, 11 February 1942; Louis Finkelstein to Mrs. Samuel Spiegel, 25 March 1942.

[354]Louis Finkelstein to Frieda Schiff Warburg, 28 November 1950.

[355]Louis Finkelstein to Mrs. Samuel Spiegel, 25 March 1942; minutes of Inner Committee, 1 April 1948. Finkelstein responded to a Women's League complaint about rabbis' indifference to its work by indicating that he would ask that a talk regarding the Women's League be added to the course in practical problems of the ministry. Louis Finkelstein to Mrs. Samuel Spiegel, 4 May 1943.

The Women's League provides a good example of the Seminary's ambivalent relationship with the Movement. Even though the Women's League affirmed the Seminary's loyalty to the perpetuation of traditional Judaism and even though it was a dedicated Seminary supporter, the Seminary chose to conduct a Women's Institute of Jewish Studies, albeit "in cooperation with a number of Jewish women's organizations, of which the Women's League [was] one."[356] This prompted the Women's League to ask for a meeting with Dr. Finkelstein to discuss the difference between the educational efforts of the Women's League and the educational programs of the Seminary's women's group. According to the president of the Women's League, Mrs. Samuel Spiegel, the sisterhoods were confused by the existence of the Seminary's group.[357] Once again, while the Seminary acknowledged and included in its work the requisite organizations of the Conservative Movement, it steadfastly refused to be limited or defined by any one of them.

Mrs. Spiegel wrote Dr. Finkelstein to seek guidance regarding use of the term "Conservative Judaism," explaining that a number of the League's members thought that their organization's name ought to contain a word describing the type of Judaism that the Women's League stood for. After all, she pointed out, their Reform and Orthodox counterparts used the appropriate descriptive term when referring to themselves. She asked whether the word "Conservative" described the type of Judaism that the graduates of the rabbinical school followed. His reply was interesting for its attempt to acknowledge the Seminary's relationship to the Conservative Movement without actually embracing it. He explained that neither Schechter nor Adler liked the term

---

[356]Conference report, "The Seminary Program and Its Problems," 8 November 1942.

[357]Mrs. Samuel Spiegel to Louis Finkelstein, 22 September 1939.

"Conservative" Judaism, although he acknowledged that Adler, in his later years, sometimes used it because it had become so common a designation for the Seminary's congregations. He explained that Schechter's and Adler's views were similar to those of their predecessors, Drs. Lesser and Morais, namely, that Judaism knows no parties.

> If someone calls us traditional, orthodox, or conservative, it is he who makes a division in Judaism, not us. However, the necessities of organized Jewish life do require some term to describe our general point of view. I think that the members of the faculty generally prefer the term "traditional Judaism." It is a correct description of us because even those congregations of ours which have introduced slight deviations from the norm have done so because, in their opinion, these deviations are themselves essential for the preservation of traditional Judaism. There may be some disagreement regarding this judgement, but there can be no disagreement regarding their sincerity or their purpose.
>
> Summarizing the whole situation, I should say that I believe the term "traditional Judaism" accurately describes the Movement of which all of us are a part. On the other hand, I see no objection to the use of the term "Conservative Judaism" if members of your Board believe it will help make their position clear.[358]

The Women's League provided the Seminary with an organizational ally within the Conservative Movement. Unlike the larger United Synagogue of America or the Rabbinical Assembly, it never challenged the role or authority of the Seminary and its leadership. To the contrary, it was deferential to Finkelstein and worked tirelessly to raise funds on the Seminary's behalf.

---

[358]Louis Finkelstein to Mrs. Samuel Spiegel, 30 September 1941.

The Federation of Jewish Men's Clubs

The Federation of Jewish Men's Clubs of the United Synagogue of America was founded in 1929 "to strengthen the Jewish home, synagogues and the Conservative Movement."[359] In the 1940s, the organization attempted to place greater emphasis than heretofore on the spiritual and religious education of club and regional leaders through the introduction of regional meetings, study programs, and the publication of educational pamphlets. By 1945, there were some eighty-eight clubs and about fifteen thousand members.[360] Although the Men's Clubs were supported by the United Synagogue throughout and even beyond the period of this study, they developed a close association with and a strong allegiance to the Seminary. This was the result of both Dr. Finkelstein's work with early presidents of the organization and, even more so, the influence of Rabbi Joel S. Geffen. Rabbi Geffen had been hired by the Seminary in 1944 as the director of the Department of Field Activities and Community Education. In 1945, he became the spiritual adviser to the Men's Clubs. For him, this group represented yet another constituency to be cultivated for Seminary support. Shortly after coming to the Seminary, he wrote to a colleague that the decision had been made to establish a Manhattan branch of the Men's Clubs, which would serve "as a medium for us to bring the Seminary to greater numbers of our people in Metropolitan New York."[361] As far as Geffen was concerned, this body needed a great deal of attention if it were to emerge as a leading organization within the American Jewish community and a strong supporter of the Seminary.

359Simon and Sperber, 1990.

360Address to Men's Clubs by Joel Geffen, 17 June 1945.

361The postwar years, in particular, saw a growth in the development of new regions. Minutes of Liaison Committee, 13 January 1947.

He observed that the Men's Clubs

> are too loosely affiliated with the synagogues, that the program of activities is stimulated too artificially, that the social aspect seems uppermost, that few organized and planned cultural programs are carried out, that the relationship to the community as a whole is rather weak, and that the growth of interest in the Seminary as the center of our religious life has been made evident, but that it is still a long way from what it should be for the healthy development of our Movement through the growing together of the Seminary, the Rabbinical Assembly, and the United Synagogue of America.[362]

Although the Federation of Men's Clubs was considered an affiliate by the United Synagogue, the Men's Clubs, like the National Women's League, preferred to see themselves as independent. The kind of tension between the organizations that this difference of opinion precipitated was evident at a 1944 Executive Council meeting of the United Synagogue, where the Men's Clubs representatives reported that, being an independent organization, their Executive Council had adopted a resolution calling on the Men's Clubs to raise $10,000 for some *Seminary* programs. The United Synagogue, maintaining that the Federation of Men's Clubs was an affiliate, responded emotionally, reminding the Men's Clubs that

> the Federation is an arm of the United Synagogue and owes its first allegiance to it, and should not embark upon enterprises with other organizations involving the raising of substantial funds; and, furthermore, that the nature of the project likewise should be discussed with and receive the approval of the Parent Body.[363]

A further indication of tension is seen in the Executive Council of the United Synagogue proposal that both the

---

[362]Joel Geffen, address to Men's Clubs, 17 June 1945.

[363]Minutes of United Synagogue Executive Council, 13 January 1944.

Women's League and the Men's Clubs appoint a committee for the purpose of deciding the relationship between themselves and the United Synagogue.

In time, the Men's Clubs grew in stature, having carved out for themselves a role within the Movement. In 1947, discussions were held to find a project for the Men's Clubs to parallel the appeal of the Women's League campaign on behalf of the Seminary. The Men's Clubs agreed to assume responsibility for funding the newly created Leadership Training Fellowship. A goal of $75,000 was set with the understanding that it needed to be raised by fund-raising events rather than by individual solicitations. Also in 1947, representatives of the organization were appointed to the Seminary's Board of Overseers by the United Synagogue,[364] and in 1949, the Rabbinical Assembly adopted a resolution that called for the establishment of a committee to work out a program of cooperation between the Rabbinical Assembly and the Men's Clubs.[365]

By 1954, the Men's Clubs had become deeply engaged in all kinds of youth work and succeeded in amassing a membership of more than thirty thousand Jewish men in the support of the Seminary, the United Synagogue, and the Rabbinical Assembly.[366]

The United Synagogue bemoaned the fact that the Men's Clubs and the Women's League were virtually independent

---

[364]Minutes of Liaison Committee, 13 January 1947.

[365]R.A., *Proceedings*, 1949; resolutions of Rabbinical Assembly Convention, June 1949.

[366]The Young People's League remained a part of the United Synagogue. Its membership had reached an all-time low of twelve affiliated chapters. Its publication efforts were described as in "a very precarious situation" with many of them in need of revision. Thus, it was not difficult for the United Synagogue to retain control of this group. Preliminary report of direction of field activities of United Synagogue, Stanley Rabinowitz, 4 October 1945.

organizations, even though both had stemmed from the United Synagogue. Considerable time and thought were expended by United Synagogue leadership toward "holding on" to these two organizational offshoots, as it had managed to do with the Young People's League.

The United Synagogue continued its struggle to define itself and to rise to the level of proficiency expected by its constituency. It remained frustrated by what it saw as actions by the Seminary that thwarted its efforts to achieve those goals. The Seminary, the United Synagogue complained, constantly failed to mention it in letters in which it thought it belonged or, even more serious, to include it in its description of the Conservative Movement.[367]

The organization's weakness and the extensive role that the Seminary played in the United Synagogue were still evident in the early 1950s in many different ways. For example, when Rabbi Albert Gordon left the United Synagogue as its director, after a period of three years, it was *Seminary* professor and provost Greenberg who succeeded him in that position for the next three years.[368] While United Synagogue president Sam Rothstein hailed the appointment as a "major step toward closer cooperation in the work of all the component parts of the Conservative Movement," the fact remained that a senior Seminary official was now in charge of the organization.[369] Not so coincidentally, it was Rabbi Greenberg who wrote to Maxwell Abbell to ask him to serve as president of the United Synagogue for the very same

---

367Maxwell Abbell to Simon Greenberg, 26 June 1952.

368Rabbi Emil Lehman served as acting director for a brief time until Rabbi Greenberg was appointed. While considering a replacement for Rabbi Gordon, the Liaison Committee considered merging the position of executive director of the United Synagogue with that of director of the Joint Seminary Campaign. Minutes of Rabbinical Assembly Executive Council, 14 February 1950.

369Karp, 1964, p. 83.

period that Greenberg was to serve as its executive director. Although Abbell was an involved leader of the United Synagogue, he was also a strong Seminary supporter. The combination of Greenberg and Abbell gave the Seminary considerable control over the United Synagogue. For example, when Rabbi Greenberg assumed the director's office, he found that his predecessor had established a commission on the formulation of a philosophy and program for the Conservative Movement.[370] Ironically, it was during the Finkelstein years when the self-consciousness of the Conservative Movement began to emerge. Calls for self-definition had become more frequent. Dr. Robert Gordis, for one, as president of the Rabbinical Assembly, remarked:

> [O]ur spokesmen have long hesitated to espouse a distinct orientation in Jewish life, preferring...to be loyal to an adjectiveless Judaism. Unfortunately, the realities have been widely at variance with our wishes; American Jewish life, democratic to the point of anarchy, is replete with clashing viewpoints and philosophies. In attempting to be all things to all men, we are in danger of being nothing to anyone.[371]

This commission was simply to have been a forum for the discussion of such views, but this kind of definitional activity was anathema to the Seminary, which believed, in the words of Dr. Finkelstein, that "to define is to exclude." Since it was the Seminary's desire to appeal to the broadest possible community, it was opposed to such an effort.[372] As Dr.

370When the idea for this commission was first raised by Rabbi Gordon, Finkelstein made it clear that before any national meeting was held, the implications of such a commission would be discussed. Albert Gordon to Max Arzt, 15 December 1947.

371R.A., *Proceedings*, 1946, p. 60.

372In an interview with Dr. Finkelstein (14 February 1984) in which I asked him about this commission, he told me that he did not see such groups as ultimately helpful to the Seminary's mission because the

Greenberg wrote, "It is not that confusion is a desideration, but we must always guard against the fallacy that life can be continued within a series of crystal clear definitions or boundaries."[373] The United Synagogue commission never met again.

A further example of the Seminary's ongoing influence on the United Synagogue was the choice of Greenberg's successor. When Greenberg decided to step down as executive director of the United Synagogue, Abbell consulted "at great length" with Finkelstein about a replacement.[374] The person selected was none other than the Seminary's executive vice president, Rabbi Bernard Segal. And so the influence of the Seminary would continue to be felt within the United Synagogue for years to come.[375]

The United Synagogue was not only in tension with the Seminary, but with the Rabbinical Assembly as well. When the Joint Prayer Book Commission was formed, it was composed of members of the Rabbinical Assembly and the United Synagogue. However, the United Synagogue's representatives were rabbis and not laymen. Now, in 1953, the leadership of the United Synagogue thought it inappropriate to have laity represented by rabbis, even if the rabbis had been chosen by the laity. Accordingly, it was decided that the Rabbinical Assembly would have its own prayer-book committee, and the United Synagogue would have a prayer-book consultative committee, which would sit in with the Rabbinical Assembly committee from time to time

---

strength of the Seminary in those days was that "we could say anybody belonged to us and the outcome of such a commission would have been to exclude individuals."

373Greenberg, 1955, p. 23.

374Maxwell Abbell to United Synagogue officers Charles Rosengarten, George Maslin, B. L. Jacobs, Ben Markowe, 5 January 1953.

375Rabbi Segal served as executive vice president of the United Synagogue from 1953 to 1970.

to give the layman's viewpoint. A somewhat similar change was made with the rabbinic placement commission, whereby the United Synagogue's representatives on this commission would now be laymen who would participate in the deliberations, but who acknowledged that candidate selection would be done exclusively by the rabbinical members of the commission. It was felt that

> [t]his entire "reform" should bring a bit of clarity into our various relationships. It will give the laity the feeling that they are personally involved; while at the same time it assigns to our [the Rabbinical Assembly's] men the work for which they possess the greatest competence.[376]

The patronizing attitude reflected in the above quotation was typical of the attitude toward the United Synagogue by the Rabbinical Assembly. Notwithstanding that the United Synagogue had undergone considerable growth since 1940, it was still possible for a lay leader in 1953 to note that "our people have very little knowledge of what the United Synagogue is doing."[377]

Perhaps the relationship of the Seminary to the Movement at the end of the period under study was best captured in an exchange of correspondence between Finkelstein and the president of the United Synagogue in 1954. The latter, Charles Rosengarten, had solicited from his people suggestions for ways of strengthening the Conservative Movement, the desire for which never really abated within the United Synagogue or the Rabbinical Assembly. One letter, from a leading layman, suggested that the local congregations and communities needed to feel a "closer identification with both the United Synagogue and the Seminary." Most communities, according to this suggestion,

---

[376]"Rabbinical Assembly News," 9 January 1953.

[377]Reuben H. Levenson to Rabbi Herbert Parzen, 30 January 1953.

felt isolated "with no strong bond to the Movement." Furthermore, "the Rabbi is so intent upon cementing relations *inside* the congregation that he dare not go out for a Seminary campaign....As a result, the Seminary and the United Synagogue are 'soft-pedaled.' "[378] Rosengarten suggested to Finkelstein that these problems, in particular, and the general problem of strengthening the Movement, could be addressed if the field staff were increased. He suggested that monies be taken for that purpose from joint fund-raising activities.[379]

Finkelstein's response was a political one in which he suggested that they meet to talk, while at the same time indicating that Rosengarten's suggestion was, at best, but one of many worthwhile areas to which additional campaign funds could be committed.[380] In another letter, Finkelstein attempted to obfuscate the matter by raising several organizational issues. For example:

> Actually, the question of whether money from the joint campaign may be invested in the manner suggested can, at the moment, not be decided because there is no one who really has authority to make such an investment.[381]

In this letter, Finkelstein said that (a) no one can decide if such an expenditure is acceptable, (b) to your suggestion I can add others from the Seminary and the Rabbinical Assembly, and (c) "after you have been in the East for a little while you will feel differently about the need to increase the field staff."[382] Rosengarten was persistent, believing that his idea to increase the field staff was the panacea to the

---

378Correspondence between Louis Finkelstein and Charles Rosengarten, 22 November 1954.

379Ibid.

380Ibid.

381Ibid.

382Ibid.

Movement's ills. In another response, Finkelstein suggested that perhaps Rosengarten should present his case to the Board of the Seminary, since it was the Seminary that would have the burden of financing the project. Finkelstein told Rosengarten that in preparing his remarks, he should consider:

> The question might easily arise whether it would not be better for the United Synagogue for example to postpone some of its youth activities [an important United Synagogue program] in order to find the means for the project.[383]

In other words, if you think the project is so critical, let the United Synagogue finance it. And so, in 1954, some fourteen years into Finkelstein's administration, there was still a feeling among his critics that the Movement lacked cohesiveness and positioning within the larger community. Furthermore, Finkelstein's attitude toward the leadership of the United Synagogue was basically the same as it had been at the beginning of his term.

The Rabbinical Assembly of America

The third major organizational unit of the Conservative Movement, in addition to the Seminary and the United Synagogue, was the Rabbinical Assembly of America. Begun as the Rabbinical Alumni Association of the Seminary in 1901, it had grown by the time of the Finkelstein administration into an independent rabbinical group, the preponderance of whose members were Seminary graduates. In fact, it was in the first year of the Finkelstein administration, 1940, that the Rabbinical Assembly changed

---

[383] Ibid.

its name to the Rabbinical Assembly of America.[384] In a letter to Arthur Hays Sulzberger, Finkelstein offered an explanation for this most recent name change:

> Several years ago the name of the organization was altered [from Alumni Association of JTSA to Rabbinical Assembly of JTSA] because a majority of its members felt that there was a considerable difference between them and the Seminary faculty. The association members did not wish to be bound by the Seminary responsibilities or to submit to the opinions of the faculty members....I do not feel any responsibility for the views of the R.A.; and on the other hand they take no responsibility for my own views.[385]

Although some of the Seminary's strongest critics were rabbis[386] and although the Rabbinical Assembly believed that the Seminary's role should be limited to that of an academic center,[387] the two organizations had a number of common

---

[384]In 1918, with the addition of non-Seminary graduates, it changed its name from the Alumni Association of JTSA to the Rabbinical Assembly of JTSA.

[385]Louis Finkelstein to Arthur Hays Sulzberger, 27 January 1943.

[386]In understanding the relationship between the Seminary and the Rabbinical Assembly, one must keep in mind chapter 5 of this volume, which clearly demonstrates the strained relationship, since many in the Rabbinical Assembly did not embrace the Seminary's mission during Finkelstein's administration.

[387]At one of the Rabbinical Assembly–Seminary Institutes on the Future of Judaism, "the men indicated that they regarded the Seminary as purely an academic institution which should avoid taking active part in organized Jewish life." Louis Finkelstein to Rabbi Mordecai Brill, 4 January 1943. Similarly, in 1953, the Seminary withdrew its participation from the National Jewish Music Council and in that same month declined an invitation to attend the convention of the *Histadrut Ivrit*, stating that by agreement it was only the Rabbinical Assembly and the United Synagogue that operated in the sphere of national community activities. Moshe Davis

interests. Both were united in their unhappiness with the United Synagogue of America; both were committed to the perpetuation of a modern, yet traditional Judaism. Moreover, the Rabbinical Assembly was the fraternity to which Seminary graduates belonged. Most significant, the Assembly's relationship with the Seminary was characterized by the ongoing debates over matters of Jewish law, by the Seminary's reliance on individual rabbis to raise funds for it within the lay community (this was particularly true in the years of the Finkelstein administration), and by its concern for the content and quality of Seminary rabbinical education.

Concerns about the quality of this education began to surface with some force in the Rabbinical Assembly in the 1930s. For example, in 1933, the social-action committee of the R.A. recommended that the Seminary establish as part of its regular curriculum

> a course in social problems which should be obligatory upon every candidate of the Rabbinate. Such a course would acquaint the student both with the field of philanthropy and social service; and with the field of social and economic justice.[388]

Operational in the 1930s was a program in the Rabbinical School that utilized congregational rabbis (who were members of the Rabbinical Assembly) as rabbinic advisers to students. In 1935, student internships with a congregational rabbi for upper classmen and a course on problems of the ministry for lower classmen were instituted.[389] As these

---

to Rabbi Emmanuel Green, National Jewish Music Council, 15 June 1953; Louis Finkelstein to Samuel J. Borowsky, 5 June 1953.

[388]R.A., *Proceedings*, 1933, p. 10.

[389] Those rabbis who participated in the adviser program commented that such a program "would have been of great value to them if they had had it in their student days" (minutes of faculty meeting, 18 December 1935).

changes were occurring, the leadership of the Rabbinical Assembly was also calling for such changes in the curriculum. In 1936, Rabbi Eugene Kohn, president of the Rabbinical Assembly, called upon his colleagues to persuade the Seminary faculty to include in the curriculum "courses that will help orient the rabbi to social problems that confront the world and, more especially, to the Jewish people in modern times."[390] This theme continued to emanate from the Rabbinical Assembly over the years.[391] Their concern about the comprehensiveness of a Seminary education expressed itself in a number of ways. For example, in 1945, members of

---

[390]R.A., *Proceedings*, 1936, p. 259.

[391]In 1941, Rabbi Israel Goldstein called for a review of the Rabbinical School curriculum and for the addition of practical courses (I. Goldstein to Louis Finkelstein, 10 June 1941). The report of the Committee on Alumni Advisors called for a plan that would enable students to become acquainted with the activities and problems of the active rabbinate ("Report of Committee on Alumni Advisors," 1942). In 1943, Rabbi Louis Levitsky informed Finkelstein of a resolution from the Institute on the Future of Judaism for a study of the Rabbinical School curriculum in order to clarify the Conservative position; that all courses be synthesized; that a Department of Religious Sociology be added, etc. (Louis Levitsky to Louis Finkelstein, 23 December 1943). In 1944, several R.A. members were appointed as a committee on revision of the Seminary curriculum (minutes of Executive Council of the R.A., 8 February 1944). In 1946, Rabbi Leo Lang commented that the rabbi is unprepared as a counselor and implicitly criticized the curriculum: "Before we can expect to lead others into wholesome Jewish experiences, and to a realization of the purposefulness of life, we ourselves must have formulated an adequate philosophy of life, must understand Judaism and how its content can be applied to current problems as they affect the individual" (R.A., *Proceedings*, 1946). In 1948, Rabbi William Greenfield said that Seminary graduates were not properly trained to interpret Jewish law (ibid., 1948, p. 126). In 1950, Rabbi David Aronson said that the curriculum needed to emphasize moral issues on Jewish law (ibid., 1950, p. 104). In that same year, the R.A. Committee on College Youth and Campus Activities recommended to the Seminary that it add courses to help rabbis relate effectively with college youths (ibid., p. 40).

the Rabbinical Assembly thought that the Assembly should pass on the fitness of the candidates to the Seminary and, more to the point, Rabbinical Assembly representatives should sit on the Admissions Committee of the Rabbinical School, implying thereby that the Seminary admitted students who were not necessarily fit for the congregational rabbinate.[392]

Indeed, the Rabbinical Assembly leadership often expressed itself in ways that would lead one to think that they were desirous of exercising considerable influence over Seminary affairs. Involvement in the curriculum was but one example. At a 1947 meeting of Rabbinical Assembly representatives and the Seminary, the Rabbinical Assembly recommended that the Seminary not be represented on the newly formed placement commission that was to place rabbis (predominantly Seminary graduates) in synagogues. They also made it clear that they did not want the Seminary to be able to call a conference of United Synagogue congregations unless it involved fund-raising. In other words, the laity of the Movement was to be off-limits to the Seminary for all activities other than fund-raising, which would leave the Seminary open to the criticism that it did not do anything for the congregations except ask for money. All these recommendations bespoke an attempt to curb the Seminary's influence and power within the Movement.

Yet another example of the Rabbinical Assembly's desire to affect Seminary life had to do with an area of internal Seminary governance. The Rabbinical Assembly had been granted three seats on the Seminary's Board of Directors.[393] It was Finkelstein's practice to meet with these representatives just prior to each meeting of the Seminary's board to discuss

---

[392]R.A., *Proceedings*, 1945, pp. 22–23.

[393]In 1949, the R.A. relinquished one of its seats to the United Synagogue (ibid., 1949, p. 86).

with them the agenda of the forthcoming meeting and to ascertain their reactions in advance of the meeting. Whenever possible, he also tried to include the president and the vice president of the Rabbinical Assembly in these meetings.[394] Although the Rabbinical Assembly had representatives on the board, it did not select them. Rather, it presented a list of possible candidates to the Seminary, from which the Seminary chose the actual representatives, thereby maintaining control over who the Assembly's representatives were.[395]

Following one such meeting, one prominent rabbi and R.A. representative to the board wrote Finkelstein a letter expressing his dismay at Finkelstein's lack of candor and process. Specifically, he was upset that although there was an agreement that the Rabbinical Assembly's Executive Committee was to be consulted by the Seminary before making any appointments to its newly formed Board of Overseers, this had not been done. Moreover, the writer was offended when Dr. Finkelstein, at the Board meeting, presented a name to serve as chairman of the Seminary Board without having consulted with the R.A. representative at their meeting prior to the Board meeting.

> I am unhappy rather about the lack of frankness on your part and, correspondingly, the lack of confidence on our part that an experience of this kind, which has now come to me more than once, creates.[396]

For Finkelstein, the issue of the Rabbinical Assembly's intervention in Seminary affairs came down to the question

---

[394]Louis Finkelstein to Louis Levitsky, 11 June 1944.
[395]Ibid.
[396]Louis Epstein to Louis Finkelstein, 30 November 1944.

of the leadership of the Seminary.[397] In a reply to the charges referred to above, he attempted to explain what had happened and why, and that he wanted to make certain that he sought "all the counsel and direction that [he] can possibly get,"[398] but that in the end,

> [w]e must think through the question of the extent to which the Seminary must, for the protection of the purpose it has to serve, be an autonomous, academic institution, as the Rabbinical Assembly must be an autonomous institution.[399]

This notion of the autonomous nature of the Seminary, the Rabbinical Assembly, and the United Synagogue was a defining characteristic of the organizational structure of the Conservative Movement.[400] All three organizations felt strongly about it from the perspective of their *own* organization, but nonetheless each was desirous of exercising considerable influence on the other. It has been suggested that

> [t]he tension...in the relationship of the Seminary to its closest sister organizations, the Rabbinical Assembly and the United Synagogue is not due to the Seminary's effort to impose its image upon them but rather the efforts of some of them to impose their image upon it.[401]

---

[397]In another instance, Rabbi Solomon Goldman was critical of Finkelstein's appointment of Saul Lieberman, who had been had brought from Israel.

[398]Louis Finkelstein to Louis Epstein, 13 December 1944.

[399]Ibid.

[400]The Seminary, Rabbinical Assembly, and United Synagogue "are in theory absolutely autonomous....[T]hey cooperate because they share common goals and common or overlapping leadership....[This] organizational structure [is] unique not only in Jewish history, but in the history of religion generally" (R.A., *Proceedings*, 1960, pp. 152–53).

[401]Ibid., p. 145.

Because all rabbinical graduates of the Seminary automatically became members of the Rabbinical Assembly, there was a shared concern by both organizations not only for the training of the rabbi but also for his welfare. This particular connection between the R.A. and the Seminary was one that brought the two organizations together, but on the other hand, served to distance them both even further from the United Synagogue, which represented the rabbis' employer. Rabbi Arzt, in his capacity as Seminary director of Field Services and Activities, had close ties to his colleagues in the congregational rabbinate and thus knew well the difficulties and indignities suffered by them. In the late spring of 1945, having received several letters of complaint from lay people about their rabbis, he was moved to write to the president of the United Synagogue, Sam Rothstein. Arzt cautioned Rothstein against allowing the laity to engage in "a wholesale condemnation of the Rabbinate" and in "break[ing] down the morale of a young rabbi and caus[ing] him to be disillusioned from the high ideals with which he entertained when he studied for the Rabbinate."[402] The correction for this, said Arzt, was

> in developing responsible and respectable lay leadership....The United Synagogue...has taken for themselves the task of educating the laity to a realization of their responsibilities. [You] must do a more effective job if Judaism is to flourish in this country.[403]

Also emanating out of their joint concern for the rabbi, the Seminary and the R.A. established a special committee in 1948 to consider the offering of the Bachelor of Divinity

---

[402]Max Arzt to Sam Rothstein, 8 June 1945.
[403]Ibid.

degree by the Seminary in order to train individuals to assist the rabbi as professionals.[404]

Jewish Law

The rabbinical graduates of the Seminary had long looked to the Seminary in general, and to its faculty in particular, for guidance in matters of Jewish law. Although so-called law committees had been organized over the years[405] under the auspices of either the Seminary, the United Synagogue, or the Rabbinical Assembly, these bodies were not deemed effective, and thus there continued to be a strong reliance on the faculty of the Seminary to decide questions of Jewish law. By the late 1940s, however, many members of the Assembly had grown frustrated with what they perceived to be the inflexible traditionalism of the faculty.

The congregational rabbi was struggling on a day-to-day basis with the serious religious crises that were affecting his congregants, and with little or no realistic guidance from anywhere as to the position of Jewish law on any of these problems. These rabbis found themselves taking liberties and making innovations on matters of Jewish law. One rabbi bemoaned what he saw as "an increasing individualistic trend [among rabbis] whereby each [one] determines the degree of modification from older patterns...resulting in a heterogeneity that is confusing the laymen" and that left the rabbis uncomfortable.[406] Their discomfort stemmed from the knowledge that their Seminary professors maintained a position different from theirs, a fact about which they felt

---

[404]Report of Special Committee on B.D. degree, 9 December 1948.

[405]In 1917, a United Synagogue Committee on the interpretation of Jewish law was constituted under the chairmanship of Seminary professor Louis Ginzberg. In 1927, a new committee was formed under the auspices of the R.A. This committee underwent a further change in 1948.

[406]R.A., *Proceedings*, 1942, p. 62.

guilty. On the other hand, the rabbis believed deeply that the changes they were engaged in were good for the Conservative Movement and for Jewish life. As one rabbinic observer noted:

> It is an embarrassing position when in those rare moments when you are alone, to see that you are doing things within the Jewish community, permitting yourself a latitude for which you have not worked out a rationale and a justification in your own thinking.[407]

This area of adopting Jewish law to practical situations in the community and the question of who was to do the adaptation had become the field most charged with tension and controversy.[408] Rabbi Max Routtenberg, president of the Rabbinical Assembly in 1949, remarked, "We are literally dooming our men to ineffectiveness and frustration by not providing them with the authority of our collective decision on all the basic issues."[409] Under the leadership of Rabbi Ira Eisenstein, the R.A. sought to challenge the Seminary's authority in this area. The emerging notion was that the members of the R.A. should take these matters into their own hands. One member agreed that just as the R.A. did not ask the Seminary for its endorsement when it issued a statement on social justice or Zionism, so it need not seek the Seminary's endorsement to make public statements on matters of Jewish law.[410] Indeed, some thought that "because of our loyalty to the Seminary, because of our respect for our teachers, because of our attitude toward the Seminary, because we want to please the Seminary, because of that we find ourselves in very embarrassing situations."[411] The rabbis

---

[407]Ibid., 1948, p. 149.
[408]Ibid., 1949, p. 36.
[409]Ibid.
[410]Ibid., 1948, p. 141.
[411]Ibid., p. 145.

felt infantilized by the Seminary in that they perceived that the Seminary expected unconditional loyalty and devotion, without itself having the obligation of looking out for the needs and welfare of the rabbis. As one rabbi put it, "The Seminary regards us as its children...[but] refuses to give us the privilege of regarding [it] as primarily our mother."[412] It was the sense of the Seminary graduates that the Seminary did not deem them qualified to make legal decisions, which was something they found demeaning and humiliating.

Following from the Seminary's long-held conviction that only an academic institution could be the center of the Movement came the desire or need to control what happened religiously within the Movement. For example, Adler in his 1933 address commented that "the course of Judaism may not rest upon the judgment of as many individuals [rabbis] as there are congregations. They should rather consult with Seminary faculty to be sure that they are not just expressing their own individual opinion."[413] On the other hand, the Seminary was not always willing to do what, in this case, the rabbis thought needed to be done. For example:

> The Seminary...insisted...that the students [live] in accordance with Jewish law. From this tradition the Seminary itself has never varied. It has not modified the prayer book, it has not changed the calendar, it has not altered the dietary laws, it has not abolished the second day of the holidays, and although some of its founders and some of its graduates have, without protest from the Seminary, attempted changes in ritual, the Seminary itself has never adopted any of these changes.[414]

---

[412]Ibid., p. 149.
[413]Adler, 1933, p. 234.
[414]Ibid., p. 260.

The result was a significant area of tension between the Assembly, its members, and the Seminary. The question was who—the Seminary or the Rabbinical Assembly—had the authority to decide matters of Jewish law. Many in the R.A. thought that if they were not qualified to exercise such authority, the Seminary should not have ordained them. In the words of one rabbi, "I refuse to remain a preacher without authority."[415]

This tension reached its climax in 1948–53, when the difficult and controversial subject of the *agunah* (chained wife) was dealt with.[416] In 1949, Finkelstein wrote to Seminary professor Louis Ginzberg and expressed his concern for what was happening within the ranks of the R.A. regarding Jewish law: "I would like to discuss with you the whole question of the Rabbinical Assembly Committee on Law....It is a very difficult problem and, frankly, I do not know the solution."[417]

The Assembly was clearly moving forward with its initiatives in this area, and because the Seminary faculty was not represented on the Rabbinical Assembly Committee on Law, the Seminary did not have any real control. That is the way the Assembly wanted it. According to R.A. president Rabbi David Aronson:

> The relationship of parent and children we must and want to maintain. But even as [God] gives freedom of

---

[415]R.A., *Proceedings*, 1948, p. 137.

[416]For an overview of the history of the various law committees, see Nadell, 1988, pp. 1–18; Nudell, 1980. Cf. also Parzen, pp. 212ff. An *agunah* is a woman who is unable to remarry because she has not received a Jewish bill of divorce from her husband, either because he has disappeared and there is no proof of death or because he has refused to give the bill of divorce to her. She therefore remains "chained" and, according to Jewish law, unable to remarry. The congregational rabbi encountered the problem time and again and felt strongly that an otherwise rigid Jewish law had to be overcome.

[417]Louis Finkelstein to Louis Ginzberg, 31 August 1949.

> decision to His children, so must our Alma Mater. A considerate mother places definite limits on how far she may direct the domestic life of her grown-up children.[418]

Finkelstein made several attempts to redress the imbalance that had developed between the R.A. and the Seminary in the sphere of Jewish law. He knew that he needed to regain some element of control over the direction that the discussions in the Rabbinical Assembly were taking in this area, lest decisions be made by the R.A. that, he believed, would have adverse consequences for the Seminary. He managed to regain the upper hand through his address at the 1949 Rabbinical Assembly convention, when he spoke of the Seminary faculty's "change of heart" regarding its involvement in the Movement and in current affairs:

> For many years the members of the Faculty of the Seminary liked to consider their work as limited to instruction and research....In the course of this year, however, the members of the Faculty have become increasingly convinced that this seclusion...is not to the best interests of Judaism. They have come to realize that three institutions through which Conservative Judaism expresses itself—the Rabbinical Assembly, the United Synagogue and the Seminary—are not separate but three phases of what is essentially the same institution....We cannot walk off each in his own direction....
>
> We on the Faculty feel, therefore, the urging of more co-thinking between ourselves and the Rabbinical Assembly particularly on questions of Jewish life. We feel too that there must be more effective co-thinking between us and the leadership of the United Synagogue....

---

[418]R.A., *Proceedings*, 1950, p. 100.

> This change of heart on the part of the Faculty is due to the influence of the Rabbinical Assembly.[419]

In addition, just prior to the 1949 convention, Finkelstein, together with Seminary professors Mordecai Kaplan and Simon Greenberg, appeared before the Executive Council of the Rabbinical Assembly and indicated a desire on behalf of the Seminary to work more closely together, not only in this area of Jewish law but in general.

> [I]n the philosophy of our Movement there need not be that dichotomy between academic aloofness and rabbinic responsibility toward their varying congregations; that there is room in our Movement for diverse points of view, and that the Seminary need not be—should not be—apart from the problems which the rabbis in the field must face.[420]

As a result of this reaching out by the Seminary, the Rabbinical Assembly proposed the calling of a special convention to take place that fall for the purpose of exploring the "far-reaching" implication of such joint action. Specifically, the convention was to consider, yet again, the relationship of the three groups that constituted the Conservative Movement and

> to discuss the future course of action which will result from a definition of our relationship [and] to discuss and, if possible, to decide, on a method of implementing a program for the formulation of a philosophy for Conservative Judaism.[421]

Although the rabbis wrestled with their discomfort in breaking away from the authority of the Seminary faculty, they nonetheless moved forward with their agenda, believing that the "defining of [their] position would enable [them] to

---

[419]Ibid., 1949, p. 36.
[420]Ibid., p. 140.
[421]Ibid.

win adherents to [the Conservative] Movement."[422] And as they moved forward, particularly in the areas of marriage and divorce, Finkelstein's concern deepened once again:

> The other matter that is worrying me very much is the [R.A.] Committee on Law. I understand that the Committee on Law is having a weekend seminar in Atlantic City for discussion of David Aronson's proposal and similar matters.[423] If that is correct, the time has come to take a firm stand with regard to the situation. Obviously, the Rabbinical Assembly cannot act as if it could make any decision whatever in regard to the basic orientation of our Movement. There are areas in which the R.A. ought to act alone; but decisions, even in matters of law, which determine our relationship with Klal Yisrael [the entire Jewish community], are in a different category. They belong to the whole Movement, and therefore are in the area of the Liaison Committee.[424]

Finkelstein knew that he was again losing control of the situation and that his usual position of permitting the constituent organizations to do whatever they liked as long as it did not hurt the Seminary had given rise to a serious problem. He knew that some action was required on his part to regain control. He proposed that there be formed a tripartite committee of which he would be chairman and the fourth vote, "to work out the areas in the philosophy of Conservative Judaism, and Jewish standards of conduct, including Jewish law, which require an overall commission, and which can be delegated to the R.A."[425] Finkelstein acknowledged that "we are touching a hornets' nest, in even taking up the matter in this way; but frankly from what I see

---

[422]Ibid., 1950.

[423]Rabbi David Aronson, past president, had authored a plan to deal with the plight of the *agunah*.

[424]Louis Finkelstein to Simon Greenberg, 10 December 1951.

[425]Ibid.

here, we need time to recapture some of our alumni and many of our constituent congregations, spiritually."[426]

Finkelstein knew that this plan was nothing more than a "holding operation," but saw little choice. To give free rein to the Rabbinical Assembly would be, to his mind, to spell "disaster" in the form of an "amalgamation with Reform [Judaism]." As Finkelstein had predicted, his attempt to regain control of this situation produced further unhappiness in the R.A. The way in which Finkelstein had proposed to "put the genie back in the bottle" was to convene a conference between the Rabbinical Assembly and the Seminary's Rabbinical School faculty to deal with the relevant issues of marriage and divorce. In typical Finkelstein fashion, he sought to broaden the agenda, stating that "the real question is whether it is possible for Jews in America to live in accordance with Jewish law."[427] He conceptualized the conference in terms of a world conference:

> The establishment of such a world conference is a basic need of our time, everywhere; and would be in effect the re-establishment of the Anshe Kneset Ha-Gadolah and just as that group built the bridge between Bible and Talmud, so our world conference, given sufficient and effective guidance, can build the bridge between Talmudic and future Judaism.[428]

The conference idea was not received with favor in the Rabbinical Assembly because, by the participation of the Seminary faculty in a joint conference, the Assembly would be giving up its independence. Rabbinical Assembly president Rabbi Ira Eisenstein was, in fact, quite annoyed by the idea

---

[426]Ibid.

[427]Minutes of meeting to consider Joint Conference on Jewish Law, 22–23 December 1952.

[428]Louis Finkelstein to Max Davidson, chairman of Law Committee, 17 June 1952.

and thought that the Seminary was being manipulative and controlling:

> About four years ago at a Convention when we reorganized the Committee on Law...Professor Finkelstein stood up in front of the convention and gave us his blessing. He said...the Seminary obviously cannot be a part of it, we must stand above these controversies, we are an academic institution, but you go with our blessing.[429]

The Rabbinical Assembly wanted their organization to be open to all views and that this desire would be precluded by the participation of the Seminary faculty in the rendering of any decision. They resented the notion that now that they were serious, the Seminary seemed to want to take back the freedom it had bestowed upon them.

> Consider how long and effectively we were frustrated [by the Seminary] in our efforts to solve the problem of the agunah....[H]ow clever and inventive was the strategy by which we surrendered control...and tied our hands. And who knows whether we ever will be able to get out of this partnership.[430]

Indeed, Finkelstein's deepest feelings about this situation were revealed in a letter to Dr. Saul Lieberman, rector of the Seminary and one of its leading authorities on Jewish law. He told Lieberman that this conference was "our last chance to deal with the problem of Jewish law effectively in this country."[431] He stressed the need for the Seminary and its faculty to get someone to take the application of Jewish law to modern-day problems seriously; otherwise, unqualified people would assume such authority. Finkelstein acknowledged that practical matters of Jewish law were more

---

[429] R.A., *Proceedings*, 1952, p. 61.

[430] Ibid., 1955, pp. 134–35.

[431] Louis Finkelstein to Saul Lieberman, 25 March 1952.

pressing for pulpit rabbis than for many at the Seminary. Yet he was astute enough to know that such a view would not sit well with members of the pulpit rabbinate. Accordingly, he discussed with Lieberman the possibility of reassigning a member of the rabbinics faculty from pure talmudic research to the handling of issues of Jewish law, for the alternative to taking such a step would be "the development of a Bet Din [court of law] of unqualified men."[432]

Procedures between the Seminary and the R.A. were negotiated, which enabled the law conference to go forward. The outcome was one that both organizations were able to accept. Following the conference, Finkelstein wrote to one Seminary participant to thank him for his participation and remarked that had the conference failed, "the future would have brought a final and irrevocable break with the Rabbinical Assembly."[433]

The rabbis of the R.A., most of whom were Seminary graduates, respected their Seminary teachers and, for the most part, were grateful for their Seminary education; yet there was a certain disappointment and frustration on their part toward the Seminary. They were disappointed that the formal Jewish education that they had received had prepared them insufficiently to handle the practical problems of the congregational rabbinate, and they did not think that their alma mater was providing the religious leadership that the Conservative Movement needed. Moreover, they believed that they should have a greater role in helping the Seminary provide that leadership. After all, they were both learned graduates of the Seminary and experienced communal leaders and were thus, to their minds, most qualified to at least share the leadership of the Movement with the Seminary.

---

[432]Ibid.

[433]Louis Finkelstein to Saul Lieberman, 26 February 1953.

Leadership Training Fellowship and the Ramah Camps

The Seminary's relationship to the Conservative Movement was also expressed through two other significant programs that it created or helped to create: the Leadership Training Fellowship; and the Ramah Camps.

Both these programs came into existence at more or less the same time as possible answers to the pressing question of how the Conservative Movement could find and train new leaders.[434] The Leadership Training Fellowship (LTF) was an effort to identify and cultivate the best young people within Conservative synagogues and lead them into Jewish public service. The idea for such a program came from Dr. Mordecai Kaplan. Initially, his plea was directed to individual rabbis to find the most capable young people in their congregations so that the rabbis, together with the Seminary, could develop these young people as future leaders. While the Young People's League of the United Synagogue was geared to all young people within the Movement, LTF was seen as an elite group. Kaplan believed that "very few Jewish young men and women of ability and character consider making Jewish public service their vocation."[435] So, Kaplan argued, the rabbinate

> must concentrate on the effort to persuade desirable young people to see in Jewish public service opportunities for a satisfying career, as well as for being identified with a great cause.[436]

Not only should future leaders be identified by the Movement, as Kaplan urged, but equally important, according to Dr. Moshe Davis (a member of the administration), the Movement should prepare them:

---

[434]Schwartz, 1976, p. 8.
[435]Mordecai Kaplan to R.A., 11 May 1945.
[436]Ibid.

> We do not train our own people. We rely virtually exclusively on the students that are prepared—and I would say ill prepared—in other institutions....Unless we start preparing our own leadership, the time may come along when we will not have that leadership.[437]

The first Leadership Training Fellowship conference, attended by 144 people affiliated with some thirty-three United Synagogue congregations, was held at the Seminary on December 26 and 27, 1945.[438] Regional chairmen were appointed to strengthen the work of the Rabbinical Assembly committee that they had established to work with Dr. Kaplan in developing this program. As a result of the opening conference, the leaders became aware of the magnitude of work that the Fellowship would require. They quickly realized that they had created something for which they were not properly prepared; it became clear that every member of the Fellowship would require individual guidance and follow-up.[439] To help deal with the size of the program, the leaders of the program proposed that sponsorship of the Fellowship be expanded to include the United Synagogue, the National Federation of Men's Clubs, and the Women's League, in addition to the Rabbinical Assembly and the Teachers Institute of the Seminary. In other words, what was being suggested was that LTF be a program of the entire Conservative Movement.

In spring 1947, LTF had a membership of 270 young people from fifty congregations.[440] Annual conferences were held at the Seminary in order to unify the organization. In addition, a monthly bulletin was started. Most significant was

---

[437]Schwartz, p. 5.

[438]Louis Finkelstein to Board of Directors, 25 October 1946.

[439]Kaplan report on the Teachers Institute–Seminary College of Jewish Studies, 1 March 1946.

[440]R.A., *Proceedings*, 1947, p. 74.

the announcement of the appointment of a full-time director, effective fall 1947. A year later, the Fellowship was able to boast of chapters in Philadelphia, Hartford, Chicago, Cleveland, New York, and Los Angeles at the newly established University of Judaism. With almost three years of activity complete, the Seminary's Teachers Institute was looking forward to increased enrollment from the graduates of this program. Given the need for increased funding to support the burgeoning Fellowship, the news that the Men's Clubs would undertake its funding for the 1947–48 year was greeted with enthusiasm.[441]

Perhaps the program's single biggest problem, however, was the lack of commitment to it by the rabbinical community. In the Fellowship's first three years, we note again that where the local rabbi gave of his time to mentor the enrolled students, the program was eminently successful. Unfortunately, too few rabbis seemed prepared to make this commitment. In June 1949, there were seventy congregations that participated out of a possible pool of more than three hundred.[442]

While the Leadership Training Fellowship never became a popular or fashionable program, it did, for the period of this study, accomplish Kaplan's original mission, which was to draw young people into service within the Jewish community. "One of the truly happy results of the magnificent Leader's [*sic*] Training Fellowship program has been the encouragement given to young men from the south, the Midwest and the far west to enter the Rabbinical School."[443]

The other activity that connected the Seminary to the Movement was the Ramah Camps. The first Camp Ramah, spearheaded by a local Chicago rabbi, was founded in 1947 in

---

[441]Ibid., p. 124.

[442]*Rabbinical Assembly Bulletin*, convention issue, June 1949.

[443]R.A., *Proceedings*, 1952, p. 31.

Conover, Wisconsin. It received support from the United Synagogue to acquire its grounds.[444] It was the very complement to LTF in that it would carry on in an even more intensive fashion over the summer the same serious learning and Jewish living in line with the Conservative Movement to which the LTF was committed throughout the remainder of the year. Initially, Finkelstein was opposed to the idea for financial reasons and for fear of exposing the Seminary to costly legal action in the event of a camp accident.[445] Nevertheless, the camp opened in the summer of 1947, with close to a hundred campers, thirty-two of whom had come from LTF.[446] The first season was so successful that Provost Greenberg, after a visit to the camp, was moved to report to Finkelstein:

> We are becoming more and more what I have recently in my own mind termed an "integrated spiritual enterprise," paralleling an integrated industrial plant

---

[444]For additional history of Camp Ramah, cf. Burton I. Cohen, 1989; and Brown, 1997.

[445]Schwartz, 1976, pp. 18, 10. Evidently, after four successful summers, Finkelstein felt better about the endeavor, for Greenberg wrote, "I am glad that you share with me more fully now than heretofore the enthusiasm in behalf of summer camps" (Greenberg to Louis Finkelstein, 12 August 1950). Although his experience helped him to make peace with the reality of the camps, he never lost his concern. As the 1955 camping season was ending, Finkelstein wrote to Seminary faculty member Seymour Siegel: "Your letter came on the Monday after I spent some hours in great concern about our Ramah camps in the East. This is nothing less than a miracle. The whole situation points to the problems that Ramah camps pose. They are very different from those posed by the Seminary both practically and morally. Obviously, accidents can happen in the Seminary. Nevertheless, here we have a staff and are part of a big city. The sending of hundreds of children to camps under delegated guardianship always gave me some tremors. Still, I suppose, we have to carry on the Ramah camps and try to avoid their perils" (Louis Finkelstein to Seymour Siegel, 22 August 1955).

[446]Nadell, p. 345; minutes of Inner Committee, 2 June 1947.

> which starts with controlling its own source of raw material, and ends with its own outlets for selling its output to the ultimate consumer. Camps like Ramah are a vital need of our Movement in the future. They give us the only real significant contact with sources of our raw material.[447]

During the course of the next year, the Seminary, whose involvement with the camp had been limited to staff hiring and program supervision, became a financial partner, loaning the camp $5,000.[448]

In spring 1948, the Seminary announced the opening of a second camp in the New England area, to be followed by another to open in 1950 in the Poconos. The Seminary retained responsibility for the hiring of staff and the content of educational and religious programs.

In the fall of 1948, Finkelstein was pleased with the development of his program to build Jewish leadership. In a letter to Sylvia Ettenberg, a founder of the Ramah Camps and member of the Seminary staff, he wrote:

> It seems that we are making headway along all fronts and that at long last it is beginning to look as though the efforts in which we are engaged both in the educational and in the congregational field will prove effective. The Leader's [*sic*] Training Fellowship is doing wonderfully! Camp Ramah is about to multiply itself into a number of them. The Teachers Institute registration, is...much greater then ever before.[449]

By 1952, Finkelstein himself spoke highly of the Ramah experience, expressing hope that the Movement might start

---

[447]Greenberg to Louis Finkelstein, 30 August 1947.

[448]Exchange of letters between R. R. Kaufman, Stroock, and Arzt, 6 April 1948, 30 March 1948, 3 September 1947, and 12 September 1947. Initially, the camp was sponsored by the Chicago Council of Conservative Synagogues and the Midwest branch of the United Synagogue.

[449]Louis Finkelstein to Sylvia Ettenberg, 24 November 1948.

up such a camp in Israel. Indeed, enthusiasm for the camping program was infectious, for anyone familiar with its operations saw it as perhaps the most important educational undertaking of the entire Conservative Movement. Maxwell Abbell wrote: "Ramah is so vital to the Conservative Movement that I have no hesitation in stating that it would be my strong recommendation that the Endowment of the Seminary help finance [it]".[450]

Finkelstein, no less impressed with Ramah than was Abbell, reminded him that "we dare not allow our enthusiasm for Ramah to hinder the development of the Seminary." The Seminary had a $300,000 deficit in fiscal 1952. Thus, it could not fund a third camp, nor could it permit Ramah to engage in independent fund-raising, thereby siphoning off badly needed funds from the Seminary campaign.[451]

In 1951, the National Ramah Commission (NRC) was established to oversee the camps' operation. Even with the appointment of this Commission, which included representatives from the United Synagogue and the Rabbinical Assembly, the Seminary maintained control of the religious and educational aspects of the camps.

The NRC was staffed by Rabbi Bernard Segal, who at the time was also the executive vice president of the Seminary. Finkelstein believed that the Commission's functions should be to promote "ideas and interest people in Camp Ramah" while leaving the task of administering the camps to the Seminary.[452]

In 1953, the NRC acquired *its* first camp in East Hampton, Connecticut, subsequently purchasing another in 1955 in California. By this time, the Ramah Camps had become important in the overall educational program of the

---

[450]Maxwell Abbell to Bernard Segal, 24 August 1952.

[451]Louis Finkelstein to Maxwell Abbell, 5 September 1952.

[452]Ibid., 23 November 1954.

Seminary and were viewed as having the potential of bringing about a revolution in the attitude of future Jewish leadership. Just as the relationship between the Seminary and the United Synagogue was characterized by bickering and issues of control, so was Ramah's relationship with the United Synagogue.

Because of their early involvement in the creation of that first camp, the United Synagogue saw itself as a key player in the Ramah movement. Indeed, the letterhead of the National Ramah Commission acknowledged that it was a commission of "the United Synagogue of America in cooperation with the Teachers Institute, the Jewish Theological Seminary of America." Realistically, however, once the first camp was launched, the United Synagogue had little to do with its operation or development. On the contrary, it was the Seminary, because of its supervision of the programs and the staff, that set educational and religious policies. In addition, the Seminary became financially involved in the purchase and renovation of the camps. With this in mind, Abbell, as president of the National Ramah Commission, sought to reorganize it in such a way as to enable the Seminary to take control over the entire Commission. Abbell was convinced that a change was in order:

> The more I think about the Ramah situation the more I am convinced it was a mistake in the first place for the Seminary not to have made it a committee like the museum etc. Perhaps it was the reluctance of the Seminary or its indifference or skepticism as to its importance and future value that influenced the decision to permit the United Synagogue to take hold of the Ramah program. Be that as it may, I have been gradually coming around to the opinion it should be under the Seminary's jurisdiction; that there is no need for any national Ramah commission; but that the Seminary should appoint a committee on Ramah similar to the committee on the Museum; that the

> Seminary or its subsidiary should own the camp properties and should be in charge of the program. I presume there would still be room for the United Synagogue to be represented on such a committee.[453]

Abbell had been engaged in a dialogue with Sam Rothstein, then president of the United Synagogue, about the organizational control of the camps. The former acknowledged that the "camp idea originated in the United Synagogue" and that it was the Chicago Council of the United Synagogue that succeeded in raising its initial funds, but because the staff was provided by the Teachers Institute of the Seminary, conduct of its operations must be under the Seminary's aegis.[454] Abbell's argument for change was based on the fact that both the Connecticut and Poconos camps were owned by a subsidiary corporation of the Seminary. The Seminary thus was entitled to be the key supervisor of the camps. Moreover, it was the intention of the National Ramah Commission to transfer both the Wisconsin and the Los Angeles camps to a corporation controlled by the Seminary. Furthermore, the Seminary, through its Teachers Institute, had made substantive expenditures in connection with the camps.[455] Rothstein, conversely, argued that since both the Commission on Jewish Education and the National Academy for Adult Jewish Studies were solely United Synagogue activities, Ramah should be the same. Abbell countered,

---

[453]Maxwell Abbell to Simon Greenberg, 15 April 1955.

[454]In fact, according to Dr. Moshe Davis, another member of the Seminary administration who was deeply involved from the beginning, Rothstein's "recollection of the early history...is not quite accurate." Davis maintains that the Teachers Institute of the Seminary "planned its future around Ramah [and] that this was done with the full authorization of Finkelstein and the Seminary Board....Furthermore, the Seminary invested heavily in Ramah" (Moshe Davis to Maxwell Abbell, 11 April 1955).

[455]Maxwell Abbell to Sam Rothstein, 6 April 1955.

explaining that the magnitude of the Ramah enterprise was already such that it could not be solely a United Synagogue program. Simon Greenberg best characterized the situation in a response to Abbell, in which he expressed his gratefulness to Abbell for confronting Rothstein and added:

> We are wasting so much of our strength in bickering and in creating organizational set-ups that are in many ways merely impedimenta [*sic*] that we simply are putting stumbling blocks in our own way. What an impossible job from an administration point of view it would be if everyone of our enterprises were to be organized along the same lines that Ramah is today organized. We simply could not begin to function efficiently [in]...any one of our...other major projects.[456]

The National Ramah Commission was ultimately changed to reflect Seminary control; however, the United Synagogue continued to participate in the deliberations.

The Leadership Training Fellowship and the Ramah Camps, the latter in particular, provide two more examples of the organizational tensions that existed between the Seminary and the Conservative Movement. While both these programs served the needs of the Movement, they were, for the most part, controlled by the Seminary, which made some members unhappy. Thus, even when the Seminary was making efforts to serve the Movement, issues of power and turf surfaced to exacerbate the already existing tensions and to impede the likelihood of a closer working relationship among these groups.

---

[456]Simon Greenberg to Maxwell Abbell, 12 April 1955.

Chapter 7
The Conservative Movement Comes Together

Efforts to bring about interorganizational cooperation led to the creation of a coordinating committee and the establishment of a joint fund-raising campaign. This campaign required the Seminary to have a closer association with the Movement, heightening already existing tensions. Reliance on the Movement for financial support was problematic. Nonetheless, both the Movement and the individual organizations realized significant growth.

Plan for Interorganizational Cooperation

Despite ongoing discord among the Seminary, the United Synagogue, and the Rabbinical Assembly, momentum for cooperation was building. This momentum was due to a number of different needs within the Movement. The Seminary needed to raise more money to fund its ambitious mission. Both the Seminary and the Rabbinical Assembly had been working for some time with the United Synagogue to help it strengthen itself. And the call from rabbis and laity for greater unity within the Movement had not ceased. In addition, Finkelstein's critics were growing ever more strident, and the Seminary needed to be at least somewhat responsive to their demands.

The development of a plan for interorganizational cooperation was a major first step toward the coming together of the Conservative Movement. Just as the Seminary held conferences for the laity, it also brought the rabbis together. As a result of these rabbinical conferences, the Seminary established the Institute on the Future of Judaism and asked Rabbi Solomon Goldman of Chicago, Finkelstein's erstwhile critic, to serve as its director. At one of the meetings of the 1942 Institute, the body recommended that yet another committee be established to study the relationship of the Seminary, United Synagogue, and Rabbinical Assembly to one another. Rabbi Milton Steinberg of New York, another Finkelstein critic, was invited to serve on this committee, which was asked to investigate three areas:

> 1) What type of organization of our congregations would be most effective and most useful and would we seek to establish if we did not already have certain institutional commitments in that direction?
>
> 2) To what extent do our present congregational organizations meet the needs?
>
> 3) How can the situation now existing be remedied so as more nearly to approach the ideal conditions described in reply to question 1?[457]

What is noteworthy is that the issue of the relationship among the organizations in general, and the problems with the United Synagogue in particular, were still around in 1943, three years into Finkelstein's administration.

Indeed, the agenda for the 1943 Institute on the Future of Judaism represented a balancing of Finkelstein's and Goldman's concerns. Goldman, as we know from his criticism of Finkelstein and the Seminary discussed in the previous chapter, wanted the Seminary to be more Movement-oriented. Thus, the Institute included a session entitled "The Intensification of the Conservative Movement." Reflecting Finkelstein's concerns, there was a session entitled "Judaism and the Contemporary Scene."

This institute succeeded in producing a detailed and comprehensive statement that spelled out an arrangement for

---

[457]Louis Finkelstein to Solomon Goldman, 11 December 1942.

a working relationship between the Seminary, the United Synagogue, and the Rabbinical Assembly, which included a plan for the integration of administrative and secretarial staff. The plan also proposed a joint fund-raising campaign that was to benefit all three organizations. At that time, each organization raised its own funds. However, the Rabbinical Assembly, in addition to raising its own support, mostly from membership dues, was also assisting the Seminary with its fund-raising efforts.

This plan for interorganizational cooperation affirmed several key points that had been, and continue to be, among the defining characteristics of the Conservative Movement, organizationally speaking. Specifically, it acknowledged that the Seminary, the Rabbinical Assembly, and the United Synagogue were "mutually independent" and that each should continue to have "complete autonomy" while minimizing friction, maximizing cooperation, and relating to one another with mutual respect. Moreover, the proposal reaffirmed the Seminary's place as an institution of learning at the head of the Movement as well as its role in both "the general system of American education" and the world of Jewish learning. The proposal also made the specific recommendation that the long-time executive director of the United Synagogue, Rabbi Samuel Cohen, be given a leave of absence and then permanently retired. Although this action had been under discussion for several years, because the Seminary and the Rabbinical Assembly saw Cohen as one of the obstacles to a better relationship with the United Synagogue, the United Synagogue leadership had managed to sidestep it.[458] Recognizing that at that moment the

---

[458]For example, Rabbi Louis Levitsky, president of the Rabbinical Assembly, wrote to Dr. Finkelstein to report on a meeting he had with the president of the United Synagogue, among others. "I indicated to Mr. Rothstein [president of the United Synagogue] that one of the terms of

relationships between the three organizations were strained and that there would be a long process in order to bring these recommendations to fruition, the proposal stated that, if necessary, the plan would be implemented by the Seminary and the Rabbinical Assembly. In other words, if the United Synagogue did not accommodate itself to this proposal, the Seminary and the Rabbinical Assembly would force its compliance. The entire proposal was the source of much discussion over the course of the next year.

In the meantime, leaders such as Rabbi Louis Levitsky, president of the Rabbinical Assembly, continued to call for coordination among the "arms" of the Movement, as the three organizations referred to one another. At the 1944 convention of the Assembly, he acknowledged in his presidential address that the process to improve relations was moving slowly. He emphasized that it was essential to

> face the American Jewish Community as a "United Conservative Judaism" with three coordinating branches, each functioning in an area assigned to it by mutual agreement....We must be big enough to face [new situations and readjustments] for the good of our common cause.[459]

Similarly, two rabbis from Texas who had been interviewed as part of a fund-raising study for the Seminary observed:

> We see at the Seminary the beginning of a Movement which can amount to a great deal in American Israel. The time is ripe for something to happen; it should

reference upon which those conversations [re: reorganization of United Synagogue] were predicated was that Dr. Samuel Cohen be retired" (Levitsky to Finkelstein, 16 June 1944). At the same time, Rabbi Levitsky was quoted at a meeting of the Seminary's Board of Directors to have said: "No cooperation with the United Synagogue would be possible while the United Synagogue retained its present executive director" (minutes of Board of Directors meeting, 22 June 1944).

[459]R.A., *Proceedings*, 1944.

> start soon. There are a dozen avenues where it can begin to work, not the least of which is the text-book material. It is time to show the congregations that the Conservative Movement is alive.[460]

Notwithstanding such idealistic sentiments, the reality continued to be one of strained relations and mistrust. The Rabbinical Assembly, for example, planned to compile a prayer book, only to find that the United Synagogue, having had full knowledge of the Assembly's intention, had announced a plan to do the very same thing. The Seminary's Board leadership remained opposed to both a joint campaign among the three organizations and to the sharing of Seminary funds.[461] Eventually, however, the Board of the Seminary did accept the idea of an allocation out of Seminary funds for both the Rabbinical Assembly and the United Synagogue.[462] A rabbinic chaplain wrote to the Seminary to complain about problems with rabbinical placement in pulpits and was told that "the major difficulty is due to the...United Synagogue....We are moving as far as we are permitted by those who think of institutional loyalty rather than of the interests of the men whose problems should be solved."[463]

After almost a year of debate within and among the three organizations, substantial progress had been made toward agreement on the 1943 proposal for interorganizational cooperation, particularly between the Seminary and the United Synagogue. At a meeting of the Seminary Board, Judge Rifkind, who had served as chairman of the Seminary's committee in negotiations with the United Synagogue, reported:

---

[460]The rabbis interviewed were A. H. Blumenthal and Sanders A. Tofield. Series of ten interviews, May 1943.

[461]Henry S. Hendricks to Lewis L. Strauss, 29 February 1940.

[462]Executive Committee Board meeting minutes, 5 January 1944.

[463]Chaplain Brill to Bernard Segal, 23 May 1944.

> Since the United Synagogue and Seminary have many objectives in common, it is advisable that both institutions follow parallel courses; and in order to achieve this and avoid duplication of effort and conflict of purpose it is recommended that an interorganization liaison committee be formed.[464]

It was also approved at this meeting that there would be a joint fund-raising campaign that would be called "Campaign for the Jewish Theological Seminary in Cooperation with the United Synagogue and Rabbinical Assembly." Furthermore, the Board of Directors of the Seminary voted to create a Board of Overseers of the Seminary, whose membership would be chosen from among Jews in Conservative congregations in consultation with the Rabbinical Assembly.[465]

The resolution of the "United Synagogue problem" was hailed by Rabbi Max Arzt of the Seminary administration as a "step [that] means that our Movement is facing a day of rejuvenation."[466] In its internal newsletter, the United Synagogue enthusiastically reported the agreement with the headline "United Synagogue, Rabbinical Assembly and Seminary implement their unity" and in the story compared it to the agreement of the big three world powers at Yalta![467] In general, the agreement was seen by most in the Movement as

---

[464]Minutes of JTS Board of Directors, 29 November 1944. Rifkind was deeply involved in the resolution of the United Synagogue problem. It was not unusual for him and Finkelstein to meet on a Sunday to discuss the formulation of policy regarding this matter (Finkelstein to Greenberg, 29 September 1944).

[465]The creation of this Board of Overseers might well have been one of the ways in which Finkelstein tried to quiet his critics. Steinberg, in particular, called for a larger role for the laity within the Seminary (cf. p. 111 of this vol.). The creation of this board at least created the illusion that this was now happening.

[466]Max Arzt to Chaplain Brill, 27 December 1944.

[467]"News of the United Synagogue," March 1945.

an extremely positive sign that would now "inaugurate a new era in the development of Conservative Judaism in this country."[468]

This agreement was a turning point in the history of the Conservative Movement, accomplishing three things: it served to further strengthen the role of the Seminary as the head of the Movement; it deepened the economic connection between the Seminary and the Movement; and it forced the Seminary to become more deeply involved with the "affairs" of the Conservative Movement, largely through the creation of the joint campaign, which obligated the Seminary to fund the Rabbinical Assembly and the United Synagogue. It was from this point forward that the three national organizations put forth what could appear to have been a unified public face. The agreement also raised expectations in the minds of Conservative Jews about the sense of the Movement that would now prevail and about the effectiveness of the United Synagogue organization that would materialize.

The new agreement was, however, far from a panacea. The lack of a clearly defined ideology, the lack of a strong sense of the Movement, and the organizational tensions were all firmly rooted in philosophical differences about the nature of modern traditional Judaism in America. Yet because the adoption of the agreement did raise expectations for many Conservative Jews, it was as if the Movement had to make up years of lost opportunity virtually overnight.[469]

Liaison Committee

The Liaison Committee was formed in 1946. This committee, which existed in one form or another for over twenty years, was made up of the top leadership of each of the three constituent organizations. The Seminary was represented by

---

[468]Robert Gordis to Joel Geffen, 16 January 1945.

[469]R.A., *Proceedings*, 1945.

its top administrative and board people, including Louis Finkelstein and Alan Stroock, chairman of the Board.[470] Shortly after its establishment, the R.A. noted that its work had yielded "cordial relations among the leadership of the three organizations and increased interest in the United Synagogue work on the part of our colleagues."[471]

The Committee provided these three organizations with the opportunity to see themselves as a unified body representative of the Conservative Movement. In the course of their work, they considered such ideas as the coordination of personnel practices of the organizations; having the salaries of the United Synagogue regional directors paid directly by the Liaison Committee rather than by the United Synagogue; the establishment of a joint press; the possibility of opening a joint midtown office; and the possibility of launching a national publication.[472] Given that each organization was subject to constituent pressures to undertake various projects—all of which were deemed urgent by someone—the committee agreed that it would weigh proposals in relation to the projected activities of each of the organizations so as to ensure that the limited resources of each organization were properly directed. Any profits realized would go into the general joint campaign fund.[473] In short, the Liaison Committee tried to function as a clearinghouse and a kind of managing partner of the Movement.

But the work of this committee did not go smoothly. For example, when the Liaison Committee considered the

---

[470] Minutes of Liaison Committee, 28 August 1946.

[471] R.A., *Proceedings*, 1945, p. 39.

[472] The Committee also recommended that a subcommittee be appointed to draw up a model budget for the three organizations to indicate the kind of information that should be included in estimating future budgets (minutes of Liaison Committee, 13 January 1947).

[473] Minutes of Liaison Committee, 17 February 1948.

establishment of joint field offices around the country, Rabbi Albert Gordon, who had succeeded Rabbi Samuel Cohen as executive director of the United Synagogue, objected.[474] He believed that as the idea was proposed, the Seminary's campaign would be the staff's first priority and that the needs of the United Synagogue would be neglected.[475] In fact, the whole idea of the establishment of field offices, particularly in Chicago, became such a source of tension that the Liaison Committee appointed a separate subcommittee to discuss the relationship of the constituent agencies of the campaign within the various communities.[476]

When the United Synagogue proposed the creation of a National Commission on Conservative Judaism, the Seminary objected, arguing that the leadership of the Movement must follow the direction of the scholars, namely, the Seminary. It was agreed that before the idea would be considered further, Dr. Finkelstein would discuss it with the president of the Rabbinical Assembly and the executive director of the United Synagogue.[477] The idea was not pursued. However, a year later, Dr. Finkelstein proposed the creation of a somewhat similar Council of Presidents of United Synagogue Congregations, to be administered by the Seminary's campaign department. Rabbi Albert Gordon bristled at the idea that a lay group would be controlled by anyone other than the United Synagogue:

> The task of building the United Synagogue on a solid organizational foundation cannot be done successfully

---

[474]In earlier discussions within the Liaison Committee, it had been suggested that ideally three men would be needed in each office with each having one of the following areas as his major concern: Seminary, United Synagogue, and Education (minutes of Inner Committee, 22 May 1947).

[475]Rabbi Albert Gordon to Max Arzt, 18 June 1948.

[476]Liaison Committee, 21 December 1948.

[477]Minutes of Liaison Committee, 13 November 1947.

> if the campaign department [of the Seminary] enters into territories and takes over any part of the work that should be done by the United Synagogue.[478]

At the very time that he was objecting to the Seminary entering *his* "territories," Gordon had instructed the United Synagogue field staff to bring to him all matters regarding rabbinic placement within the congregations—an area that was clearly identified as the "territory" of the Rabbinical Assembly. This act forced the executive vice president of the Rabbinical Assembly to point out that there was, in fact, a *joint* placement commission that included representatives of the United Synagogue and, moreover, that said commission was under the auspices of the Rabbinical Assembly.[479]

Given the general lack of financial resources and the joint campaign commitment to raise more, the Liaison Committee spent a good deal of time reviewing the budgets of the three organizations and seemed to pay particular attention to the fiscal problems of the United Synagogue. For example, in 1947, the Liaison Committee involved itself with the financial problems of the United Synagogue Commission on Education and the possibility of a retrenchment.[480] The committee agreed that the budget of the United Synagogue could be changed only by the Liaison Committee.[481] When there were discussions about the creation of a national publication to be published by the United Synagogue for

---

[478]Rabbi Albert Gordon to Louis Finkelstein, 27 April 1948. The National Commission on Conservative Judaism was not formed. The Council of Synagogue Presidents was established by the Liaison Committee. Louis Finkelstein to "Dear Friend," 4 May 1948.

[479]Bernard Segal, executive vice president of the Rabbinical Assembly, to Max Arzt, Louis Finkelstein, 9 June 1948.

[480]Minutes of Liaison Committee, 13 November 1947.

[481]Louis Finkelstein to Rabbi Albert Gordon, 29 August 1947.

members of the Conservative Movement, it was the Liaison Committee that had to discuss how it would be financed.[482]

The Liaison Committee produced the "Proposed Outline for Principles Guiding the Organizational Relationship Between the Seminary, the United Synagogue, and the Rabbinical Assembly."[483] This document attempted to devise structures that would promote mutual understanding among the three organizations. For example, since not all organizations were represented appropriately, if at all, on one another's governing councils, it was proposed that there should be unofficial representatives from each organization on one another's governing bodies. Such individuals would be intimately acquainted with their own organization's thinking and workings, thereby making them effective representatives as well as intermediaries. They would not, however, be official representatives of any organization.[484]

There already existed, and the "Proposed Outline" sought to continue, an Inner Administrative Staff Committee, which included as equal members the executive heads of the Rabbinical Assembly and the United Synagogue as well as a member of the Seminary administration. This body was to serve as a constant liaison among the three groups, supplementing the work of the Liaison Committee.

As a whole, the "Proposed Outline" revolved around the joint campaign, "since all of our activities are dependent upon

---

[482]Minutes of Inner Committee, 10 March 1947.

[483]"Proposed Outline for Principles Guiding the Organizational Relationship Between the Seminary, the United Synagogue, and the Rabbinical Assembly," 1948–49.

[484]Ibid. At the time of this proposal, three members of the Seminary's Board of Directors were named by the Rabbinical Assembly, while its Board of Overseers had ten representatives chosen by the Rabbinical Assembly and fifteen chosen by the United Synagogue. The Seminary had five representatives on United Synagogue's eight-hundred-member Board of Directors.

the success of our fund raising effort."[485] However, it was in connection with the campaign that the Liaison Committee came under self-criticism. Between 1944 and 1949, the proceeds of the joint national campaign were allocated annually by the Liaison Committee.[486] This "Proposed Outline" also suggested that there be a change to a distribution based upon a predetermined percentage. The United Synagogue was to receive 10 percent and the Rabbinical Assembly 3 percent of the net campaign revenues.[487] It was felt by the United Synagogue and Rabbinical Assembly that the Committee did not have the authority to judge each item in each organization's budget and thus did not have the authority to determine the budget of any organization. To continue having the committee allocate the monies the old way would

> inevitably lead in the future, as it has been in the past, to initiating discussions of the relative merits of items in one budget as against items in another budget. It would lead...to tensions due to real or implied criticism by members of the Liaison Committee of the manner in which one or another of the national organizations spent its funds.[488]

The proposal also dealt with the structuring of regional offices and the conduct of educational activities and laid out a complicated system of who could do what, when, and under

---

[485]Ibid.

[486]The allocations were made after subtracting the Seminary's fund-raising costs from the total campaign income. Determining those costs was fraught with tension and disagreement. For example, Maxwell Abbell wrote to the Seminary's accounting firm to complain that not enough of the cost for campaign staff was charged off to non-campaign lines for work unrelated to the campaign (Maxwell Abbell to Samuel L. Kuhn, 18 November 1949).

[487]United Synagogue Board meeting minutes, 15 March 1949.

[488]"Proposed Outline," 1948–49, p. 7.

what conditions in each region. The United Synagogue, more so than the Seminary, felt that its program was being threatened each time the Seminary reached out to lay leadership. As was pointed out by a special United Synagogue committee formed to consider its overall program, budget, and financing:

> It is only insofar as we are able to make it clear to our affiliated congregations and to their membership that *we* [emphasis mine] are providing a service which is of direct benefit...that we shall have performed our real function.[489]

A look at an agenda for a meeting of the Liaison Committee in 1955 showed little change in the character of the committee or the nature of the Movement. The items on the agenda included a discussion of the relationship of the National Women's League to the Liaison Committee, space problems at the Seminary where all the organizations discussed here had their offices, and a report on a proposed manpower study.[490]

Seminary Finances and the Joint Campaign

Finkelstein's first year in office (1940–41) was financially difficult. For the first time in thirteen years, the Seminary did not have sufficient scholarship funds for all its rabbinical students, and the year concluded with a $10,311 budget deficit.[491]

The Seminary continued to struggle for some time to meet its annual budget, and this struggle caused frustration and strain within the administration. In the spring of 1941,

---

[489] Ibid.

[490] Louis Finkelstein to Mandelbaum, 2 November 1955.

[491] "First Report of the President of JTSA for the Academic Year 1941–42," June(?) 1942. Louis Finkelstein to Sol Stroock, 10 December 1940.

Finkelstein had a difficult talk with Rabbi Mordecai Kaplan about the latter's role in the Reconstructionist Foundation. As was explained earlier, Kaplan was the father of the Reconstructionist school of thought, which was an outgrowth of Conservative Judaism. In 1940, the Reconstructionist Foundation was established completely independent of the Seminary to promote this new philosophy. Although Kaplan was a senior member of the Seminary's faculty and dean of the Seminary's Teachers Institute, he was staunchly associated with the Foundation and its work, as were many students and graduates of the Seminary. Finkelstein thought that the time had come for Kaplan to withdraw from the Foundation's campaign because, although it was small, it was hurting the Seminary in that it appealed to the same group of Rabbinical Assembly rabbis and was based on personal loyalty to Kaplan. Kaplan agreed to withdraw.[492] However, when Finkelstein probed with Kaplan the idea of making the Teachers Institute a separate corporation, since a good part of the Seminary's annual debt stemmed directly from the Institute, Kaplan would agree only if the Institute became the owner of the building in which the Institute functioned. Kaplan knew Finkelstein would never agree because the building to which he referred represented one-third of the Seminary's physical plant and its sole classroom facility. After an unpleasant exchange in which Kaplan protested that he had tried to be helpful with the Seminary's fund-raising efforts, he agreed to cooperate with Finkelstein in a campaign on behalf of the Teachers Institute.[493] The conversation with Kaplan was one of several Finkelstein had with the Seminary

---

[492]Memorandum of conversation with Kaplan and Marx, written by Finkelstein, 21 March 1941. Kaplan told Finkelstein that for three years in the early 1920s, he had turned over to the Teachers Institute the salary paid to him by his congregation.

[493]Ibid.

administration in an attempt to muster support for fund-raising.

Although the Seminary continued to struggle to meet its annual budget, the Rabbinical Assembly's campaign on behalf of the Seminary continued to grow. It was in the area of fund-raising that the Seminary and the Rabbinical Assembly had one of their strongest ties. From a disappointing $66,000 in the initial year, this campaign grew close to $500,000 in 1944–45. Finkelstein was moved to note to the Seminary's Board that "the Rabbinical Assembly...is largely responsible for the success of the Seminary membership campaign."[494] In fact, the campaign was so successful that it had begun to result in difficulties for the Assembly, leading Finkelstein to consider whether the Seminary could be helpful to it by sharing some of the Assembly's expenses. Finkelstein explained, however, that "the larger increases were more than offset by (a) the increased cost of living and the increased cost of labor; (b) the decrease in income from investment funds; and (c) the necessity of spending part of this income on the process of raising it."[495] Nonetheless, at least one Rabbinical Assembly representative felt that the Assembly should receive a share of the money that the Seminary raised each year, since according to this view, it was the rabbis who did the work.[496] Indicative of the weakness of the R.A.-Seminary relationship was this rabbi's suggestion that if the Seminary did not see fit to share the campaign revenues with the Assembly, they might have to conduct their own

---

[494]Report to Board of Directors, 6 June 1941.

[495]Pages associated with conferences on Jewish affairs, 8 November 1942. Finkelstein believed that the fund-raising activities should, for the most part, be self-supporting.

[496]For example, when the Seminary held a Midwest conference, it had visiting rabbis speak in each of the Chicago congregations on the Sabbath. Louis Finkelstein to Solomon Goldman, 26 February 1942.

campaign, which would leave them little time to fund-raise for the Seminary.[497]

However, the Seminary knew that every congregational rabbi was a key to an expanded fund-raising effort, and this knowledge was confirmed by outside experts. A public-relations firm told the Seminary that the first objective of a public-relations program was "to activate the Rabbinate [and] to equip them with material which should be distributed by them."[498] The ambivalence toward fund-raising shown by the Seminary's leadership in the 1920s and 30s persisted. The 1943 report by the firm noted that as far as the Seminary was concerned,

> the objectives of the program were not to undertake an immediate fund-raising campaign for the Seminary [but] rather...a broad program covering general relations between the Seminary and the Jewish people of the country.[499]

Just as the Seminary's relationship with the Rabbinical Assembly was deeply influenced by its need for money, so was its relationship to the entire Conservative Movement characterized as much by its economic needs as it was by a shared religious ideology and philosophy. For all intents and purposes, the Seminary saw the Movement, its constituents, and its constituent bodies primarily as sources of support. In an interview with Dr. Finkelstein, I asked him if he ever wondered why the Movement needed the United Synagogue. He responded, "No, we need them to raise money for the

---

[497] I. Goldstein to Louis Finkelstein, 10 June 1941. In 1943–44, the Seminary gave a $2,000 allocation to the Rabbinical Assembly. Louis Levitsky to Louis Finkelstein, 14 June 1943.

[498] Louis M. Cottin to Max Arzt, public-relations critique and proposal, 1943.

[499] Ibid.

Seminary!"[500] In a subsequent interview, he said that Schechter only wanted the United Synagogue "as a base of financial support."[501]

The Seminary thought that it deserved the Movement's support because, for the most part, it was its graduates who served the congregations identified with the Movement. It did not believe that it should have to do very much else to get that support. As one R.A. president noted:

> [In the past] the Seminary has come to the congregations of the country, and the approach has been a unilateral one. We have come to these congregations and said, "The Seminary needs this; American Judaism needs that; give us the funds." We have not so far been in the position to come to the congregations and enter upon a bilateral agreement by which, if the congregations give us the funds we should be able to come to them in turn and say, "We will be able to give you certain programs, certain textbooks, certain activities which will make your congregation alive."[502]

To the Seminary, the Movement was seen as a donor who gave support with little asked for in return, rather than as a customer who paid for a product and expected something back.[503] As far as the Seminary was concerned, its "customer"

---

[500]3 January 1984 interview.

[501]14 February 1984 interview. This very point was noted by Rabbi Israel Goldman, who was president of the Rabbinical Assembly, 1946–48: "I think that the greatest achievement of Dr. Finkelstein and the men surrounding him...was that they have discovered the Conservative congregation....It occurred to Dr. Finkelstein that [they] w[ere] an untapped reservoir, not only of income, but of strength" (R.A., *Proceedings*, 1946, p. 214).

[502]Ibid., 1945, p. 181.

[503]Board chairman Alan M. Stroock acknowledged that it was often said that once the Seminary graduates its rabbis, it has no contact with them other than to ask for money. By way of explanation, Stroock quoted

was the entire Jewish community as well as the elites of academia, government, and commerce. Ideally, the Seminary wanted full financial support from the Movement without giving it or its component parts much of a voice in Seminary affairs. In the words of one rabbi speaking on behalf of his colleagues:

> Many of us...are afraid of the very fertile mind of this man called Louis Finkelstein. What will he think of next? Tomorrow's newspaper may bring us information about a new project which he has started—a project which commits the Conservative Movement to a course of action or to a specific goal, and for which we are expected to find the funds! Even if the project is a perfect one, we wonder with varying degrees of indignation why we were not consulted about it.[504]

Thus, the joint campaign, which was part of the 1944 agreement to bring the three organizations closer together, created yet another area of tension between the Seminary and the Movement. The terms of the original joint campaign proposal set a goal for the 1943–44 year of at least $400,000, of which the R.A. and the United Synagogue were to receive whatever each spent in the preceding year, less any other income they might receive in the 1943–44 year.[505] The

---

Seminary professor Israel Davidson in describing the annual commencement exercises as "a sort of marriage ceremony between the graduates and the rabbinate. When they are handed their diplomas, the president [of the Seminary] as much says, 'Do you, Mr. Candidate, take the rabbinate as your lifelong companion, for better or for worse?' And when the candidates accept their diploma, they as much say, 'We do, until death do us part.' And...it is best to leave newly joined couples alone to work out their own salvation" (commencement address, Alan Stroock, 22 October 1944).

[504]R.A., *Proceedings*, 1955, pp. 133–34.

[505]$306,000 was raised. Draft of letter from Hendricks to Lehman proposed by Finkelstein, 7 August 1944.

original proposal, almost half of which was devoted to details about the campaign, called for audited statements and monthly accountings lest there be any thought of dishonesty among the participants.[506]

The bulk of the $400,000 was to go to the Seminary, since the budgets for the Rabbinical Assembly and the United Synagogue, despite their recent growth, were relatively small, and because the United Synagogue, in particular, had other sources of income. The sum represented a significant increase in the Seminary's expenditures. In fiscal 1942, the Seminary expended $274,445, but in the 1943 fiscal year it planned to expend $461,500, of which only $72,375 was to come from endowment income. The increases in the budget were for a number of different items, ranging from $25,000 for the Institute for Religious Studies to $27,500 for various reserve funds.[507] If the 1943–44 campaign did not succeed, the institution would fall short almost $150,000.[508]

To help ensure a successful campaign, the Seminary reached out to members of the Rabbinical Assembly and asked them to preach a Passover sermon about the Seminary. The letter to the men said that "unless such a message...is brought to our people this Pesach, and unless we immediately capitalize on the interest it is bound to generate, our current...campaign will fall...short...and our plans for the greater Seminary will be frustrated."[509]

---

[506]Institute on the Future of Judaism, spring 1943.

[507]Draft report on all aspects of the Seminary, 3 August 1944.

[508]Finkelstein must have been quite hopeful because in the middle of the year, he wrote to Frieda Schiff Warburg: "Our income has now increased to such an extent that it will provide amply for necessary alterations in the [museum] building" (Finkelstein to Warburg, 6 January 1944).

[509]Max Arzt to "Dear Colleague" (with Passover sermon), 21 March 1944.

The expansion of the Seminary's activities, described fully in chapter 4 of this volume, together with this new possibility of raising funds for three organizations instead of one, forced the Seminary to consider a more aggressive fund-raising plan in which greater effort would be expended on development initiatives in search of larger goals. So in spring 1943, the Seminary hired the John Price Jones Corporation to assist it in considering the possibility of mounting a capital campaign for $10–20 million that would expand its fund-raising efforts beyond the membership of Conservative synagogues.[510] At this point, the Seminary had incurred a $10,000-plus deficit for fiscal year 1941 and a $15,500 deficit in fiscal year 1942. No deficit was projected for 1943. The Seminary's income came from two primary sources: its endowment income and its annual campaign. In fiscal 1942, $91,000 of its income came from the former and $163,000 from the latter. The campaign itself had grown from $23,000 from twelve hundred donors in 1936 to $170,000 from ten thousand donors in 1943. The Seminary's desire was to increase its budget threefold to $750,000 and to have an endowment of at least $10 million, which would yield an annual income of $375,000.[511] A feasibility study was conducted by John Price Jones, which entailed interviews with twenty-eight individuals around the country. The outcome, in addition to a number of specific recommendations, was that "a large-scale endowment campaign was impracticable."[512] Among the report's recommendations was that a department of development should be established "to realize the promotional and fund-raising possibilities described in [the] report."[513] Once again,

---

[510]John Price Jones to JTS Board of Trustees, 7 June 1943; R. F. Duncan to John Price Jones, 21 April 1943.

[511]Memo re: John Price Jones project, 1943.

[512]John Price Jones to JTS Board of Trustees, 7 June 1943, p. 7.

[513]Ibid.

the Seminary was advised to work closely with its rabbinic alumni, this time by forming a Development Council of Alumni.

Finkelstein was disappointed by the consultant's report because he knew that without such a campaign he could not go forward with his expansion program.[514] In a letter to the development consultant, he acknowledged that he was having difficulty with the Executive Committee of the Board regarding the conduct of a capital campaign and that "the fact that we cannot run an endowment fund campaign, which I had urged so strongly, has of course encouraged the opposition to any type of expansion whatsoever."[515] Finkelstein continued to lobby the Board over the summer, and at the November 1943 Executive Committee meeting, he proposed that the Executive Committee recommend the following to the Board of Directors:

> 1) Authorization for himself...to undertake an immediate effort, looking to the raising of the sum of $1 million for the establishment of a fourth building on the Seminary quadrangle, to house a synagogue and Auditorium, and possibly enlarged museum, and also to provide a fund for the maintenance of this building.[516]
>
> 2) that the Executive Committee be empowered to undertake, at the same time, preliminary commitments looking to the inauguration of a large fund-raising campaign as a basis for the expansion of the Seminary, in the hope that as much as $10 million must be raised

---

[514]Finkelstein believed that to accomplish the expanded program, $750,000–800,000 a year would be needed in addition to a $10 million reserve fund. Louis Finkelstein to Duncan, 8 July 1943. Only Alan M. Stroock, Board chairman, and Arthur Oppenheimer, treasurer, were in favor of the campaign.

[515]Louis Finkelstein to R. F. Duncan, 8 July 1943.

[516]Adler had built three buildings in 1929–30: a library, a dormitory, and a classroom building.

> for the Seminary in the year beginning April 1 [1944], the understanding, however, being that, unless the preliminary effort for the Seminary Building and its maintenance fund is successful, a larger effort will not be undertaken.[517]

This time, Finkelstein was more successful, and the Executive Committee made the above recommendations in a modified form to the Board of Directors, who, "after considerable discussion," accepted them.[518] As a result of this decision, the Seminary created a joint committee to plan a nationwide appeal: the National Planning and Campaign Committee. Finkelstein was also ultimately authorized to rehire the development consulting firm, which he did, to prepare the Seminary during April, May, and June 1944 for a large-scale fund-raising campaign in the fall.[519]

In the meantime, the Rabbinical Assembly was doing what it could to enhance the campaign. It had established its own national committee to strengthen the Seminary's membership effort, which in turn appointed regional chairmen from within the R.A. One of its members was editor of the *Seminary Progress*, a newsletter for friends of the Seminary.[520] In addition, the Rabbinical Assembly's leadership spoke publicly of the Seminary in the most supportive terms. For example, at the 1944 Convention, Rabbinical Assembly president Rabbi Louis Levitsky said that the Jewish Theological Seminary

---

[517]Executive Committee Board minutes, 17 November 1943.

[518]Board of Directors meeting minutes, 12 November 1943. Instead of $10 million plus $1 million for a fourth building, the adopted motion called for a minimum $5 million to be raised beginning 1 April 1944, $1 million of which would be for a fourth building.

[519]John Price Jones proposal, 30 March 1944, at a cost of almost $20,000.

[520]*Seminary Progress* (January 1943).

> has become established in the minds of American Jews as that fountain from which all Jews draw refreshing. The usefulness of the Seminary as a source for stabilizing and dignifying and continuing Jewish life in America has been recognized by Jews in all walks of life and of all shades of religious opinion.[521]

In addition, the Assembly established its own newsletter for the Rabbinical Assembly Committee on Seminary Affairs with "the purpose of keeping members of the Rabbinical Assembly abreast of developments in and around the Seminary especially during [the] current campaign."[522] Members of the Assembly also went out to congregations other than their own to speak on behalf of the campaign. The Rabbinical Assembly Committee on Seminary Affairs also set up a speakers' bureau that provided speakers to anyone interested in hearing about the Seminary. A guide, "Five Important Steps in Campaign Procedures," which instructed the rabbis exactly how to conduct the campaign, was produced.

The campaign that year (1944–45) was a success, and the Seminary had a surplus of income over expenditures of $33,000; however, this was not made public. The accountants "hid" the money in new reserve funds.[523] Presumably, the Seminary thought that it would hurt the campaign if it were known that it had sufficient funding, and therefore it chose not to release this information. The official audit for that year showed a surplus of only $4,633.57.[524]

Finkelstein utilized every opportunity to market the Seminary's expanded program to the members of the Rabbinical Assembly because he knew that many of them had

---

[521] R.A., *Proceedings*, 1944, p. 286.

[522] Rabbinical Assembly Committee for Seminary Affairs, newsletter no. 1, 25 October 1944.

[523] I. B. Block to Louis Finkelstein, 11 October 1945.

[524] Audit statement for 1944–45, 25 October 1945.

difficulty in comprehending why the Seminary needed so much money. For example, Rabbi Ira Eisenstein had commented that "for the last several years some of us were very much in the dark as to the need for such an expanded program as had been presented to us."[525]

Each time Finkelstein addressed a group of Rabbinical Assembly members, he was careful to acknowledge the role of the R.A. in the Seminary's campaign achievements:

> The success of the Seminary, through the Rabbinical Assembly, in raising much larger sums in the last four years than anyone anticipated gives promise that the[se] [larger] sums [are] attainable, since we are beginning to realize the strength and power of our Movement throughout the country.[526]

Similarly, the Seminary set aside funds to make it possible for rabbis to attend the 1944 Rabbinical Assembly Convention because it recognized that the rabbis were becoming increasingly important to the campaign and it was thus critical that they knew and understood the expansion plan.

On the other hand, progress with the development consultant in the capital campaign had moved more slowly then either side had anticipated. At the end of the initial three-month agreement, progress had been made on only three of the five agreed-upon goals. The consultant acknowledged that it had been more difficult than first imagined to set forth the case for the Seminary in a compelling manner and also indicated that the key to creating a fund-raising organization was having lay leadership of the highest quality; the Seminary was having difficulty attracting such individuals.[527] At the end of the summer of 1944,

---

[525]R.A., *Proceedings*, 1945, p. 177.

[526]Draft of minutes, Finkelstein before Executive Council of Rabbinical Assembly, March 1944.

[527]Outline of campaign plan, 23 June 1944.

Finkelstein severed the contract with the company, and in doing so indicated that the Seminary Board was not willing to go along with what the consultant had suggested as the next step:

> Our men feel that while we made progress there is little likelihood under the present circumstances that the effort we have undertaken will succeed in its present form. They feel that there may be some possibility of our annual fund raising to be increased through a little more energy on their part, and perhaps even some capital funds being raised through the organization we have in hand. But they do not think that there is a likelihood of any large contributions such as might justify a supplementary organization.[528]

The idea of a large-scale endowment campaign was not scuttled, however. The Seminary presented the idea in great detail to members of the Rabbinical Assembly.[529] The case statement and sourcebook, which the consultant had developed, were completed and also shared with them. Similarly, many of the suggestions for including the rabbis in the campaign and for reaching out to the larger community were incorporated in these communications. The outreach plan had several parts. The first goal was to enlarge the circle of Seminary friends through such techniques as dinners, at which Finkelstein would tell the Seminary story without fund-raising.[530] Then, after the circle had been widened and the new friends had been cultivated, they would be solicited for gifts.

In the meantime, the Seminary fund-raising campaign, which as a result of the joint agreement had become in 1944 "The Campaign for the Jewish Theological Seminary of

---

[528]Louis Finkelstein to John Price Jones, 25 August 1944.
[529]Max Arzt to the R.A., 28 May 1945.
[530]Henry Hendricks to Irving Lehman, 15 August 1944.

America, in Cooperation with the Rabbinical Assembly and the United Synagogue," had been making strides. Between 1942 and 1945, the amounts raised more than doubled.[531]

While the Seminary was appreciative of the Assembly's work, it had become clear to Finkelstein that their efforts were not enough to take the Seminary where Finkelstein and his leadership wanted it to go. He wrote to Board member Lewis Strauss: "We just cannot build this institution in the way you, Arthur Sulzberger and I conceived it, if it has to be an inverted pyramid, wobbling, as it were, on the support of the Rabbinical Assembly alone."[532] Moreover, the Seminary leadership believed that the rabbis were capable of doing far more than they were doing. They thought that the Seminary and the needs of the Movement were not the rabbis' first priority. Dr. Arzt, the Seminary's chief fund-raiser, bemoaned that "if we write to three hundred rabbis, we get twenty-four replies. Something is wrong with that."[533] He related the experience of walking into the office of one congregational rabbi who had requested three thousand campaign pamphlets only to find the entire three thousand "gathering dust." At the 1945 convention, Arzt concluded his remarks to his colleagues pitifully: "I plead with you to teach your people to have respect for our program and to cooperate with us."[534]

With the start of the capital campaign, the total campaign goal for 1945–46 grew to just under $3 million.[535] This sum

---

531The Rabbinical Assembly was quite proud of these results and commended itself for having "laid the groundwork for the growth and development of the Seminary as a great center of Jewish life and learning" (R.A., *Proceedings*, 1945, pp. 17–18).

532Louis Finkelstein to Lewis Strauss, 6 May 1945.

533R.A., *Proceedings*, 1945, p. 192.

534Ibid.

535This new campaign received the support of the Rabbinical Assembly in the form of an adopted resolution at its 1945 convention (R.A., *Proceedings*, 1945, p. 27). Another resolution demonstrated the R.A.'s

consisted of an operating budget of $943,484, which reflected the Seminary's expanded program, and $1,947,000 for Endowment and Reserve funds, this being the first year of a five-year $10 million goal.[536] There were a number of expenses in the budget that could remain unexpended should the campaign fall short. The expectation was that whereas until then most of the fund-raising had been done by the Seminary and the rabbis, now lay leaders would be more deeply engaged. To this end, it was suggested that each region of the Movement establish a society called "Seminary Associates," which would be composed of lay leaders with an interest in the Seminary. The Seminary Associates group was intended to be the nucleus of regional Movement-wide councils, with representatives from each Movement organization represented.[537]

While the campaign continued to grow, it did not achieve the lofty goals that had been set for it.[538] In fact, Finkelstein reported his concern with the progress of the campaign to a meeting of the Rabbinical Assembly's Executive Council: "The Campaign has not been going as well as anticipated [because] the members of the R.A. [*sic*] are not giving sufficient support to the new...expanded drive."[539]

This was to become a recurrent theme over the next several years. For 1945–46, the Seminary incurred a deficit of $26,953.47, since the campaign fell short of its goal as did the income of the first year of the endowment fund drive.[540]

---

support by calling for each congregation to receive a photograph of Dr. Finkelstein, suitable for framing and permanent display in a prominent place in each synagogue (ibid., p. 28).

536Current budget of JTSA, 1945–46.

537R.A., *Proceedings*, 1945, p. 18.

538In 1945–46, the campaign raised $545,353.61, plus $750,000 in endowment funds.

539Executive Council of the Rabbinical Assembly, 22 January 1946.

540Audit report, 30 June 1946.

Finkelstein was not altogether unsettled by this deficit, for just a couple of months later he wrote that "the Seminary has no real difficulty in meeting its annual budget."[541] However, the increased revenue over previous years' campaigns that did result was extraordinarily helpful in strengthening the United Synagogue and the Rabbinical Assembly. The budgets of both those organizations had grown significantly over the past six years as a result of their providing new or improved service to their constituencies.[542] So although the Rabbinical Assembly, or at least many of its leading members, were critical of the Seminary's expansion program, and although there were still significant tensions between the organizations of the Conservative Movement, there was an almost universal recognition of the fact that the Movement was stronger and more cohesive than it had been when Dr. Finkelstein assumed the presidency of the Seminary in 1940.[543]

Accordingly, all those concerned with the Movement saw great potential for the growth of the individual organizations and of the Movement as a whole. There was a unanimous feeling that the financial goals of the campaign were realizable because they had only begun to tap the reservoir that was the Conservative congregations and, in addition, Jews were already giving large sums to other Jewish charitable causes. The fact that expectations met with only limited success did not stop the Seminary from expanding its budget, exclusive of the sums to be funneled to the Rabbinical Assembly and United Synagogue, nor did it stop it from dreaming about

---

541Series of letters about the establishment of Bernard Baruch Foundation (Finkelstein to Proskauer, Proskauer to Sarnoff, Sarnoff to Baruch, November 1946).

542The R.A.'s budget was $2,000 in 1940 and $23,000 in 1946. The United Synagogue's budget went from $12,000 to over $100,000. R.A., *Proceedings*, 1946, p. 206.

543Cf. R.A., *Proceedings*, 1946, pp. 64ff.

large sums and increased programming as is evidenced from the multiyear endowment campaign. When Finkelstein assumed the presidency of the Seminary, the operating budget for that first year was $235,552, whereas by 1946–47 the budget had grown, only in small measure because of the joint campaign, to $2,156,738.16 plus $2,647,000 for endowments.[544] While the Seminary's rabbinical school accounted for approximately 50 percent of the 1940–41 budget, it represented only about 15 percent of the total budget in fiscal year 1947.[545]

But the programmatic expansion and larger campaign goals did not of themselves guarantee positive results. There were still any number of problems with the campaign, as was exemplified by this list put forth at the 1947 Rabbinical Assembly Convention:

> 1) A great many of our colleagues are still unacquainted with our enlarged program and do not realize the extent to which the United Synagogue and the Rabbinical Assembly share in our overall campaign efforts together with the Seminary.
>
> 2) Many of our colleagues fail to realize that until a greater number of responsible laymen come to the forefront in assuming responsibility in organizing and leading in campaigns—[the rabbis] must therefore assume a greater share of this undertaking.

---

[544]The Seminary's concern over the size of its existing endowment funds was significant enough to have Governor Herbert Lehman chair a committee whose purpose was to consider the problem. The committee conducted a study and found that in larger universities, 40–50 percent of their income came from their endowment while in the smaller schools, the figure was 30–35 percent. The committee ascertained that the proper ratio of endowment to annual expenditures was 10 to 1. At the Seminary, the endowment at that point was less than twice its annual expenditures. Greenberg newsletter, 10 December 1948.

[545]Complete budget of JTS 1946–47, 26 December 1946.

> 3) Once a parlor or dinner meeting has been held many of our colleagues fail to follow through in contacting the balance of their members. Since we do not have a field staff that can go into every community and spend a great deal of time we must ask our colleagues to assume the personal interest of the follow up.[546]

In addition to these problems, the campaign workers experienced difficulty in obtaining congregational lists so necessary to do their work. They also found that not enough of the rabbis were convincing their congregations of the importance of assuming responsibility for the Joint Campaign by making it a regular part of the congregation's business.[547] The basic issue underlying these comments, that is, stronger rabbinical support, was echoed by the United Synagogue Executive Director:

> I believe...that if the Rabbinical Assembly [made] clear that the United Synagogue is basic in the development of a Conservative Movement and that its services are necessary toward the proper development of our congregations and our organizations...funds will be forthcoming.[548]

By spring 1947, the national chairman of the Rabbinical Assembly told his colleagues that the "Seminary's financial situation [was] most unsatisfactory. To put it bluntly, if the present trend is not radically changed soon our entire Movement will find itself in a perilous position."[549] How unfortunate that would be, he reflected, given the fact that the United Synagogue and the Rabbinical Assembly "are finally making themselves felt throughout the land."[550]

---

[546]R.A., *Proceedings*, 1947, pp. 46–47.
[547]Ibid., p. 47.
[548]Ibid., p. 362.
[549]Max Klein to R.A. membership, 1 April 1947.
[550]Ibid.

By early summer 1947, it appeared that the regular campaign would fall short of meeting its goal and that some $300,000–400,000 would have to be borrowed to meet expenses. A telegram was sent to the entire Rabbinical Assembly membership, asking them to bring in as much money as possible because of an apparent $400,000 deficit.[551] At the June meeting of the Rabbinical Assembly's Executive Council, it decided that a couple of members of the Assembly would work with the Seminary "to devise ways and means of stimulating the members of the Rabbinical Assembly to conduct campaigns in those communities where they thus far have not been held."[552] The lack of rabbinical support affected the campaign in another way. When lay donors observed or learned of this problem with the rabbis, they found it demoralizing:

> I embarked upon the venture [of raising funds for the Seminary] like Sir Galahad of old—full of enthusiasm and dreams, but the latter have been foundered upon the rock of the indifference and open hostility of the very graduate of the Seminary, without whose aid you cannot enthuse the laity.[553]

There were those rabbis, however, who did work on behalf of the campaign. A number of them constituted themselves as visiting teams, together with laymen, and

---

[551]Telegram to Rabbinical Assembly, 4 June 1947. The endowment campaign was conducted in a very low-key fashion and separate from the regular campaign to cover the annual operations of the three organizations. The endowment campaign did not seek large initial gifts. It tried for general annual contributions and testamentary bequest awards of $10,000. Greenberg newsletter, 13 May 1949. The audited deficit for fiscal 1947 was $135,785.16. Summary statement of General Fund Direct and Allocated Expenses and Income for 1946–47, 14 November 1947.

[552]Minutes of Rabbinical Assembly Executive Committee, 3 June 1947.

[553]Maxell Abbell to Martin J. Feld, 29 April 1948.

traveled "anywhere from ten to 1,000 miles from their own cities to visit communal leaders of other cities."[554] By 1949, even the reports of the R.A. Commission on the Seminary Campaign acknowledged that the rabbis must expend greater effort in the mobilization of their congregations and in interesting key donors in the Seminary. The members of the Rabbinical Assembly were also reminded that the monies raised also supported the work of the Rabbinical Assembly:

> Let us not forget that we lean very heavily on the sums of money given to the Seminary because our pension plan, our placement bureau and our numerous other committees would be drastically thinned out if the Seminary did not meet its budget.[555]

Given the lack of full support from the Conservative rabbinate and the insufficient number of campaign field staff, additional steps had to be taken to bring the Seminary and the needs of the Movement more successfully to the general Jewish population in a systematic way. In keeping with the Seminary's desire to reach out to all Jews regardless of denominational affiliation, the Seminary held a "Big Gifts Dinner" at a New York hotel, which was conducted on a nondenominational basis. The sponsoring committee included both Reform and Orthodox Jews in addition to Conservative Jews, all of whom felt a "responsibility for the Seminary as an institution of higher learning."[556] And in 1949, Friends of the Jewish Theological Seminary of America was launched, with the intent of establishing a regional network. The country was divided into twenty-two regions, with each region having as its basic components twenty-five congregations belonging to the United Synagogue. The

---

[554]"Seminary Record," April 1948.

[555]R.A., *Proceedings*, 1949, p. 84.

[556]Louis Finkelstein to Governor Lehman, 23 January 1947.

expectation was that each region, which would also welcome all other laymen, would

> constitute a year-round nuclei for heightening lay understanding of the Seminary's role in building a dynamic Judaism...[and would] maintain a core of interested volunteer workers who [would] lead the annual effort to marshal public support of the Seminary and its affiliated independent groups.[557]

The underlying concept for this group was that it would involve the grassroots population in a meaningful way.[558] The thought was that each year a leadership group from within the Friends of the Jewish Theological Seminary of America would come to New York and participate in deliberations regarding the Seminary's budget, the campaign goal, and what portion of that goal they felt they could raise in their respective regions.

But even with all these additional efforts, the campaign continued to struggle not only for the reasons already mentioned, but also because of the competition from other Jewish philanthropic projects. The campaigns of the United Jewish Appeal had been having an adverse effect on the Seminary's campaign in many communities for several years.[559] Moreover, the other fund-raising efforts on behalf of

---

557"Seminary Record," March 1949.

558Minutes of the United Synagogue Board of Directors meeting, 12 June 1949. They indicate that there was a recognition that the United Synagogue should identify itself more clearly with the campaign, but there is little evidence that this happened even though the organization was so dependent on support from the campaign.

559Minutes of Executive Council of Rabbinical Assembly, 22 January 1946. In fact, in 1946, Finkelstein indicated that the UJA campaign was one factor that had contributed to a disappointing Seminary campaign. Moreover, the UJA had adopted a resolution in that year "urging that all fund-raising be submerged or postponed in favor of the One Hundred Million Dollar UJA effort" (Max Arzt to the R.A., 24 January 1946).

Israel, which became a state in 1948, were a significant competitive force. This is evidenced in a resolution adopted at the 1949 convention of the Rabbinical Assembly, which read, in part:

> Standing firmly for the support of Jewish life in the State of Israel, we declare with equal firmness that the needs of our own community must not be tabled at this crucial moment. We cannot approve of giving that priority to one Jewish need which would relegate to a secondary place religious and cultural upbuilding of American Judaism. Just as we look upon the reconstruction of Israel as the sine qua non for the survival of world Judaism, we regard the religious and cultural vitality of American Judaism as equally historic in importance.[560]

By 1949, the situation had become a severe crisis. Specifically, the audited deficit for the year ending June 30, 1949, was $285,978.92. The president of the Rabbinical Assembly wrote to the membership telling them that he had been authorized by their Executive Committee to appoint a special committee of past Assembly presidents to deal "with the problem of financial emergency facing the Seminary."[561] Finkelstein himself wrote to the entire Rabbinical Assembly that "our whole Movement is confronted by one of the gravest financial crisis in its history."[562] Again and again, the appeal for help went out primarily to the rabbis rather than the laity and primarily to the Rabbinical Assembly and virtually not at all to the United Synagogue of America. The rabbis were seen as the gatekeepers, the individuals who could bring people and money to the cause; they were the only ones, individually and organizationally, who had

---

[560]Resolution of Rabbinical Assembly convention, June 1949.

[561]David Aronson (president of the R.A.) to the R.A., 15 September 1949.

[562]Louis Finkelstein to the R.A., 12 October 1949.

demonstrated any commitment whatsoever, with the exception of the Women's League, to raise funds on behalf of the Seminary.[563]

The Rabbinical Assembly special committee was formed and met on September 13, 1949,[564] when the committee decided to call a special conference of the Rabbinical Assembly in late October "to consider the financial crisis in our Movement and specific plans which the Committee w[ould] submit for meeting this crisis."[565] The Assembly had already called a special convention for December to deal with matters of Jewish law that were of concern to the Rabbinical Assembly and the Seminary, so there was some concern about the ability of the membership to attend both gatherings. As it turned out, both events were held. At the October conference, the R.A. voted that "each of its members w[ould] be expected to contribute toward a $100,000 fund to be raised for the Seminary from its

---

563In fall 1949, Dr. Emil Lehman of the United Synagogue submitted to Finkelstein a seventeen-page comprehensive proposal for a totally different kind of joint campaign. Though carefully considered to cover virtually every detail, his plan was unwieldy in that it proposed including the local synagogues to share in the campaign revenue and was highly political because it called for the establishment of an independent campaign organizational structure that presumably would have made the Seminary the equal of the United Synagogue and the Rabbinical Assembly (Emil Lehman to Louis Finkelstein, 28 September 1949). Eighty percent of United Synagogue members contributed nothing to the Seminary (Maxwell Abbell, address to fourth annual meeting and conference of the National Planning and Campaign Committee, 30 April 1950).

564David Aronson to Rabbinical Assembly, 15 September 1949. Twenty-six men attended. The committee's membership was expanded to include members of the R.A. Executive Council and several members at large.

565Ibid.

rabbinical alumni."[566] Following the special conference, the Rabbinical Assembly wrote to those members who had been unable to attend and advised them of the self-imposed tax. They indicated that it was everyone's intention to make 1950 a special campaign year and to strengthen the financial structure of the Seminary so that "it can carry out its far-flung program of activities without being under the stress of emergency."[567] The hope was that this magnanimous gesture on the part of the rabbis would energize the entire Jewish community.

During this conference, the Rabbinical Assembly asked the Seminary to provide it with a more detailed review of the Seminary's budget. The outcome was the formation of a budget committee of the four-hundred-member National Planning and Campaign Committee. Accordingly, the Seminary's 1948–49 and its projected 1949–50 annual budgets received a fairly public scrutinizing by the rabbis and lay people who attended the 1950 annual meeting of the National Planning and Campaign Committee. Prior to that review, the newly formed budget committee, acknowledging that it had looked forward to studying the budget "with avid appetite and sharpened pencils," perused it again.[568] The fact was that members of the Assembly continued to wonder where all the money from these escalating budgets was going.[569] Perhaps now with their colleagues going over the

---

566Greenberg newsletter, 7 November 1949. "Quotas were fixed at definite salary percentages, ranging from 1–2 percent for men receiving $5,000, to 10 percent for those receiving $15,000 or more." Cf. also *Seminary Progress* (December 1949).

567Leon Lang and Manuel Saltzman to R.A. colleagues, 29 November 1949.

5681948–49 actual budget and 1949–50 proposed budget, 22 June 1950.

569The growth of the campaign was also a concern of some members of the Board and possibly of Finkelstein as well. In a meeting that

budget they would learn the answer. However, all seemed to be "legitimate and reasonable." The proposed budget for fiscal 1950 was $1,972,000, up from the previous year's actual budget of $1,488,419. The committee acknowledged that the proposed 1950 budget was somewhat of a wish list, highly dependent on a successful campaign. The implication was that, since it was not likely that all the money would be raised, it was also unlikely that a number of the expenses, which they questioned, would ever be realized. Indeed, the Seminary budgets from 1945 onward tended to be wish lists with which to interest donors and welfare funds. There were any number of items in each budget that which could go without allocation if the campaign goal was not achieved without seriously jeopardizing the institution's core activities.

Prior to the special conference that the Rabbinical Assembly had called to deal with the Seminary's financial condition, Finkelstein met with a small group of R.A. leaders. He wanted their permission for the Seminary to contact their respective synagogues to request that they lend their rabbi to the Movement for field and administrative work either in the Seminary or the United Synagogue or the Rabbinical Assembly, for as much as a month at a time.[570]

One rabbi explained the crisis to his congregation and the need for the rabbis to tax themselves, as follows:

---

included Board members Judge Rifkind and Stroock as well as Finkelstein, they expressed the concern that the Seminary in its growth not lose its distinctive message that made it a unique institution. According to Rifkind, an institution's greatness was not a function of its size but rather of what it stood for. "A campaign qua campaign would be destructive [but] to the extent that the campaign succeeds in being a medium of education does it deserve to succeed." The group seemed to conclude that the Seminary's campaign was a vehicle for education and not just a vehicle to raise money, so the size of the campaign was allowed to continue to grow.

[570]Louis Finkelstein to Rabbinical Assembly, 11 November 1949.

> [T]he overwhelming direction of Jewish philanthropy has been and still is being geared to overseas and Israel. In the particular case of the Jewish Theological Seminary moreover, the drift and spiritual lassitudes of the American Jewish community forced it to undertake an expanded program for dynamic Judaism....An entire cycle of new activities was created, each project more vital then the next. The result has been to place the Seminary in the forefront of Judaism's struggle for survival on the American continent; but the price that was exacted meant a fearful drain on its financial resources.[571]

The above analysis was very much on target, since the continuous funding crisis was due to a simultaneous expansion of program and activities with the concomitant increase in expenditures. The campaign, which the Seminary expected the rabbis to conduct within their synagogues and local communities, demonstrated an annual growth of approximately 10 percent a year, but the annual budget increases were so great that this grassroots campaign could not possibly keep up with them; thus, the escalating deficits.[572]

After a large deficit in 1949 and an impending deficit for fiscal year 1950, the Seminary, to emphasize the seriousness of this matter, went so far as to distribute special prayers dealing with the Seminary. Not relying on prayers alone, however, the Seminary did an analysis of its contributions and discovered that a significant portion of the fifteen thousand donors made contributions in the $50–500 bracket. In other words, there were comparatively few large donors or small donors ($10–20 contributions). It was decided that a mass

---

[571]Special R.A. campaign to raise money for Seminary, 1949–50.

[572]$516, 078 in 1944–45; $545,353 in 1945–46; $685,237 in 1946–47; 1947–48 not available; $796,249 in 1948–49. Audit statement 1944–45, 25 October 1945; audit statement 30 June 1946; 1947 complete budget plan; summary statement for 1946–47, 14 November 1947.

appeal for small donations would be begun. Finkelstein and Greenberg were already at work getting $1,000-and-over givers.[573] In order to be helpful, the faculty of the Seminary offered to take a 5 percent pay cut but were politely turned down.[574]

Because the deficits were not only a concern of the faculty but also of the Board of Directors, Arthur Oppenheimer, Seminary treasurer, wrote to Chairman Stroock in fall 1947 to express concern about the shortfall and the Board's responsibility for permitting it.

> I am so afraid that we are going along in our merry way accumulating deficits without considered approval....It looks as if we will have to invade our capital this month [October] by an additional $50,000, making $125,000 in all this fiscal year.[575]

The full participation and commitment of Board members was also a problem. While there were a number of dedicated and hardworking Board members, there were several who took little interest in the institution. In the same letter, Oppenheimer remarked that if the Executive Committee meetings were as poorly attended as the director's, "the whole thing will fall right back in our laps."[576] One such uninvolved Board member was Saul Blickman. Stroock wrote to him imploring him to come to the next meeting and made it clear that he had a serious responsibility as a Board member to help the institution through this difficult period:

> Those of us who are in daily touch with the affairs of the Seminary have been very much concerned by the paucity of attendance at most Board meetings. This not

---

573 Rabbinical Assembly Executive Council, 14 February 1950.
574 Louis Finkelstein to Saul Lieberman, 28 December 1949.
575 Arthur Oppenheimer to Alan M. Stroock, 24 October 1949.
576 Ibid.

> only indicates a lack of interest on behalf of Board members generally, but places upon a handful of us a responsibility for a large budget and a dangerously increasing deficit....The course which the Seminary is following is an extremely precarious one, and if our decisions prove to be wrong, the public will hold all of the members of the Board responsible, and not just those who happened to attend the meetings at which the decisions were made.[577]

By the 1950 Rabbinical Assembly Convention in late spring, the special campaign among the rabbis had received pledges totaling $46,000, less than halfway to the goal of $100,000.[578] Similarly, the overall campaign was also running behind its goals. As of March 30, 1950, the deficit was $320,000 and the Seminary had "invaded principal funds in the amount of $238,000."[579] The institution was now on an austerity budget. Arthur Oppenheimer had informed the Seminary staff and faculty that the Board had voted emergency measures. Expenses were curtailed wherever possible.[580] Because of the recurring deficits, which by then totaled approximately $800,000, the free endowment funds were almost depleted.[581]

In fall 1950, the financial picture was not significantly brighter. The Seminary's Board of Directors had decided to form a committee to consider the best means of presenting

---

[577] Alan Stroock to Saul Blickman, 4 November 1949.

[578] R.A., *Proceedings*, 1950, p. 61. A total of $55,000 was raised from 325 members. Ibid., 1951, p. 82; this rabbinical self-tax was continued into the 1950–51 year, but at 25 percent of the schedule established for 1949–50. Israel Goldman to R.A. colleague, 1 November 1959.

[579] Arthur Oppenheimer to Max Arzt, 24 April 1950.

[580] Approximately $61,000 was saved from several reductions. Report of Rabbinical Assembly Committee on Seminary budget, 22 June 1950.

[581] Abbell address, fourth annual meeting of the National Planning and Campaign Committee, 30 April 1950.

the needs of the Seminary to the public.[582] Concern was also expressed about whether the Seminary's endowment funds were properly invested so as to yield the maximum gain. Maxwell Abbell wrote Dr. Greenberg to complain about how endowment funds were raised in his hometown of Chicago. He also told Finkelstein that if those funds were invested prudently, they would yield an additional $100,000 a year.[583] Abbell also suggested that the Seminary follow the University of Chicago and Northwestern University and invest in real estate.[584]

Finkelstein told members of the Rabbinical Assembly Executive Council and Rabbinical Assembly Commission on the Seminary that he was now convinced that it was impossible for the Seminary to carry on its expanded program based on such an "uncertain financial base." He proposed the launching of a $10 million endowment campaign to culminate in 1954, which would mark the fiftieth anniversary of Solomon Schechter's coming to America.[585] The Rabbinical Assembly thought that such action warranted yet another special convention of the Assembly to give it proper consideration.[586] Due consideration was given by a special meeting of the Rabbinical Assembly, which happened to take place during a convention of the United Synagogue. The endowment campaign was authorized.[587]

582Sol M. Stroock to Lewis L. Strauss, 15 November 1950.

583Maxwell Abbell to Louis Finkelstein, 20 December 1950.

584Maxwell Abbell to Simon Greenberg, 24 November 1950; Maxwell Abbell to Louis Finkelstein, 20 December 1950; Maxwell Abbell to Louis Finkelstein, Oppenheimer, Rifkind, Stroock, 28 December 1950.

585The Seminary seemed to have been engaged in an ongoing campaign for endowment funds, for the $15 million endowment campaign announced in 1944 had, technically speaking, just ended, albeit unsuccessfully.

586Minutes of R.A. Executive Council, 10 October 1950.

587Minutes of R.A. Executive Committee, 4 December 1950.

Continuing to rely on the rabbis for the success of the campaign as well as for outreach into the communities, the Seminary created a Rabbinical Cabinet in the summer of 1951 "for the purpose of creating a group of rabbis which would be intimately informed of the program of the Seminary and which would aid in its campaign for funds."[588] The group also traveled on behalf of the Seminary to large and small communities, cementing links between congregations and the Movement in one community while raising funds in another. Nonetheless, the lack of complete support by the rabbis for the Seminary campaign continued to mystify the leadership. At the beginning of fiscal 1950, a member of the Seminary administration predicted a year-end deficit of between $100,000 and $125,000. This deficit would have been less were it not for a policy to set aside 5 percent of the cash income to repay funds borrowed from the endowment to cover earlier deficits.[589]

Just as Finkelstein's forward planning had been undeterred by lack of funds in the past, so he now seemed unfazed by the recurrent deficits. He told Dr. Greenberg that the faculty of the Rabbinical School must be expanded and faculty salaries in that school must be increased if the school was to be properly maintained. He expressed confidence that on a forthcoming fund-raising trip to Chicago, he would raise the matter of the anticipated deficit and the need to raise faculty salaries, hoping that significant funds would be raised to meet those needs.[590] Equally interesting and almost

---

[588]R.A. *Proceedings*, 1952, p. 88. Louis Finkelstein to Arthur Sulzberger, 11 March 1942.

[589]Simon Greenberg to Joel Geffen, 19 July 1950.

[590]Louis Finkelstein to Greenberg, 30 January 1952. Seminary professor Abraham Joshua Heschel wrote to Finkelstein regarding a reduction in teaching hours, to which Finkelstein responded that the most important problem that faculty faced was adequate salaries and that this

simultaneous with the foregoing, Finkelstein entered into discussions regarding the establishment of a branch of the Seminary in Washington, D.C., in the belief that American Jewry needed a symbolic center of culture in Washington that the Seminary could fill.[591] It was not that Finkelstein did not appreciate the gravity of the situation; rather, he continued to focus on the larger picture of building the Seminary. He was very much aware of the significance that this small theological institution was raising in excess of $1 million a year, for that was a great deal of money for that kind of institution. Moreover, he believed that the fund-raising problem was purely a technical one; that is, the money was available, but it was just a matter of figuring out how to get it. In fact, in 1951, there was a reorganization of the administration in order to provide Finkelstein with more time for fund-raising and the larger concerns of the Seminary. As a result of this change, Finkelstein assumed the title Chancellor and President of the Faculties; and Drs. Greenberg and Arzt, Vice Chancellor.

---

problem had to be resolved before he could deal with teaching hours. Louis Finkelstein to Abraham Joshua Heschel, 26 March 1952.

[591]"Seminary Bulletin," 4 March 1952. While he did not establish a Seminary branch in Washington, he did launch the Seminary Israel Institute, whose purpose was: to strengthen the spiritual and cultural bonds between the State of Israel and America; to offer Americans an interpretation of the spiritual and cultural values of the State of Israel; to foster an understanding of the political role of the State of Israel as intermediary between Orient and Occident; and to help develop a recognition of the State of Israel as a spiritual center for Jews everywhere (Seminary *Register*, 1966–69, p. 169). In 1952, the Seminary also established the Seminary College of Jewish Music–Cantors Institute with funds raised by the Cantors Assembly. See minutes of United Synagogue, 12 June 1949; R.A., *Proceedings*, 1949, p. 114. Two years later, the American Jewish Historical Center was established at the Seminary (*Seminary Progress* [January 1954]: 5).

While Finkelstein was planning to increase the budget, Seminary treasurer Oppenheimer was busy cutting it. He requested that the internal Business Administration Committee meet and determine where cuts could be made "so that it will not have to be done arbitrarily and even more drastically later on."[592] Finkelstein himself circulated a memorandum to all Seminary staff in which he reminded everyone that the Seminary had been "functioning on an austerity program, because of its precarious financial situation." This particular communication informed them that any new expenditures had to be presented first to the internal Business Affairs Committee and then to the Executive Committee of the Board of Directors.[593]

He wrote another memorandum to members of the administration to request that a portion of their secretary's time be contributed to the campaign department. In that memorandum, he said:

> It appears that unless we can find some way to operate our institution with still greater efficiency, our whole structure will have to be subjected to a basic revaluation [*sic*] involving the curtailment and elimination of some of our activities.[594]

The institution's poor financial condition at the end of 1952 was exacerbated by an inactive Rabbinical Assembly Seminary Fund Campaign. Virtually nothing had been done with it during the year and, in fact, the *Proceedings* of the Rabbinical Assembly for 1952 contain no report on that fund or the Seminary campaign, for the first time in many years.

---

[592]Arthur Oppenheimer to Florence Slobin, July 1952. The Committee met and was congratulated by Oppenheimer for their work. Arthur Oppenheimer to Jessica Feingold and Florence Slobin, 20 June 1952.

[593]Spring 1952, memos about deficit and cost-cutting measures.

[594]Ibid.

Despite its budget cutting, the Seminary concluded the 1952 fiscal year with a significant deficit of $300,000 and an even larger one projected for fiscal 1953.[595]

In the last three years (1953–55) covered by this study, the personal participation of the individual rabbis in the Seminary Fund continued to be problematic and, what is more, proved frustrating to those who sought greater support from them. In 1953, the Rabbinical Assembly leadership took to writing their delinquent members and noted their "defection" and the "shame" they should feel over having neglected to make a contribution. "Since so little had been raised" that year, the Assembly appointed representatives in each region to approach the recalcitrant men.[596] In 1954, an attempt was made to "change [this] rather sorry record of personal support."[597] The Rabbinical Assembly believed that if it established a regular, rather than onetime, campaign among the members as a part of the overall fund-raising effort, a better level of participation would result. Although the collections from the 1953–54 year were up somewhat from previous years, the fact remained that it seemed that there were "about 200 rabbis [out of 568] who [did] not consider the cause of the Seminary, the United Synagogue and the Rabbinical Assembly worthy of any gift whatsoever."[598]

During the 1954–55 campaign, the number of men who contributed to the campaign improved, with 63 percent of the Rabbinical Assembly responding, although the overall

---

[595]By February 1953, the deficit was estimated over $400,000. L. B. Reed to Louis Finkelstein and Arthur Oppenheimer, November 1952. However, the final figure was expected to be $250,000. Joel S. Geffen to Benjamin H. Garb, 19 June 1953.

[596]R.A. Executive Council, 16 December 1953, p. 3.

[597]R.A., *Proceedings*, 1954, p. 98.

[598]Ibid., p. 99; about $20,000 was raised in 1953–54.

level of giving did not change substantially. The less than stellar results reduced the R.A. chairman of the campaign to preaching to his fellow colleagues:

> If we, the rabbis, are not willing to support the campaign which makes our work possible, then we are really proclaiming to the world that we are not interested in the Conservative Movement. What disturbs us very much is the number of excuses and rationalizations which we hear from our members about their failure to make even a token contribution....I plead with you to rethink your position on this campaign.[599]

Despite the poor response from within the Conservative Movement, the Seminary continued to reach out often to it for fund-raising. In 1954, the Seminary embarked on a special campaign, together with the United Synagogue and the Rabbinical Assembly, to raise $500,000 over five years for the establishment of two chairs in memory of two of the Seminary's great faculty members—Professors Louis Ginzberg and Alexander Marx. No individuals were to be asked to contribute, so as not to compete with the regular campaign. Instead, the sum was "to be raised entirely through treasury gifts from congregations served by members of the Rabbinical Assembly."[600]

Finkelstein told a member of his administration that some of the Seminary's extension or outreach work would probably have to be cut during 1952–53 and 1953–54 and, even more significantly, that the Seminary would have to limit the number of students it admits because "we cannot bankrupt

---

[599]R.A., *Proceedings*, 1956, p. 82.

[600]Louis Finkelstein to Alan Stroock, 12 March 1954. In its first year, the campaign received $165,000 in pledges from ninety-two of the 663 United Synagogue congregations. R.A., *Proceedings*, 1955, p. 256.

the Seminary even to produce rabbis."[601] Indeed, the Executive Committee of the Board instructed the administration to find every possible means to reduce the outlay of expenses. To assist the institution in this budget-cutting effort, it engaged the S. D. Leidesdorf firm, a management-consulting company, to effect whatever economies it could. The thrust of their efforts was focused on combining certain departments and operations of the Seminary and the other Movement organizations, all of which maintained space at the Seminary.[602]

When the Seminary announced its five-year expansion campaign in 1946, it spoke of turning the museum into a "Center of Letters, Art, and Music; of opening branches of its Teachers Institute in the United States and Canada as well as establishing new sites around the country for the Institute for Religious and Social Studies."[603] Because of the recurring deficits, none of these plans came to fruition.

Throughout the period under study, the Seminary's relationship with the Conservative Movement was strongly characterized by its economic needs. From the first fund-raising campaign in conjunction with the Rabbinical Assembly in 1939 up to 1955, the Seminary devoted enormous efforts and resources to raising money from the constituents of the Movement. Even at the end of this period, the Seminary entered into yet another fund-raising activity, connected, perhaps more than all of its preceding ones, with the organizations and individuals of the

---

[601]Louis Finkelstein to Moshe Davis, 29 August 1952; Louis Finkelstein to Benjamin Stern, 29 April 1953. In a letter to Seminary professor Alexander Sperber, Finkelstein acknowledged that the financial difficulties precluded him from inviting other scholars to lecture at the Seminary, 27 March 1953.

[602]Liaison Committee minutes, 17 December 1951.

[603]Max Arzt to the R.A., 7 March 1946.

Movement. This effort, begun in 1955, was called the National Enrollment Plan. The idea of this effort was that the Seminary would collect a sum of money from every congregational member of each United Synagogue congregation. In other words, the intent was to establish a truly grassroots campaign on behalf of a "National Conservative Movement." In theory, the potential in financial terms was enormous—if it worked. Although this campaign did raise some additional money, it, like virtually all other Movement-related campaigns, fell short of its potential.

Finkelstein's First Fifteen Years

After what seemed to be fifteen years of endless bickering and politicking by and among the organizations of the Conservative Movement, what, if anything, changed? What did not change in any substantive way was the level of tension within the Movement and among its organizational arms. Indeed, the very issues and tensions that existed at the beginning of this study were just as visible at its close. Notwithstanding a more entwined relationship among the Seminary and the Rabbinical Assembly and United Synagogue, and the campaign to raise funds for all three of them, they continued to lack sufficient resources to accomplish their respective missions. The Movement was every bit as unhappy with the Seminary's outreach programs, including its radio and television work as well as its interfaith activities, as it was at the time of their inception.

The frustration over the lack of a well-developed philosophy of Conservative Judaism was probably even greater at the end of this period than it was at its beginning, and this was not for lack of attempts by the rabbis and others to identify basic principles around which all Conservative Jews could unite. For example, in 1947, the United Synagogue published a paper by Dr. Mordecai Kaplan entitled "Unity and Diversity in the Conservative Movement," in which Kaplan identified four unifying principles of Conservative Judaism: the importance of the Land of Israel, commitment to the Hebrew language, use of the scientific approach to the study of Jewish texts, and the primacy of religion as the expression of collective Jewish life. In this paper, he acknowledged that "[d]espite this underlying unity...[there are] three distinct groupings that go to explain the definite evidence of diversity within the Movement."[604] In the words of one rabbi: "There have been many interpretations and there have been many statements as to what Conservative Judaism is, whether we accept one or all of them."[605] At that time, Conservative Judaism was in reality "both doctrinally and from the standpoint of practical directions...still inchoate and amorphous."[606]

Dating from Finkelstein's 1927 paper "The Things That Unite Us" to Greenberg's paper "Standards for the Conservative Movement in Judaism" in the 1950s, the Movement was characterized by a recognition that there was more than one type of approach to understanding Judaism, and thus a sense of complete unity evaded it.

In addition to the dissatisfaction over the lack of a clear ideology, both the rabbinate and the laity remained unhappy over the Seminary's continued lack of a complete commitment to and involvement in the Movement and its work. Organizational sensitivities, certainly on the part of the Rabbinical Assembly and the United Synagogue, as regards the Seminary's dominance of the Movement, continued to exist. In 1955, one rabbi noted:

> Our problems with the Seminary derive from three other matters: (1) the fact that the Seminary is

---

[604] *Conservative Judaism* 4, no. 1 (October 1947): 2.
[605] R.A., *Proceedings*, 1955, p. 156.
[606] *Conservative Judaism* 4, no. 1 (October 1947): 1.

> responsible for the raising of funds for our Movement; (2) the public affairs activities of the Seminary; and (3) the suspicion that the Seminary's officials strive to dominate the R.A.[607]

However, despite the lack of Movement cohesiveness, the three organizations—Seminary, Rabbinical Assembly, and United Synagogue—did manage from time to time to join together to act in a unified and coordinated way on behalf of Conservative Judaism. As early as 1940, the United Synagogue and the Rabbinical Assembly formed a joint commission on Jewish education.[608] Several years later, these two organizations formed the joint prayer-book commission in order to publish liturgical texts for the congregations of the Movement.[609] Most significantly in this area, the Seminary, at the behest of the Rabbinical Assembly, began the National Academy for Adult Jewish studies in 1940 "in answer to the need for a broad yet cohesive program of adult education in America."[610] The Seminary constructed an adult study curriculum of basic Jewish topics, had the course materials prepared by members of the Seminary faculty or graduates of the Seminary, and published them for distribution to synagogues around the country. Finkelstein believed that

---

[607]R.A., *Proceedings*, 1955, p. 133.

[608]In 1947, the Teachers Institute of the Seminary was given three seats on the commission.

[609]Finkelstein reported to Seminary Board of Directors: "There is a good deal of confusion and misunderstanding regarding the Jewish prayer book, simply because no authoritative edition and translation of the service has yet been published. After consultation with our faculty, I have been able to obtain the cooperation of Dr. [Louis] Ginzberg and Professor [Alexander] Marx in the creation of a Prayer Book Commission, with Professor Ginzberg as Honorary Chairman and myself as Chairman. We are discussing with the Rabbinical Assembly the manner in which the body will cooperate with us" (report to Board of Directors, 6 June 1941, p. 7).

[610]Seminary *Register*, 1944–45, p. 39.

> a broad knowledge of historical Judaism will bring psychological reassurance to the Jew of today by showing him the present crisis in its proper perspective. A study of the Bible, Talmud, medieval and modern Hebrew literature, will indicate the manner in which Judaism can be saved in periods of crisis.[611]

Each congregation that chose to run an "institute" could be chartered to do so by the National Academy. By 1948, 140 congregations had established at least a course of study, if not a complete institute, in conjunction with the Academy.[612]

In 1945, in keeping with the desire for the arms of the Movement to work more closely together, the board of governors of the National Academy for Adult Jewish Studies was reorganized to include representatives of the other arms of the Movement. In addition, the United Synagogue formed a committee of adult Jewish education to facilitate the work of the Academy, although the Academy itself remained under the auspices of the Seminary until 1953.[613] The formation of the United Synagogue Committee was the result of discussions during a meeting of the Board of Governors of the Academy, in which they discussed how the work of the Academy might be strengthened in congregations across the country.

From 1940 to 1955, the Movement as a whole grew considerably. The Rabbinical Assembly had grown to six hundred members; the United Synagogue had now affiliated more than six hundred congregations; there were several new organizations that were created, such as the Cantors Assembly, which had a membership of two hundred, and an

---

[611]1940–41, announcement for National Academy for Adult Jewish Studies.

[612]Seminary *Register*, 1948–49, p. 107.

[613]By 1953, the Academy had fallen on hard times. It was being led by a part-time volunteer director because there were no funds to pay a director. Rabbi Simon Noveck to Simon Greenberg, 23 June 1953.

Educators Assembly of eighty, as well as an organization of synagogue administrators. The Seminary, despite its financial woes, had grown on virtually all fronts. A number of joint committees and commissions, in addition to those previously mentioned, had been created, which, in addition to their substantive accomplishments, helped bring about considerable consultation between the organizations—far more than had existed in 1940. And, of course, there was far greater funding for the Movement and its arms than there had ever been before. The Conservative Movement had definitely established itself on the American scene as a vital religious force. Indeed, Judaism and Jewish learning had become integrated into mainstream America.

Chapter 8
Understanding the Finkelstein Years

> Finkelstein's leadership of the Seminary was very much in keeping with the ideas on which the Seminary was established and with the needs of the period. The very nature of the Seminary was such that conflict with the Conservative Movement was inevitable. Finkelstein wanted to use knowledge to build bridges of communication within and between the Jewish and non-Jewish communities.

What was it that compelled Finkelstein to shape the Seminary's mission along the lines that he did? Given the severity and lasting nature of the criticism that he encountered, would it not have been easier, and perhaps more beneficial financially, to have pursued a different path for the Seminary's growth? Clearly, the avenue that he chose only served to heighten the tension between the values of the religious Movement and the values of the Academy. Such a tension is inherent in the life of virtually all institutions of theological education, given their desire to be loyal both to the values of higher education and the beliefs of the religious community with which they are associated. However, his highly visible role in the American community and the institution's broad outreach to men and women of different religions, races, academic disciplines, and denominations exacerbated it within the Seminary and the Conservative Movement.

To understand why Finkelstein pursued the path that he did, it is necessary to look at the early legacy of presidential leadership that he inherited as well as the zeitgeist during the first half of his administration under study. It is also instructive to see the Seminary's mission and the institution's relationship to the Conservative Movement in the context of theological higher education. Specifically, was the Seminary's experience an anomaly, or was it similar to that of other theological institutions of its time? Was the tension between it and its religious community inevitable or could it have been prevented?

The Schechter-Adler Legacy

Finkelstein took the helm of an institution that already had a rich history and whose basic ethos and values had been clearly articulated and established at the very beginning of its reorganization in 1902. There were four basic tenets that constituted a significant part of the legacy that Finkelstein inherited and that guided him in his work:

> 1) the Seminary was not to embrace a particular faction of Judaism in order that it might reach out to all Jews;
>
> 2) the Seminary must be a force for reconciliation and unity so that it did not widen the already existing divisions within both the Jewish community and the community at large;
>
> 3) the Seminary was to work to make Judaism and Jewish scholarship and their contributions to Western civilization understood and acceptable in the world at large;
>
> 4) the Torah must be at the center of any community of Jews.

Although Solomon Schechter acknowledged that the Seminary represented a "conservative position"[614] and that it was to operate "in the midst of many Movements,"[615] he spoke of that position as a "spirit"[616] spelling "conservative" with a small *c* rather than a capital *C*, which would have

---

[614] Schechter, *Seminary Addresses*, p. x.
[615] Ibid.
[616] Ibid., p. xiii.

placed the emphasis on the *kind* of Judaism rather than on Judaism itself. Schechter did not want the Seminary to "become partisan ground or a hotbed of polemics."[617]

When Cyrus Adler assumed the presidency of the Seminary upon Schechter's death, he remained loyal to this institutional philosophy, believing that since the Seminary was not the creation of any particular party in Judaism, it was going to stay that way.[618] In one of his addresses to the Rabbinical Assembly, he was asked to explain the Seminary's position vis-à-vis Conservative Judaism. He remarked that he was not certain that he could do what was asked of him, "since the parties named have never...absolutely defined themselves."[619] He referred to "Conservative" as "a general term which nearly everybody uses but which is, I believe, technically applied to those congregations which have departed somewhat in practice from the Orthodox, but not to any great extent in theory." In that speech, he also acknowledged that the Seminary was cognizant of the divisions that existed among American Jewry,

> but recognizing all these possibilities of divergence, the Seminary still aim[ed] to teach a form of Judaism to which all people could come so far as fundamental values are concerned,...a common language, the understanding of a common history and a common literature are the strongest factors for keeping together the Synagogue—stronger in our opinion than any set of resolutions or platforms. Short of the very simple words of our charter we have laid down no platform and adopted no creed.[620]

---

[617]Ibid., p. 11.

[618]Adler, 1933, p. 251. He concedes that "this statement may seem a little strange in these days of party strife, and yet it represents an actual fact."

[619]Ibid.

[620]Ibid., p. 261.

Even in terms of the curriculum, Schechter saw the Seminary as graduating *rabbis* rather than *Conservative* rabbis:

> You must not think that our intention is to convert this school of learning into a drill ground where young men will be forced into a certain groove of thinking, or, rather, not thinking.[621]

He applied the same thinking to the creation of the United Synagogue—the preamble to whose constitution reads, in part:

> It shall be the aim of the United Synagogue, while not endorsing the innovations introduced by any of its constituents, to embrace all elements essentially loyal to traditional Judaism.[622]

As previously noted, Finkelstein remained loyal to that view, envisioning the Seminary as a place that was to be welcoming to Jews of all beliefs. "[The] strength of the Seminary in those days [1940s–1950s] was [that] we could say anybody belonged to us."[623] Finkelstein explained that the Seminary always held out the hope of bringing Orthodoxy under its wing, and "so [it was felt,] let's not be too Conservative; let's not prevent [Orthodox Jews] from coming [over to us. It was] always our hope that there would be a united Jewish community."[624]

621Schechter, *Seminary Addresses*, p. 23.

622Waxman, 1964, p. 145.

623Interview with Dr. Louis Finkelstein, 14 February 1984.

624Ibid. In fact, in 1929, there were serious discussions between the Seminary leadership and the lay leadership of the Rabbi Isaac Elchanan Theological Seminary (Yeshiva University) regarding the possibility of a merger. For detailed exposition of this, see Dash-Moore, 1981; Rothkoff, 1972; Nadell, 1988. In 1939, Finkelstein told Stroock that he was still "very much in favor of trying to unite any effort upon which we might embark...and a vast majority of the Jews...would profoundly welcome a display of unity on the part of the religious groups" (Louis Finkelstein to Sol Stroock, 19 June 1939). Also in 1951–52, there were discussions between Orthodox leaders and the Seminary about establishing a Joint

Accordingly, the Seminary tried to position itself as the umbrella institution under which American Jewry would gather. It maintained this position, despite its having become intimately involved with the general Conservative Movement. For example, the Seminary synagogue was not similar to the typical Conservative synagogue in the suburbs; rather, it was more typical of an Orthodox synagogue. Within the Conservative movement, the rabbi of each synagogue was recognized as that synagogue's spiritual leader and religious decisor, and within the broad platform of Conservative Judaism he was free to set the pattern of observance for that synagogue. To attract all elements of traditional Jewry, the Seminary insisted on maintaining a synagogue with a significant tilt to the right.

The second basic tenet in the legacy that Finkelstein inherited was that Schechter envisioned the Seminary as a "force for reconciliation" within the Jewish people. According to Schechter, "the ultimate goal at which we are aiming is union and peace in American Israel."[625] Testimony to the importance of this concept for him was the fact that he made it the topic of his address to the first graduating class of the Seminary in 1904. While Schechter accepted the reality of his day, namely, that there were divisions and factions within American Judaism, his concern was that the Seminary and its graduates not add to them: "I in no way wish you to constitute yourselves into a sort of *Synagoga Militans*, and to widen the gap which is already deep enough to divide Israel into regular sects."[626] When Schechter spoke of union, he did not mean "one of mere organization" but rather a union "on

---

Court of Law. Minutes of Steering Committee of Joint Conference on Law, 17 January 1955.

[625]Schechter, *Seminary Addresses*, p. xiii.

[626]Ibid., p. 76.

principle and the recognition of vital facts, decisive in our past and indispensable for our safety in the future."[627]

This idea of unity was also carried into the Finkelstein administration, as was illustrated by Dr. Greenberg in his inaugural address on the occasion of his being named provost:

> Some sixty years ago when the Seminary first came into being, its role as a factor making for "unity and reconciliation" was envisioned as referring exclusively to the religious life of Israel whose unity was being threatened by a rising wave of sects and parties. Today [1947] that role must be envisioned in broader outline....To be a factor for unity and reconciliation within the ranks of Israel, between Israel and mankind and among the peoples of the world, that must be our Seminary's goal today.[628]

Even the "broader outline" to which Greenberg referred had its roots in the belief of the early Seminary leaders, for the Board of the Seminary told Adler that there were certain "principles or beliefs which they believe[d] to be true and important in relation to the position of the Seminary." One of those principles was:

> The dissemination of traditional Judaism can be one of the most important, if not the most important, factor in making for understanding between Jews and others, and for alleviating the difficulties which beset Jews everywhere.[629]

Similarly, Louis Marshall, Schechter's Board chairman, had written in 1924 that the essence of the Seminary's mission was the "perpetuation of Judaism as a living religion and as a

---

[627]Ibid., p. xiv.

[628]Greenberg, 1947, p. 5.

[629]Memo from Development Committee to Cyrus Adler, May 1938(?).

great influence upon civilization.[630]

With regard to the third basic tenet in this legacy, Schechter was adamant that, since Judaism was rooted in Torah and learning, only an academic institution and its leaders could properly serve as the guiding force of the Movement. He articulated this belief succinctly: "Any attempt to place the centre of gravity outside of the Torah must end in disaster."[631] The teachings of the Torah must guide one's life, and not any other philosophical system, whether ancient or contemporary. Accordingly, only those who are fully acquainted with these teachings may serve as leaders of the community and, in this case, those individuals were the faculty of the Seminary. Finkelstein translated Schechter's belief more bluntly: "[You] can't be at the mercy of people who know nothing."[632] The Seminary's position was strengthened by the reality that it was the oldest and strongest organization within the Movement.

The fourth tenet that constituted this historical legacy was a commitment to see to it that

> Jewish learning and Jewish scholarship and the knowledge of Judaism's literature...become recognized factors in the march of human intellect [and that] Jewish science should occupy a position among other sciences worthy of its long history and its influence upon mankind, holding an independent resting place, resting on its own merits, free from all patronage of malicious theologians and sulky divines.[633]

Thus, Finkelstein inherited a legacy laid down by Schechter and perpetuated by Adler, which neither achieved totally, but which both Schechter and Adler used effectively

---

[630]Reznikoff, Louis Marshall: Selected Papers, 1957, p. 884.
[631]Schechter, *Seminary Addresses*, p. 25.
[632]Finkelstein interview, 3 January 1983.
[633]Schechter, *Seminary Addresses*, p. 2.

to shape the Seminary's mission. All that Finkelstein did can be traced back to these four founding tenets. For example, his insistence on the Seminary being the fountainhead of the Movement is directly tied to the fourth tenet; the creation of the Institute for Religious and Social Studies and the Conference on Science, Philosophy, and Religion is directly tied to the third tenet; the creation of the *Eternal Light* radio and television programs and the building up of the library are directly tied to the second tenet; and the purportedly nondenominational character of the Rabbinical School curriculum, as well as the projection of the Seminary's image to the public, are directly tied to the first tenet. In short, he embraced these four principles and built upon them to create his own set of goals, which he thought best suited the times in which he was leading the Seminary:

> 1) to strengthen among the Jews themselves the concept of Judaism as a religion;
>
> 2) to enhance cooperation between Jews and other religious groups in order to strengthen the religious consciousness of the nation as a whole, and the importance to democracy of the Judeo-Christian tradition;
>
> 3) to stress the importance of combining all intellectual forces [literary, scientific, philosophic, and religious] to preserve civilized life in our generation.[634]

Accordingly, the expansion program that Finkelstein created was very much in character with the culture of the institution

---

[634]Louis Finkelstein to Sol Stroock, 4 December 1940. As a result of the capital campaign feasibility study, the John Price Jones Company recommended that the case for the Seminary to the public be based, *inter alia*, on the Institute for Religious Studies and group tensions, and explaining to Jews and Christians the meaning of Judaism. John Price Jones to JTS Board of Trustees, 7 June 1943.

and bespoke the values by which its founders and early leaders shaped it:

> I do not think it is an accident that the Seminary should find itself pushed, as it were, out of the Jewish scene and on the world scene. It did not do it out of choice. It was not that all of a sudden we got a brainstorm and decided we must go ahead and try to help build peace in the world. *It is because the institution itself was built on these very foundations* [italics mine] of peace and understanding people who are different, encouraging differences and being grateful for differences.[635]

But the historical legacy that Finkelstein inherited had another piece that also proved to have a profound impact on the development of the Seminary and its relationship with the Movement: the creation of the United Synagogue of America. Just as Schechter and Adler had laid the foundation for the way in which Finkelstein shaped the Seminary's mission, so did they set in motion a relationship with the Movement that would only further exacerbate the tension between the Movement and the Seminary over its mission.

By creating the United Synagogue to ensure the support of those synagogues served by Seminary graduates, Schechter sowed the seeds of the dependent relationship between the Seminary and the Movement that came to fruition during Finkelstein's administration. In doing so, he gave the national organizations reason to believe, implicitly at least, that it should have a say in Seminary affairs. If Schechter established this relationship with the creation of United Synagogue, Finkelstein perpetuated it and enlarged upon it with the creation of the Joint Campaign in 1944 and by the Seminary's continually increasing reliance on the rabbis to raise funds for it. In creating the United Synagogue out of a need to add a base of supporters for the Seminary, Schechter actually

---

[635]R.A., *Proceedings*, 1945.

veered from his own basic tenet. According to his biographer, Schechter was committed to the idea that

> [the Seminary] should be endowed in such a way as to make it entirely independent of all outside opinion, so that it could pursue its way on lines mapped out for it, without any fear of interference.[636]

Schechter took exception to what he thought was the reproachful attitude toward the Seminary's inability to "form large constituencies." In his mind, "no institution of higher learning could ever expect the support of the people."[637] Thus "an appeal to the public at large is of little use....Relief...can only be expected from the trustees."[638]

Not only did Schechter stray from the idea of independence, but Finkelstein virtually tossed it aside by creating a large constituency and a broad-ranging appeal to the public at large. Thus, it was the result of limited financial resources in the administrations of Schechter, Adler, and Finkelstein that led the Seminary to do the very thing it refrained from executing since its inception, namely, to identify with a particular segment of the Jewish population and to link its success to its support. In so doing, the Seminary relinquished a good deal of the independence it held so dear and heightened the conflict over its mission.

The Seminary's Board of Directors accepted the legacy of Schechter and Adler and thus had no difficulty in giving Finkelstein their full support as he guided the Seminary in accord with that legacy. Like Finkelstein, this board was also the subject of considerable criticism by his detractors. In keeping with their desire that the Seminary be the very embodiment of Conservative Judaism, the critics complained

---

636Bentwich, p. 194.
637Ibid.
638Ibid., p. 195.

that there were virtually no Conservative Jews on the Board. On the contrary, they argued that most of the Board members were Reform Jews with little or no attachment to Conservative Judaism.[639] There are those who had argued that a board of this kind served merely as a "rubber stamp" for whatever Finkelstein wanted to do, and it would certainly not encourage him to bring the Seminary closer to the Conservative Movement. Most of the Board members in Finkelstein's administration, and certainly in Schechter's time, were enamored with the outward-looking approach and the desire to establish Judaism and Jews within the mainstream. "Judaism," wrote Board member Judge Rifkind,

> has at least this obligation to the American people: to make an affirmative contribution to the molding of character and shaping of conduct on the part of its adherents which would promote the whole nation's welfare....To my mind this represents a more important avenue for the development of conservative [*sic*] Judaism than the ritual problems upon which it appears to be engaged.[640]

Stroock, too, looked with favor upon Finkelstein's loyalty to the Schechter tenets. In a commencement address, he touted the Seminary's prowess as *the* institution to lead the Jewish community and noted that one thing that qualified it for that role was the fact that "among all the intellectual divisions, subdivisions and opposing forces which [were] to be found among Jews...the Seminary alone ha[d] at all times refused to follow a party line."[641]

---

[639]As Rosenblum observes, "The motivation and expectations that moved these powerful men to mount the substantial efforts they mobilized on behalf of the Seminary" remain a matter of conjecture (Rosenblum, 1970, p. 36).

[640]Judge Rifkind to Louis Finkelstein, 4 January 1947.

[641]Alan Stroock, commencement address, 22 October 1944.

Stroock was thus proud that the Seminary had been, and continued to be, "sponsored by men and women of varied degrees of adherence to traditional Jewish practices and the widest variety of synagogue affiliation."[642] Finkelstein was no less taken with this reality. The fact that the Seminary's Board of Directors included such diversity of men and women was a further indication of the support for the Seminary's mission within the Jewish community.

> The Seminary...has always had on its Board of Directors leaders who were interested in it as an institution of learning and as a center for religious and spiritual influence transcending differences of attitudes in Judaism and also among different creeds. So it came about that men like [Jacob Schiff], Louis Marshall, Irving Lehman, and others felt attached to the Seminary though they did not altogether subscribe to the mode of worship which we follow in our synagogue and in our daily life.[643]

When Finkelstein became head of the Jewish Theological Seminary, he entered into the presidency of an institution the parameters of whose mission had been relatively well demarcated by his predecessors. As a product of the Seminary, first as a student, then as a member of the faculty and administration, Finkelstein was no doubt accepting of the basic tenets promulgated by Schechter and Adler. To Finkelstein, the destiny of the Seminary and Jewish learning were inextricably linked more with the fate of Judaism and the Jewish people than with the development of the Conservative Movement. Accordingly, he had little difficulty building his presidency and the program of the Seminary around the Schechter-Adler legacy.

---

[642]Ibid.

[643] Louis Finkelstein to Frieda Schiff Warburg, unsent letter, 14 June 1946.

Understanding the Critics and the Criticism

So why the criticism of the Seminary's mission? Why the unhappiness with Finkelstein's leadership and the dominant role of the Seminary within the Movement? The answer is deceptively simple. It is because the Movement's organizations, most particularly the Rabbinical Assembly and the United Synagogue, and their leaders never really accepted these cornerstone tenets as guiding principles for either the Seminary or the Movement. Because of the Seminary's dominant stature dating from 1902, these organizations and their leaders were never able to do anything about those beliefs other than to be critical of what they led to, namely, the mission of the Seminary and the organizational structure of the Movement. The Seminary was the leader of the Movement, but not necessarily by anyone's choice other than its own. The reality was that the Movement was being led by a leader in the form of both a person (Finkelstein) and an institution (the Seminary) that was, at best, only begrudgingly accepted as such. To make matters worse, the Seminary embraced different values and sought to accomplish different goals from those of its critics. There simply were different images and thus, different expectations, of both the Movement and the Seminary.[644] Whenever such a situation exists, discord is inevitable and lack of unity the result. While the Seminary was aware of how it was perceived by its different constituencies, it was not prepared to redefine itself according to the terms of the Movement leaders.

---

[644]Bruning, 1975, p. 47. It is not unusual for various constituent groups to have differing perceptions of the goals, purposes, and philosophy of the institution. In a study of eighteen Lutheran colleges, it was also shown that "constituency groups vary not only in the degree to which they desire certain goals, but also in their perception of how well their expectations are being met" (Strommen, 1976, p. 198).

While critics like Solomon Goldman and Milton Steinberg wanted the Seminary to embrace and favor the synagogue and its leadership, the Seminary under Finkelstein chose to embrace the broader (not necessarily synagogue-affiliated) community and its leadership. Dr. Mordecai Kaplan described the tension between the critics and the Seminary as being between intensification and expansion. Was the Seminary to intensify its work internally? That is, was it to concentrate on the Conservative Movement, or was it to concentrate on expansion outward toward the entire Jewish community? More broadly expressed, was the Seminary to emphasize merely the Conservative Movement, or rather the perpetuation of Judaism and the survival of the Jewish people in America? Clearly, Finkelstein and the Seminary opted for the broader community over the more limited congregation, for expansion over intensification, for concern about the core of Jewish life over a concern for the status of the organizations of the Conservative Movement. Finkelstein believed that "you can't have a little Seminary and do anything to save American Judaism."[645] His critics, however, were not interested so much in saving American Judaism as they were in developing the Conservative Movement and defining Conservative Judaism in the process.

Although the differences between Finkelstein and his critics centered on Seminary goals, Finkelstein tended to minimize the substantive nature of these differences, labeling them instead as "misunderstandings and confusions" that could be ameliorated by better communication.

> I look out and find that among the many misunderstandings and confusions in Jewish life, there is none greater than the misunderstandings and confusion of what we are trying to do at this institution....Maybe we have done an injustice to our

---

[645]R.A., *Proceedings*, 1946, p. 230.

> fellow Jews in not getting them to understand what it is that we are trying to do. You cannot be too far ahead of your Army or your lines of communication will be snapped....So, I think that one of the first things that we must think of in the years ahead of us is this business of communication between ourselves and the fountain from which we have sprung.[646]

In truth, Finkelstein's idea of communication was not necessarily a dynamic one. Rather, he understood communication as not having ample opportunity to convince others of his thinking.

That thinking included an understanding of the Jewish tradition that was different from the way in which his critics understood Judaism. To Finkelstein, Judaism was a way of life that looked outward, and Jews had an obligation to be part of the society in which they lived while bringing to bear on that society the spiritual and moral tradition that is unique to Judaism.

> The time will come [said Kaplan] when Jewry will be grateful to Dr. Finkelstein for having widened the horizons of Jewish life in the country, and having taught the Jewish people to realize that it must serve the general community and bring to bear the best in its tradition upon the development of the general life about us.[647]

In other words, for Finkelstein, to engage in the larger world was central to being Jewish; it was not something that a Jew should consciously choose to do or not to do.[648]

> Either you make up your mind that Jews won't survive the exile or you make up your mind they are going to

---

[646]Ibid., 1945.

[647]Ibid., p. 202.

[648]I thank Jessica Feingold, an aide to Dr. Finkelstein for more than thirty years, for this insight. Interview, 6 January 1992.

> survive in a ghetto or they are going to survive in close contact with their neighbors. There is nothing else.
>
> Either you expect Judaism to perish or it is going to survive in a locked room or it is going to survive in the open world.
>
> I begin with the assumption that we can't get the locked room, and even if we could get it, I don't know whether it would be good to get it. I begin with the assumption that we don't want Judaism to perish. Therefore, we must find the way in which Judaism can live outside.[649]

To be a Jew was to be concerned with democratic values as Finkelstein was; to be a Jew meant to be concerned about the moral fabric of society as Finkelstein was; to be a Jew meant to be troubled over the group tensions that existed in Finkelstein's time as he was.

> I have always felt that the primary contribution which the Jews, as a group, have to make...is that of preserving their religious heritage, and indicating how that heritage could contribute, and is contributing, to the advancement of civilization.[650]

Finkelstein looked upon his critics in the Movement as isolationists because they opposed his open approach to society, which they thought was promoted at the expense of the Conservative Movement. He believed that "we just cannot be isolationists."[651] The narrowness of the views of his critics was apparent to others as well. One member of the Seminary Board wrote to Finkelstein, "As you know, the problem of getting the American rabbi to acquire a broader

---

[649] R.A., *Proceedings*, 1946, p. 232.

[650] Louis Finkelstein to Judge Proskauer, 20 October 1943, in which Finkelstein resigns from the American Jewish Committee.

[651] Louis Finkelstein to Lewis Strauss, 6 May 1945.

view of our responsibility as Jews is constantly on my mind."[652]

Just as Finkelstein differed from his critics over their understanding of the Jewish tradition, so did they differ over the nature of the Seminary's purpose. While each chose to describe the institution as an "academic institution,"[653] they defined the term in very different ways. For the Seminary, being an academic institution meant loyalty to the time-honored higher-education principle of academic freedom. Indeed, Finkelstein was quite proud of the wide diversity of views that characterized the Seminary's faculty, and he attributed the institution's ability to sustain that diversity to the principle of academic freedom.

However, some of the Seminary's critics were unhappy with the appearance of the institution's neutrality, which was a natural outcome of its adherence to academic freedom. Goldman, for example, was critical of a speech given by Chairman Stroock that implied that the Seminary was a neutral institution. In his speech, Stroock had merely reiterated the founding beliefs of Schechter and Adler to the effect that the Seminary refused to follow a party line or to align itself with "political ideologies" or assimilationist doctrines.[654] In his reply to Goldman, Finkelstein said that Stroock "did not say or imply that the Seminary was a 'neutral' institution. What he did say was that it is an academic institution, which is precisely the view you took."[655] Goldman and others understood the Seminary to be an academy, not in the sense of the Western university with its adherence to academic freedom and dispassionate objective scholarship, but rather as what Cuninggim described as the "embodying

[652]J. Solis-Cohen to Louis Finkelstein, 9 October 1945.
[653]Louis Finkelstein to Rabbi Mordecai Brill, 4 January 1943.
[654]Alan Stroock, commencement address, 22 October 1944.
[655]Louis Finkelstein to Solomon Goldman, 4 December 1944.

college," that is, an institution whose primary allegiance was to the tenets of its church rather than the norms of higher education. For critics like Goldman, the Seminary was seen as an end in itself. It only had to mirror the beliefs and practices of the Movement and train its leaders. For Finkelstein, the Seminary was closer to what Cuninggim called the "consonant" college; that is, one that "affirms its church-relatedness quality as an unassertive ally would do."[656]

For Finkelstein, however, the Seminary was not an end in itself, but rather a vehicle for preserving Judaism and improving society. Whatever can give the individual Jew a better understanding of his or her faith, so that he or she will cleave to it firmly and consciously, helps humanity by helping to maintain one of its principal servants.[657] Judge Rifkind described the Seminary "as a spiritual powerhouse, comparable to the small powerhouse on the Niagara River which (although tiny in itself) has transformed a mighty rush of water into something useful for civilization."[658] Because Finkelstein did not believe that the Seminary was an end in itself, there were any number of times when Finkelstein did something that he thought would enhance the general quality of life without seeking direct benefit for the Seminary. For example, the Conference on Science, Philosophy, and Religion held its meetings at Columbia University, and while the participants knew of Finkelstein's affiliation with the Seminary, he did not capitalize on the conference's work for the benefit of the Seminary as much as he might have. Another example: while he was going to Boston in 1955 for the newly launched Spiritual Statesman Program, he indicated that a fund-raising meeting could not be set up if it were to have "any connection whatever, no matter how remote, with

---

[656]Op. cit., 1978, p. 3.

[657]Finkelstein, 1960, 1:xxix.

[658]Jessica Feingold to Frieda Schiff Warburg, 3 May 1954.

the meeting for Spiritual Statesmanship....[W]e would much rather hurt our campaign than hurt our program."[659] Feingold has said that Finkelstein did not want to utilize his activities in the world at large for institution building or the gain of money.[660] He feared that any such activity might not only damage the programs but also would detract from his first priority, which was to improve the society. This self-effacing posture no doubt cost the Seminary much good publicity and additional revenues when these very programs were a lightning rod for criticism of Finkelstein and the Seminary.

Finkelstein was as committed to the development and perpetuation of a Judaism that was at once traditional and modern as were his critics. However, what separated them from him was a considerable difference of opinion over how that was to be achieved. As indicated, his critics believed that the way to accomplish the goal was to look inward, devoting all energies and resources to the strengthening of the Movement. But Finkelstein understood that (a) the chances of building the Conservative Movement and disseminating Conservative Judaism would be greatly enhanced if the surrounding culture was hospitable to religion in general and to Judaism in particular[661] and (b) there was little point in trying to save American Judaism as long as there were strong societal forces working to destroy the very values that were necessary for the free exercise of religious beliefs.

Finkelstein was not interested in goodwill, but in the transmission of knowledge. In fact, the reason that he was not interested in the Conference of Christians and Jews was because he saw it as being concerned only with goodwill. He explained to Rabbi Goldman that the purpose of the

---

[659]Louis Finkelstein to Harry Levine, 23 February 1955.

[660]Interview with Jessica Feingold, 6 January 1992.

[661]Finkelstein, 1960, 1:xxx. "For the disappearance of Anti-Semitism, Judaism looks to a world in which religion will have been vindicated."

Conference on Science, Philosophy, and Religion was to "attempt to reconstruct the intellectual atmosphere of our time in such a way that it might be consistent with democratic ideals as well as with religious life."[662] Indeed, it was not just knowledge of Judaism that Finkelstein wanted to disseminate, nor was it just Jewish group tensions that he wanted to resolve; he was also committed to breaking down group tensions wherever they existed, whether between Catholics and Protestants, between scientists and religionists or between academics who had become so overspecialized that they cut off any possibility of a cross-fertilizing dialogue.

Wherever men differed widely, he wanted to bring them together to exchange ideas, information, and opinions and, above all, to have them learn from one another. Finkelstein believed that the Seminary was well suited to play such a catalytic role, in part because the relatively small size of the Jewish population effectively ruled them out of the power struggles that occupied other faiths and disciplines.[663] This was, he thought, done *not* at the expense of the Conservative Movement but ultimately for its good. "[Our] interest in maintaining the tradition of Jewish scholarship does not free us from our responsibilities as citizens of the world," he told Goldman.[664] Finkelstein saw an inextricable connection between religion and democratic values, for he believed that there could be no democracy without belief in God. He attributed Hitler's success in Europe to the absence of religion in the conquered countries. Accordingly, it was of paramount importance to restore the American people's belief in God in order to safeguard American democracy.[665]

---

[662]Louis Finkelstein to Solomon Goldman, 11 November 1940. Interview with Jessica Feingold, 6 January 1992.

[663]Report to Board of Directors, 6 June 1941.

[664]Louis Finkelstein to Solomon Goldman, 11 November 1940.

[665]Louis Finkelstein to Abraham Meyers, 8 August 1940.

The critics, however, were myopic in their thinking and failed to see the connection between what they wanted and what the Seminary was doing. To Finkelstein, the growth of Judaism of any kind and the survival of the Jews were part of a larger problem, namely, the nature of the society in which Jews and Judaism had to live. He believed that the cause of Judaism and the cause of the Western world, particularly America as a free people, were identical. Certainly by the early 1950s, he thought that Jews were no longer a persecuted minority, but instead part of the imperiled majority. In what seems to be a reference to his colleagues in the Conservative Movement, among others, he said, "The waste of effort, the friction, and the controversies which this institutionalism involves are doubtless one of the most serious social problems of our age."[666] This notion of the importance of looking beyond one's immediate needs received affirmation from the Seminary's Board. Judge Rifkind remarked:

> [H]e frequently goes to meetings of Jews, [but] the Seminary is the one place where he attends Jewish meetings. At the Seminary he finds concern for the fundamental spiritual and religious problems....Jews...are especially well equipped to think through current world problems, because the Jewish tradition was forced long ago to grapple with a series of crises and catastrophes.[667]

Finkelstein and his critics simply had different images of the Seminary and of its relationship to the Conservative Movement. Therefore, each of them evaluated all that the Seminary did by a different set of expectations, inevitably leaving the critics dissatisfied with Finkelstein and critical of the institution.

---

[666]Ibid.

[667]Jessica Feingold to Frieda Schiff Warburg, 3 May 1954.

The Zeitgeist: 1940–55

Those "current world problems" that Rifkind referred to also played a role in the development of Finkelstein's vision and the evolution of the Seminary's mission. Finkelstein's own intellectual approach to Jewish history made him an astute observer of his own times and of the relationship of Jews and Judaism to the issues of the day.

Finkelstein assumed the presidency of the Seminary in 1940, as the nation was beginning to emerge from the drought of the 1930s. The chief topic of discussion among Jews and non-Jews in the opening years of the 1940s was the question of war and peace. The question that everyone was trying to understand was, what would be the complexion of the world after the war, and for Jews, what would be their place in it? Because the future was so unclear and because civilization seemed to be crumbling in Europe, the first few years of the decade were trying times. The postwar upturn in ecclesiastical prosperity that was to occur later in the decade was not yet apparent. To the contrary, Jewish leaders thought that the interest of Jews in Judaism was most unsatisfactory. This was no doubt due to the carry-over of the assimilationist and disaffiliation trends of the 1930s. Accordingly, Jewish life in the early 1940s was still characterized by a pervasive lack of religious observance, a lack of synagogue attendance, and diminishing enrollment in religious schools. In sum, all signs pointed to a general apathy toward religion. Finkelstein bemoaned the fact that during the interim of the two world wars, the Jews,

> [l]ike all other religious groups...failed...to stress sufficiently the spiritual problems of mankind, or of our own groups; we have failed to organize American Judaism on a religious basis; we have failed to meet the problem of religious education of our children; we have permitted our synagogue to become weaker; we have

> done virtually nothing to explain Judaism either to those of our own people who have not received an intensive Jewish training, or to the community at large.[668]

Some even thought that the rabbinate itself lacked religious feeling and fervor. One Conservative rabbi wrote Finkelstein, "I believe it is time to say that we have a major problem of making those people who preach religion get some of it themselves."[669]

By the mid-1940s, however, signs of ecclesiastical as well as economic prosperity became noticeable.[670] The tax situation helped to spur that prosperity. Because of the 15 percent personal and 5 percent corporate exemptions for charities, many people were searching for causes to be included among their benefactions.[671] Glazer called the upturn in religion "The Jewish Revival."[672] Indeed, the postwar revival that continued into the mid-1950s probably had a

> more marked effect on Judaism than on any other religious faith in America. Nowhere had disaffiliation and alienation been so prominent a religious trend during the first three decades of the twentieth century as among the Eastern European Jews.[673]

It was in this very period that the Seminary launched its "Ten-Year Plan to Reclaim Jewish Youth" because it recognized that there never was a time when religion had more public respect. The Ten-Year Plan noted, "The war has brought into focus a definite change to deeper reverence for

---

[668]"Preparing for the Post-War Situation of American Jews," draft of Finkelstein speech, 1943.

[669]Chaplain Isaac Klein to Louis Finkelstein, 16 July 1943.

[670]Allen, 1972, p. 167.

[671]1946, undated campaign material.

[672]Glazer, 1972, p. 106.

[673]Ahlstrom, 1972, p. 980.

religious values. There is a notable resurgence of religious life among our Christian neighbors and among us Jews as well."[674]

The 1940s and early 1950s saw the migration of Jews from the inner cities to the suburbs and small towns, placing Jews in closer proximity to their non-Jewish brethren than they had ever been. These new relationships sensitized Jews to more than the differences or similarities in material possessions. It also sensitized them to their Jewish identity. "The religious behavior of the Christian neighbor began to impinge on the consciousness and conduct of the Jewish suburbanite...forcing them to become self-conscious about religion."[675] "A national public-opinion poll showed that 18 percent of Jews attended services once a month, as against 65 percent of the Protestant respondents and 85 percent of the Roman Catholics."[676] "Emulation, thus [was] at least one factor in the revival."[677] Hence, the Jews of the 1940s were ripe for nurturing, but that nurture had to be subtle and unthreatening for they were coming to their Jewishness out of a background of ignorance and disaffiliation. Moreover, the Americanization trend of the 1930s made them very self-conscious, to the point where they were not ready to display their Jewishness in a highly visible way. "There was a vast chasm between serious religious thinkers and American congregational life. Practicality and social activity predominated at the local level."[678] Finkelstein thought that Judaism was the "unknown religion of [that] time."[679]

---

[674]Seminary's "Ten-Year Plan to Reclaim Jewish Youth to Religious and Ethical Life" (author unknown), 9 June 1944.

[675]Louis Finkelstein to list of individuals, August 1944.

[676]Ahlstrom, p. 981.

[677]Ibid.

[678]Ibid., p. 983.

[679]Finkelstein, 1960, p. xxvi.

> Its adherents live in the same cities and houses as members of other creeds; they travel in the same subways and buses; they correspond, visit, converse, and do business with their fellow Americans of all groups. Jews may be loved as individuals and respected for their gifts. Their prophets are also the prophets of Christendom and Islam. The Holy Land is equally sacred to the members of the Jewish, Christian, and Islamic faiths. Neither Christian nor Moslem theology is intelligible without a study of its Jewish antecedents. But only the rare American or European of any faith appreciates the character of the ancient Jewish tradition, is aware of its distinctive teachings and nature, and seeks to understand the relation of the modern Jew to his predecessor of biblical and talmudic times....[T]his lack of faith in Judaism as a contemporary and permanent factor in civilization carries over into Judaism itself. Its own children sometimes doubt its meaning and its future.[680]

Thus, with the creation of the *Eternal Light* radio and television programs, he helped the non-Jew better understand the Jewish religion, while at the same time introducing Jews to their own heritage. By appealing to both groups, he was accomplishing two of his basic goals while simultaneously serving as a catalyst for religious dialogue between the non-Jew and his Jewish neighbors. These programs aimed at enhancing the dignity of Judaism in the eyes of all people.

While the postwar years were ones of religious ferment, this period was not entirely positive, for immediately upon the defeat of Hitler and Japan came the Soviet Union bent on world conquest, and with it the beginning of the cold war. By 1950, the United States was forced to hold off a Communist attack against South Korea, which ultimately led to war a few years later. So "dreams of victorious relaxation ended almost

---

[680]Ibid.

as soon as they began."[681] Between the cold war, the threat of atomic attack, and the United States' newfound role as chief guardian of the non-Communist world, the stress and anxiety for Americans increased significantly, leading them to feel that something was missing in their lives. In addition, there was the added stress of a new postwar culture: fascination with the automobile and the greater mobility it made possible, and a love affair with the all-new so-called modern conveniences resulting from the new technological age. Taken together, all this produced a moral climate that bordered on despair.

Moreover, the new suburban lifestyle put a strain on the democratic values of tolerance and brotherhood. As a result of the shift from homogeneous communities to heterogeneous ones, in which ethnic groups and later, racial groups, were mixed, group tensions within the country were exacerbated. Thus, a resurgence of obscurantism and anti-Semitism invaded many a suburban community. Indeed, there was a pervasive sense of drift; traditional values were said to be deteriorating. Group tensions thus became a concern to many groups, but most certainly to the Jews.[682] Finkelstein believed that it was the most urgent problem of postwar America.[683]

This was the zeitgeist in which Finkelstein led the Seminary and the Conservative Movement for the first fifteen years (1940–55) of his administration. The notion, put forth by his critics, that the Seminary should be identified more closely with the Conservative Movement, that it should help define Conservative Judaism, thereby exacerbating existing

---

681 Allen, p. 174.

682 This was ascertained to be so when the John Price Jones firm toured the country conducting its feasibility study for a capital campaign. R. F. Duncan to Louis Finkelstein, 29 April 1943.

683 Louis Finkelstein to Frieda Schiff Warburg, 6 January 1944.

group tensions within the Jewish community, and that it should abstain from its outreach to the public, was reflective of a "head in the sand" mentality! With a dominant culture racked by group tension, the last thing a leader would have wanted to do at that time would have been to emphasize group individuality. Kaplan articulated that position best: "There is nothing more dangerous for our people than to react to the antagonism of the outside world by closing itself up in its own shell."[684] Greenberg concurred:

> This is not a time for mending denominational fences nor for stressing doctrinaire convictions which separate one Jewish group from another. What greater service can we of the Seminary bring to our people than that of being a mighty symbol and a powerful factor for a renewed sense of unity in Israel.[685]

Yet the annals of the Conservative Movement during this period, most particularly the *Proceedings of the Rabbinical Assembly*, are filled with debate around this tension and its offshoots. Indeed, the record reflects a virtual preoccupation with such questions as: Who should lead the Conservative Movement? Is there a Movement? Should the Movement define itself? Or, put slightly differently, *exactly* what does Conservative Judaism stand for and believe in? These issues were the subject of major convention debates among the rabbis on several occasions during this same period. The anthology, *Tradition and Change: The Development of Conservative Judaism*, includes no fewer than six major addresses between 1941 and 1952 that deal with these questions in one form or another. It is ironic that the section that contains these six addresses also contains a seventh one: Finkelstein's 1927 address entitled "The Things That Unite Us."

---

[684]R.A., *Proceedings*, 1945, p. 202.

[685]Greenberg, 1947, p. 6.

The Seminary and Its Critics in the Context of Theological Higher Education

That the Seminary's mission during Finkelstein's administration had a significant outreach component was not at all unusual for theological institutions of the 1940s and 1950s. The Pacific School of Religion (PSR) in California and the Union Theological Seminary (UTS)[686] in New York, which is located across Broadway from JTS, are but two examples of such institutions that pursued similar paths.

PSR was "enthusiastically involved" in major concerns of public interest. Like the Jewish Theological Seminary, it was concerned with postwar aims and what it might do to help rebuild society. After a number of conferences with experts, PSR decided to establish the Post-War Rehabilitation School in 1943.[687] It also was an observer of the theological and philosophical issues that were being raised by the new intellectual winds sweeping across the Western world and saw itself as a participant in their resolution.[688] Thus it saw itself, like JTS, as having a share in "shaping [a] new order of things."[689] The institutions were also similar in that PSR, like JTS, tried to balance a loyalty to the higher standards of scholarship as well as to its church while attempting to transcend denominationalism. Indeed, it did not, as one

---

[686]Another example is Fuller Theological Seminary in Pasadena, California. In the vision of its cofounder, "the church" had to play an integral role in Western civilization: "It must not withdraw itself to a separated community again." The mission for Fuller Seminary, as for JTS, included "the task of saving Western civilization in addition to training pastors and missionaries" (Marsden, 1987, pp. 63, 62).

[687]Hogue, 1965, p. 125.

[688]Ibid., p. 68.

[689]Ibid., p. 61.

might today, see these three emphases as being mutually exclusive.[690]

PSR also experienced a need for greater financial support. Like JTS in the early 1940s, it sought help from those closest to it—the local parishes that were often served by its graduates. PSR established a Friends campaign, which called on the school's president to travel about making the case for the school.[691] This fund-raising effort was expanded in 1948 with the Sponsorship Program, in which lay leadership visited churches and friends of the school in all parts of the far West.[692]

Another similarity between PSR and JTS was the existence of tension over the emphasis placed on scholarship as opposed to the religious experience. Just as the Seminary's critics complained that JTS students were not being properly trained, so the students at PSR complained that the heavy academic pressure forced the Christian religious experience to be neglected.[693]

Union Theological Seminary in New York City shared a similar history with JTS and PSR, particularly during the presidency of Henry Van Dusen, beginning in 1945. Van Dusen, like his counterpart across Broadway, was noted for his "big spiritual ambitions, his big ecclesiastical statesmanship as well as for the big impact he had on the Seminary and his interpretation of the Christian Gospel and its application to the whole of life."[694] Like PSR and JTS, UTS envisioned itself "an ecumenical seminary, one expanding in

---

[690]Ibid., p. viii.
[691]Ibid., p. 132.
[692]Ibid., p. 135.
[693]Ibid., p. 146.
[694]Handy, 1987, p. 213.

size and services the better to address the needs of the complex and expansive postwar years."[695]

Just as Finkelstein and the Seminary that he inherited were dedicated to achieving unity within American Judaism, so Van Dusen believed that the times called for Christian unity. In an address entitled "The Role of the Theological Seminary," he asserted:

> Unity is laid as an inescapable obligation upon the Protestant Churches because none of their greatest problems can be adequately met, none of their most claimant tasks can be effectively discharged, by individual churches or separate Communions, but only by the total resources of the whole Church of Christ....The halting of secularism, the reclamation of education, the confrontation of Government, the amelioration of social disease and disorder, the reaching of the unchurched...to each there is only one answer: the massed Christian strength of all churches directed unitedly upon common responsibilities.[696]

UTS also saw the need to expand if it was going to accomplish its work. This expansion was evident in several areas, not the least of which was the larger number of students whom it had been attracting since the end of the war, a trend that continued for several years. By 1948, Van Dusen had drafted his plans for UTS's growth, noting that in order for them to be achieved, a larger endowment would be necessary. UTS, like JTS, turned to its alumni and friends to provide financial support for these plans.

Under Van Dusen's leadership, UTS thrived. It expanded on all fronts, such as building a first-rate faculty and becoming "an important theological center for the mainline Protestant Churches."[697] Given the heightened interest in

---

[695]Ibid.

[696]Ibid.

[697]Ibid., p. 220.

religion that evolved in the 1940s and the strong leadership of Van Dusen and Finkelstein, as well as McGiffert and Fisher at PSR, all three institutions grew significantly.

Insight into the understanding of this tension between the values of the academy and the values of the religious community, with which each of these three institutions struggled, comes from a 1968 study, *University Goals and Academic Power.*[698] That study showed that institutions like JTS, UTS, and PSR—that is, institutions that are concerned with prestige in the academic community and with an emphasis on graduate students,

> manifest an elitist pattern of perceived goals: they emphasize developing the student's intellectual and scholarly qualities; they carry on pure scholarship; they see themselves as centers for disseminating ideas and preserving the cultural heritage.[699]

These qualities certainly describe JTS. Thus, the study would seem to support the idea that the institution's behavior was very much in keeping with its founding beliefs. The Seminary's critics, however, would have preferred an institution that was more oriented to *serving* the needs of the Movement. Moreover, institutions that manifest such a "service" orientation in their perceived goal structure are ones that are relatively unproductive, low in prestige, and lacking strong emphasis on graduate work.[700] In other words, an entirely different kind of institution would have been needed to meet the demands of the critics.

Gross and Grambsch help one to see that much of the tension that existed between the Seminary and the organizations of the Movement was the result of the Seminary having set for itself goals to which, for the most

---

[698]Gross and Grambsch, 1968.

[699]Ibid., p. 111.

[700]Ibid.

part, the leadership of the Movement did not subscribe. This study of university goals also reveals that with regard to the relations between power structure (Seminary) and goal emphasis, the dichotomy that emerges is one not between administration and its internal groups, but rather between outsiders—in this case, the Movement. Here again, it is the dissonance between the elitist goals of the Seminary and the "service" goals of the Movement that emerges as the underlying basis for tensions that existed between the Conservative Movement and the Seminary.[701]

Thus, it would seem that for the Seminary to have satisfied the needs of the Movement as the Movement perceived them would have required that the Seminary abandon the very beliefs on which it was founded; it would have had to be a very different institution. Short of such an institutional transformation, the tensions and ambiguities described above would, according to that study, seem to have been inevitable.

Indeed, "when what *is* differs markedly from what [is] fe[lt] *should be*, a state of dissatisfaction, tension and even conflict will exist."[702] In the case of the Seminary and the Conservative Movement, that is precisely what happened. Usually, however, in such instances "there is an underlying assumption...that when a person feels great frustration and dissatisfaction because of goal incongruence, he will move to another institution."[703] However, in this particular case, there was no other institution to move to, for, as explained earlier, the Seminary was the only training institution for Conservative rabbis in existence at that time.

Another study, *Church and College: A Vital Partnership*, has observed that a number of constituent elements characterize

[701]Ibid., p. 115.
[702]Ibid., p. 36.
[703]Ibid., p. 37.

an effective and successful relationship between an academy and the religious body with which it is affiliated or closely identified.[704] These elements include:

> 1) a common history
> 2) agreement of theological answers to basic human questions
> 3) a respect for the different roles and responsibilities of the other group
> 4) a desire among both groups to work together
> 5) close personal relationships between leaders in each group
> 6) a sense of ownership on the part of key persons in each group
> 7) formal channels for developing concepts, policies, and understandings and for changing these
> 8) a mechanism for agreements and making decisions on issues affecting the relationship
> 9) money, of some amount, given by the religious group to the academy
> 10) an understanding of the way in which various groups of persons can provide links between the two groups
> 11) a common concern about the future.

These elements, however, assume the existence of a certain equality of position between the church and the academy. This was not the case with the Jewish Theological Seminary and the Conservative Movement and would not be the case in any situation where the academy believed that, by virtue of being the academy, it must be at least first among equals, if not completely in charge.

Clearly, some of the above elements characterized the relationship between the Seminary and the Conservative Movement, while other elements were conspicuously missing. For example, there was certainly a common history between

---

[704] West, 1980, pp. 129ff.

the two entities. On the other hand, there was a lack of respect for the different roles and responsibilities of the other group(s). While each paid lip service to the other's role and each spoke of the desire to work together, there were frequent incursions by one group into the program areas of the other and frequent examples of a group working independently of the other(s).

Accordingly, one could not say that there was a mutual desire among the three groups to work together—certainly not toward the same ends. Of course, the Seminary wanted to work with the Rabbinical Assembly or the National Women's League on Seminary fund-raising, but it had little desire to work with the United Synagogue on programs for the Movement.

Although the leadership of the organizations worked somewhat closely together, it could not be said that there ever existed close personal relationships among the elected leaders of the constituent organizations. In fact, one would have to conclude that the relationship among the Seminary, the United Synagogue, and the Rabbinical Assembly manifested few of these eleven elements. Granted that there were "channels for developing policies" and mechanisms, of a sort, for making agreements. They were, however, cumbersome and so tinged with mistrust and tension as to be of only limited effectiveness.

Perhaps most significant was the absence of a common concern about the future, the eleventh of these elements. Finkelstein and the Seminary were concerned about the future of Western civilization, while their critics were more narrowly preoccupied with the future of the Conservative Movement. The absence of this one element, perhaps more than all the others, is further testimony to what has been described in this study, namely, a less than effective academy-Movement relationship.

The Bridge Builder

If there is a single phrase with which to describe Finkelstein and the Seminary, it is a term that he himself often used: "bridge builder." Virtually every one of his initiatives was driven by the desire to build bridges in order to reduce tension, ignorance, hate, and confusion and in order to fashion better human beings and through them to bring about a better society, all of which would only more likely enhance the perpetuation and survival of Judaism. To a member of the Board of Directors, he wrote:

> We are training a group of men who will, I think, prove effective spokesmen for Judaism, and as effective spokesmen for Judaism, will also prove helpful in *building bridges* [italics mine] across all kinds of differences in the world.[705]

> Jews have a job to do in this world—and the job is to act as *bridgers* [italics mine] and conciliators.[706]

When dealing with the threat of the Rabbinical Assembly vis-à-vis the handling of Jewish law, Finkelstein commented:

> [J]ust as [the men of the Great Assembly] built the bridge between Bible and Talmud, so [we]...given sufficient and effective guidance, can build the *bridge* [italics mine] between Talmudic and future Judaism.[707]

When the Seminary opened its College of Jewish Music–Cantors Institute, Stroock proclaimed in his convocation address that "the Seminary now turns its energies and its resources toward building yet another *bridge* [italics mine] of

---

[705]Louis Finkelstein to Frieda Schiff Warburg, 18 September 1945.

[706]Cincinnati Enquirer, 24 June 1945.

[707]Louis Finkelstein to Max Davidson (Law Committee chair), 17 June 1952.

spiritual communication, a *bridge* [italics mine] of music."[708] Upon his return from one of his customary summers in England and Israel, Finkelstein spoke of

> the great need in the world to discover new *bridges* [italics mine] of spiritual communication among men [for] if ideas are to be a unifying force rather than a divisive force, they must be freely exchanged among men.[709]

And so Finkelstein shaped a Seminary in the tradition of his predecessors, who sought to build bridges throughout the world community. His emissaries in that undertaking were to be the graduate rabbis who were trained not as salesmen to sell a particular brand of Judaism, but as "bridge builders" between disparate elements in the general American community.

In the words of one rabbi who recalled Schechter's call for the Seminary to be a reconciling influence in American Jewry, setting itself against those tendencies that make for disunion, for divisiveness, for separation:

> I have tried, in my humble way, to act up to that role, and to perform the function which I conceive to be the role and function of every true and loyal Seminary man. And so, I did organize the Rabbinical Association of Boston....[W]e [Seminary graduates] s[a]t around the table with the graduates of Yeshivas, the Orthodox men and the graduates of the two Reform schools and together we deliberate[d] and we work[ed] for the advancement of the cause of Judaism.[710]

---

[708]Alan M. Stroock at Seminary convocation, 14 September 1952. Implied in this quotation is the notion that cantors and even lay people may ultimately serve as effective spokespeople for Judaism alongside the Seminary-trained rabbi.

[709]JTS press release, 4 August 1952.

[710]R.A., *Proceedings*, 1947, p. 386.

Knowledge was Finkelstein's main building material in the construction of his "bridges." Accordingly, building the Seminary as a center of scholarship and Jewish learning was what essentially motivated all that Finkelstein attempted to do. With the destruction of the major European centers of Jewish learning, the Seminary saw itself as the continuing link in the pursuit of Jewish knowledge and the training of Jewish scholars and religious leaders.

Finkelstein accomplished all that he did, according to Kaplan, "in a more strenuous time and under more difficult conditions than those with which Dr. Schechter had to cope."[711] Schechter maintained that "amid all these Judaisms and no Judaisms, my colleagues and I are called upon to create a theological seminary that should be all things to all men, reconciling all parties and appealing to all aspects of the community." According to Kaplan, it is exactly this—"the reconciling of all parties and appealing to all aspects of the community"—that Finkelstein had accomplished.[712]

Professor Salo Baron, dean of American Jewish historians, remarked in the early 1940s:

> If ever...the Jewish people has been in need of a far-sighted and courageous leadership, it is in these days of great crisis. If the leaders, in particular of American Jewry equipped with the knowledge furnished them by the methods of modern social and historical sciences and imbued with the accumulated wisdom of the ages of rabbis and thinkers, will undertake to look courageously into the realities as they are and to adopt measures which they will consider best...then they may yet be destined to render a historical service.[713]

---

[711]Ibid., 1945.

[712]Ibid.

[713]Baron, p. 15.

Finkelstein brought to bear that farsighted and courageous leadership during this period (1940–55) of his presidency of the Jewish Theological Seminary and, in so doing, rendered that "historical service."

Finkelstein continued to serve as the head of the Jewish Theological Seminary for another seventeen years, resigning in 1972. As head of the Seminary, and titular head of the Conservative Movement, he transformed the Seminary from a local rabbinical school into a major institution of Jewish scholarship, professional training, and communal outreach.

In the process, he became recognized and respected as the spokesman for Judaism in America. Indeed, he was a charismatic figure, admired by all who knew him. During his tenure, the Conservative Movement became the largest Jewish denomination in the United States. In 1986, the Seminary renamed the Institute for Religious and Social Studies, Finkelstein's beloved vehicle of ecumenism, the Louis Finkelstein Institute.

Amazingly, during the period under study, Finkelstein was also able to compile a prodigious bibliography of articles and scholarly publications—in excess of 337.[714] It was this deep and prolific scholarship that powered his public leadership.[715] After stepping down as head of the Seminary, he continued to pursue his passion for scholarship, publishing additional scholarly works. He died in 1991 at the age of ninety-six.

---

[714] Schmelzer, 1977; Hamelsdorf, 1985.

[715] Seminary chancellor Ismar Schorsch to Seminary professor Menahem Schmelzer, 2 March 1993.

Chapter 9
Conclusion

Deriving conclusions from this study is made difficult by the fact that the Jewish Theological Seminary was then, as institutions of theological education go, *sui generis*. What distinguished it at the time from its Christian counterparts was the fact that it both trained *and* ordained its students. Hence, it fulfilled the role of both academy and "church," which would be the two institutions that would fulfill these roles in virtually all mainstream Christian denominations. What separated JTS from many of its Christian counterparts was the fact that it was also the sole training institution within the Conservative Movement.[716] There was simply nowhere else in the world where one could be ordained as a Conservative rabbi. When a denomination has more than one training institution, it is possible for each one of them to cultivate a unique emphasis, with one, perhaps, favoring rigorous academic training and another emphasizing spiritual development and pastoral preparation. Notwithstanding its early Jewish and interdenominational mission, the Seminary, by virtue of being the only academic institution serving the Movement, had to be all these things to all who were members of that Movement.

Notwithstanding JTS's uniqueness, certain conclusions may be drawn from its history and experience between the years 1902 and 1955. The founding tenets on which the Seminary was reorganized in 1902 and their continued underlying role in the institution's evolving mission, called for

---

[716] It also distinguished itself from the Reform Movement in that, unlike the Hebrew Union College, which was established by the Union of American Hebrew Congregations (the Reform Movement's lay body), JTS founded the United Synagogue, the synagogal body of the Conservative Movement.

the institution to work on several different levels simultaneously. On the one hand, it was an academy, and within that construct of mission, it tried to function on at least two levels: pure scholarship and intellectual activism. On the other hand, it established for itself the role of fountainhead for a specific religious group. Here, too, it attempted to perform on at least two different levels: that of the Conservative Movement and that of the broader, general society. Working on all four levels simultaneously exacerbated the ambiguity and tension that already existed inside and outside the institution. While this broad, fluid, and ambiguous positioning of the Seminary was, in some ways, a key to its survival and success, the pursuit of all four fronts simultaneously resulted in a lack of understanding for the work of the institution. Lindbeck, in his analysis of university-related divinity schools, once observed that "the range of subjects dealt with may not have to be reduced, but it may have to be integrated by a defensible *raison d'être.*"[717]

What better example of Lindbeck's conclusion than Finkelstein's leadership of the Seminary? Finkelstein attempted to have an academic institution serve as the fountainhead of a religious movement, while simultaneously maintaining a set of institutional values that were sufficiently separate and apart from that movement—at best, a difficult and taxing challenge. One must remember that Finkelstein was not terribly threatened by the criticism or the tensions that were generated against the Seminary. On the contrary, he told me in a 1989 interview that the tension between the congregational rabbis and the Seminary was "healthy."[718] Is it possible to convince all concerned parties that the ambiguity

---

[717]Lindbeck, 1976, p. 5.

[718]Interview with Finkelstein, 4 January 1989: "That is the way it must be because those who study more are going to be more observant, and the ideal is to rigorously observe the laws of the Torah."

and tensions, which existed then and continue today, are quite normal, given the ethos of this academy, and therefore one should not take them so seriously? Obviously, for Finkelstein, it was possible; for all other concerned parties, it was not. Nevertheless, the ideal goal would be to achieve a solid understanding between the leadership of the academy and the movement that it represents.

Finkelstein's tenure also shows the observer that a leader in a similar situation must (a) be strong and (b) have a clear sense of direction. I believe that Finkelstein was able to accomplish as much as he did, and serve as long as he did, because he was both forceful and resilient; that is to say, his thinking was not easily swayed by the demands of his critics, and he did not allow himself to be consumed by any momentary fad. On the contrary, he was clear in his own mind about what he wanted to accomplish and was armed with the determination to see his plan through to completion. Finkelstein was not the originator of the conflicts that existed within the Conservative Movement; rather, they were endemic to the very nature of the institution. Thus, what Finkelstein's tenure illustrates is how one mediates such conflicts: at times successfully, at other times not. To aid him in his effort toward building a consensus among the various organizations of the Movement, as well as within the Seminary itself, were such men as Greenberg, Arzt, Geffen, Davis, and, later, Mandelbaum.

Even when Finkelstein may have been the cause of some of the conflicts, he always resisted further exacerbating them. One can only imagine what the state of the Seminary would have been had he acted in a more authoritarian fashion. On the contrary, Finkelstein modeled transformational leadership, articulating a captivating vision that addressed the personal needs of many Jews and non-Jews at that time. Accordingly, today's leaders need to exercise a similar mediating style of leadership, constantly rising above the petulant arguments of their critics, in order to maintain a sense of organizational cohesion and respectful leadership. Indeed, such leadership qualities are needed not only for the *Seminary* to remain viable, but also for the Movement to survive in the twenty-first century for, in truth, I do not believe that either can survive without the other.

Accordingly, the chasm between the Seminary and the Movement should never again be as wide as it was in Finkelstein's time. Finkelstein, the "bridge builder," was single-minded in bridging group differences in virtually all areas except one—the entire Conservative Movement itself. Greater effort needed to be expended on the part of the Seminary to integrate the parts of the Movement for purposes other than fund-raising. It was unrealistic then, and is even more unrealistic today, for the Seminary to depend on the constituents of the Movement for support without sufficiently "servicing them." Finkelstein indeed began to develop a role for the Seminary as "broker" for the broader community, but he did not carry it far enough; that is, he did not successfully achieve the bridging of authentic scholarship with the needs of the people—at least not with those people who constituted the Conservative Movement. Finkelstein's Seminary simply did not reach out to mainstream Conservative Jews with its unique, albeit complex, message or with the message of Conservative Judaism. Granted, in the first years of the Finkelstein era, a denominational message was not a desideratum for a number of reasons; however, that was probably not the case in the second half of Finkelstein's presidency and certainly is not so today. A more direct, systematic, and integrated appeal to members of the Conservative Movement is a must in order to mediate the sense of ambiguity and mission conflict that continues within the Movement. The ideology and underlying philosophy that is Conservative Judaism is itself fraught with ambiguity and creative tensions. Thus, if Conservative Judaism is to be understood by its adherents in a way that enables them to feel connected to it, and as a result to feel a sense of commitment and loyalty to the Seminary and the Movement's other national organizations, then the religious and philosophical meaning of Conservative Judaism must emanate from the Movement's fountainhead, clearly, forcefully, and, most important, frequently. Indeed, if the Seminary is to remain viable into the next century, it will have to take the Movement more seriously than did Finkelstein.

Whether the Seminary can do so successfully, while still maintaining its elitist image as a premier academic institution, remains a question. In truth, it is really several questions, for implicit in this larger query is the question of whether the Seminary *should* strive to maintain the image of an elite academy, or if instead should change its image to serve the Movement through the professional training of religious and educational leaders. If the Seminary desires to remain a premier graduate school, the question is whether it has, or can acquire, the resources and the determination to sustain that goal while simultaneously expanding its outreach to the Movement.

However, the Seminary is not the only catalyst for change within the Conservative Movement, for, in truth, it matters little what the Seminary and its leadership desire if the Movement and its leaders are not prepared to accept *and support* the Seminary and its chancellor as the head of the Movement. The Seminary cannot be a successful leader of the Movement unless and until the Movement is prepared to accept it wholeheartedly as such. As long as there is a power struggle between the Rabbinical Assembly and/or the United Synagogue with the Seminary for the right to be the leader of the entire Movement, the institution's ability to lead, regardless of the best of its intentions, is doomed to fail. Indeed, the centralization of power within the Reform Movement at a single address is often cited as an explanation of why it is perceived as a strong, well-led movement.

One of the conclusions that emerges from this study is that at the root of the tensions between the Seminary and the Movement lies the desire for power. When one strips away the debate over denominationalism versus nondenominationalism, between having or not having a clear definition of Conservative Judaism, the Seminary being an academy of independent thinkers or an academy where the Jewish message and lifestyle are hammered out in direct confrontation with the secular world, one is left with three organizations fighting for power. While this desire for power is predicated on a belief held by each of these organizations that it has a rightful claim to be leader of the Movement, whether it be as perceived builders of the Movement (the rabbinate), or the body politic of the Movement (the laity and their congregations), the struggle with the Seminary comes down, nonetheless, to a thirst to control the Movement and direct its course. Obviously, Schechter's founding tenet, that only an academy of Torah scholars could be the head of a Jewish community, was never accepted by the rest of the Movement. Until it is accepted, or until there is unanimity by the participants as to who or what organization should be the Movement's leader, there will be no real unity. Moreover, any efforts made to achieve such unity will amount to little more than tilting at windmills, strengthening the perception that the Conservative Movement is weak and without focus. In time, adherents of Conservative Judaism will diminish, as will the numbers of Conservative synagogues—all to the detriment of the Jewish Theological Seminary. Until this critical issue is resolved, leadership of the Movement will be at best symbolic and therefore ineffective.

Finkelstein understood clearly that the Seminary *qua* academy was not in and of itself a viable commodity because too few in the community could understand, let alone appreciate, why the scholarship of its faculty was so important. Furthermore, the Seminary, as a school training religious functionaries, was also of limited attractiveness within the community, given that there were other institutions that trained rabbis and cantors, even if they were not of the Conservative persuasion. Accordingly, Finkelstein realized that in order to support both pure scholarship and professional training, there must be a third element that would bring the institution to the attention of the community in ways that it could understand its mission and find it exciting. It was here that Finkelstein placed much of his effort creating new and provocative outreach programs, which served to promote, in the public eye, both himself and the institution. The need for this third element, if you will, is as necessary today as it was then. It calls for an imaginative linking of the Seminary's scholarship and training mission to the issues of the day, thereby demonstrating that the Seminary and Conservative Judaism have something meaningful to say about society's problems and challenges.

Bibliography

A. Unpublished Material

Cyrus Adler Papers. New York: Jewish Theological Seminary.

Cohen, Gerson D. Interview, 29 July 1985. New York: Jewish Theological Seminary.

Feingold, Jessica. Interview, 6 January 1992.

Finkelstein, Louis. Interviews, 3 January 1983; 14 February 1984; 4 January 1989. New York: Jewish Theological Seminary.

Fisher, Ben C. "What Does It Mean to 'Sponsor' a Church-Related College/University?" Remarks delivered at the 1982 annual meeting of the Center for Constitutional Studies, University of Notre Dame Law School, South Bend, Ind., March 1982.

Gallin, Alice. "What Does It Mean to 'Sponsor' a College or University?" Paper presented at the Center for Constitutional Studies, University of Notre Dame Law School, South Bend, Ind., 23 March 1982.

Gordis, Robert. Interview, 22 May 1985. New York: Jewish Theological Seminary.

Jewish Theological Seminary of America, Ratner Center for the Study of Conservative Judaism. Records of the Jewish Theological Seminary, R.G. 1, General Files. (At the time I used these materials, they were unprocessed; they have subsequently been organized.)

Nudell, George. "The Clearing House: A History of the Committee on Jewish Law and Standards." Research paper, February 1980.

Rosenblum, Herbert. "The Founding of the United Synagogue of America, 1913." Ph.D. diss., Brandeis University, 1970.

Solomon Schechter Papers. Archives of the Library of the Jewish Theological Seminary, New York.

Schwartz, Shuly Rubin. "Ramah—the Early Years, 1947–52." Master's thesis, Jewish Theological Seminary, 1976.

Simon, Charles E., and Joe B. Sperber. "The Federation of Jewish Men's Clubs 1929–1989." February 1990.

B. Official Reports

"For the Perpetuation in America of Ancestral Judaism." Pamphlet. N.d., but believed to be from 1926–27.

Jewish Theological Seminary Association. *Certificate of Incorporation. Constitution and By-Laws*, New York, 1886.

Jewish Theological Seminary of America. *Documents, Charter and By-Laws.* New York, 1903.

———. *Audit Reports 1939–55.* New York.

———. *Minutes of the Board of Directors.* New York, 1940–48.

———. *Register.* New York, 1902–60.

Rabbinical Assembly (R.A.). *Proceedings.* New York, 1928–60.

Shriver, Donald. *The President's Report.* Union Theological Seminary, New York, 1981.

C. Published Material

Adler, Cyrus. *I Have Considered the Days.* Philadelphia: Jewish Publication Society, 1943.

———. *Lectures, Selected Papers and Addresses.* Philadelphia: n.p., 1933.

———, ed. *The Jewish Theological Seminary of America: Semi-Centennial Volume.* New York: Jewish Theological Seminary of America, 1939.

Ahlstrom, Sydney E. *A Religious History of the American People.* New Haven: Yale University Press, 1972.

Allen, Lewis Fredrick. *The Big Change: America Transforms Itself, 1900–1950.* New York: Harper and Brothers, 1972.

Anderson, Richard E. *Strategic Policy Changes at Private Colleges.* New York: Teachers College Press, 1977.

Arzt, Max. "Conservative Judaism as a Unifying Force." *Conservative Judaism* (June 1949): 10–20.

Baldridge, J. Victor, David V. Curtis, George P. Ecker, and Gary L. Riley. *Policy Making and Effective Leadership*. San Francisco: Jossey-Bass, 1978.

Baron, Salo W. "The Effect of the War on Jewish Community Life." Harry L. Glucksman Memorial Lecture at Columbia University, New York, 1942.

Ben-Horin, Meir. "Solomon Schechter to Judge Mayer Sulzberger: Part I. Letters from the Pre-Seminary Period (1895–1901)." *Jewish Social Studies* 24 (October 1963): 249–86.

Benjamin, Aaron. *The Jewish American*. 24 May 1940.

Bentwich, Norman. *Solomon Schechter*. New York: Burning Bush Press, 1964 (repr. from 1938 original, Philadelphia: Jewish Publication Society).

Blau, Joseph L. *Judaism in America: From Curiosity to Third Faith*. Chicago: University of Chicago Press, 1976.

Brown, Michael. "It's Off to Camp We Go: Ramah, LTF, and the Seminary in the Finkelstein Era." In *Tradition Renewed: A History of the Jewish Theological Seminary of America*, ed. Jack Wertheimer, vol. 1. New York: Jewish Theological Seminary, 1997.

Bruning, Charles R. *Relationships between Church-Related Colleges and Their Constituencies: A Review of the Literature*. New York: Lutheran Church in America, Department of Higher Education, Division for Mission in North America, 1975.

Bucher, Glenn R. "The Academic Revolution and Church-Related Education: Can the Schizophrenia Be Cured?" *Change Magazine* (July/August 1982): 8–10.

Burtchaell, James Tunstead. *The Dying Light: The Disengagement of Colleges and Universities from Their Christian Church*. Grand Rapids, Mich.: Eerdmans, 1998.

Carnegie Commission on Higher Education. *A Classification of Institutions of Higher Education.* New York: McGraw-Hill, 1973.

Cohen, Burton I. "A Brief History of the Ramah Movement." In *The Ramah Experience*, ed. Sylvia C. Ettenberg and Geraldine Rosenfeld. New York: Jewish Theological Seminary and National Ramah Commission, 1989.

Cohen, Naomi W. Introduction to *Cyrus Adler: Selected Letters*, ed. Ira Robinson, vols. 1 and 2. Philadelphia/New York: Jewish Publication Society of America/Jewish Theological Seminary of America, 1985.

Cuninggim, Merriman. "Varieties of Church-Relatedness in Higher Education." In *Church-Related Higher Education*, ed. Robert Rue Parsonage. Valley Forge: Judson Press, 1978.

———. *Uneasy Partners: The College and the Church.* Nashville: Abingdon, 1994.

Dash-Moore, Debra. *At Home in America: Second-Generation New York Jews.* New York: Columbia University Press, 1981.

Davis, Moshe. *The Emergence of Conservative Judaism.* Philadelphia: Jewish Publication Society, 1963.

———-. "Jewish Religious Life and Institutions in America." In *The Jews*, ed. Louis Finkelstein. 3d ed., 2 vols. New York: Harper and Row, 1960.

DeJong, Arthur J. *Reclaiming a Mission: New Directions for the Church-Related College.* Grand Rapids, Mich.: Eerdmans, 1990.

Emet ve-Emunah: Statement of Principles of Conservative Judaism. Jewish Theological Seminary of America, Rabbinical Assembly, United Synagogue of America, 1988.

Fierstein, Robert E. *A Different Spirit: The Jewish Theological Seminary of America. 1886–1902.* New York: Jewish Theological Seminary of America, 1990.

Finkelstein, Louis, ed. *The Jews: Their History, Culture and Religion.* 3d ed., 2 vols. New York: Harper and Row, 1960.

———. "The Jew in 1950." *Conservative Judaism* (May 1950): 1–5.

———. "Necrology, Cyrus Adler." Proceedings of the American Academy for Jewish Research, 1940, pp. x, 1–2.

FitzGerald, Paul A. *The Governance of Jesuit College in the United States, 1920–1970.* Notre Dame, Ind.: University of Notre Dame Press, 1984.

Friedlander, Israel. *Past and Present: Selected Essays.* New York: Burning Bush Press, 1961.

Ginzberg, Eli. *Keeper of the Law: Louis Ginzberg.* Philadelphia: Jewish Publication Society of America, 1966.

———. "The Seminary Family: A View from My Parents' Home." In *Perspectives on Jews and Judaism: Essays in Honor of Wolfe Kelman*, ed. Arthur A. Chiel. New York: Rabbinical Assembly, 1978.

Glazer, Nathan. *American Judaism.* 2d ed., rev. Chicago: University of Chicago Press, 1972.

Goldsmith, Emmanuel S., Mel Scult, and Robert M. Seltzer, eds. *The American Judaism of Mordecai M. Kaplan.* New York: New York University Press, 1990.

Gordis, Robert. *Conservative Judaism: An American Philosophy.* New York: Behrman House, 1945.

Goren, Arthur A. *New York Jews and the Quest for Community: The Kehillah Experiment, 1908–1922.* New York: Columbia University Press, 1970.

Greenberg, Simon. "A Force for Reconciliation and Unity." Address at convocation marking his inauguration as provost of JTSA, New York, 30 March 1947.

———. *The Conservative in Judaism: An Introduction.* New York: United Synagogue of America, 1955.

———. *Foundations of a Faith.* New York: Burning Bush Press, 1967.

Gross, Edward, and Paul V. Grambsch. *University Goals and Academic Power.* Washington, D.C.: American Council on Education, 1968.

Guthrie, David S., and Richard L. Noftzer Jr. eds. *Agendas for Church-Related Colleges and Universities.* San Francisco: Jossey-Bass, 1992.

Hamelsdorf, Ora, ed. *A Supplement to a Bibliography of the Writings of Louis Finkelstein.* New York: Jewish Theological Seminary, 1985.

Handy, Robert T. "The American Religious Depression, 1925–1935." *Church History* 29 (1960).

———. *A History of Union Theological Seminary in New York.* New York: Columbia University Press, 1987.

Harris, Isidore. *Jews' College Jubilee Volume.* London: Luzac, 1906.

Hartstein, Jacob I. "Yeshiva University: Growth of Rabbi Elchanan's Theological Seminary." In *American Jewish Year Book* 48 (1946–47). Philadelphia: Jewish Publication Society, 1946.

Higham, John. "Social Discrimination Against Jews in America, 1830–1930." *Publications of the American Jewish Historical Society* 47 (September 1957): 1–33. Also in *The Jewish Experience in America,* ed. Abraham Karp. Selected Studies from the Publications of the American Jewish Historical Society, vol. 5: At Home in American Jewish Historical Society. New York: Ktav, 1969.

Hobbs, Walter C., and Richard L. Meeth. *Diversity Among Christian Colleges.* Arlington, Va.: Studies in Higher Education, 1980.

Hoffnung, Arthur. *The University of Judaism at Forty—Historical Memoir.* Los Angeles: University of Judaism, 1991.

Hogue, Harland E. *Christian Seed in Western Soil: Pacific School of Religion through a Century.* Berkeley, Calif.: Pacific School of Religion, 1965.

Hunt, Thomas C., and James Carper, eds. *Religious Higher Education in the United States: A Source Book.* New York: Garland, 1996.

Johnson, Barry. *Polarity Management: Identifying and Managing Unsolvable Problems.* Amherst, Mass.: HRD Press, 1992.

Kaplan, Mordecai M. *A University of Judaism—A Compelling Need.* New York: United Synagogue of America, 1946.

Karff, Samuel E., ed. *Hebrew Union College—Jewish Institute of Religion at One Hundred Years.* Cincinnati: Hebrew Union College Press, 1976.

Karp, Abraham. *The Jewish Experience in America* (vols. 4 and 5). New York: Ktav, 1969.

————-. *Haven and Home: A History of the Jews in America.* New York: Ktav, 1985.

————-. "Solomon Schechter Comes to America." *American Jewish Historical Quarterly* 52, no. 1 (September 1963): 42–62.

————-. *A History of the United Synagogue of America 1913–1963.* New York: United Synagogue of America, 1964.

————- "The Conservative Rabbi—Dissatisfied But Not Unhappy." In *American Jewish Archives: The American Rabbinate: A Centennial View.* November 1983.

Libovitz, Richard. "Kaplan and Cyrus Adler." In *The American Judaism of Mordecai M. Kaplan*, ed. Emmanuel S. Goldsmith, Mel Scult, and Robert M. Seltzer. New York: New York University Press, 1990.

Lindbeck, George, Stanfield K. Deutsch, and Nathan Glazer. *University Divinity Schools: A Report on Ecclesiastically Independent Theological Education.* New York: Rockefeller Foundation, 1976.

MacEoin, Gary. "Notre Dame's Father Hesburgh." *Change Magazine* (February 1976).

Mandelbaum, Bernard. *The Wisdom of Solomon Schechter*. New York: Burning Bush Press, 1963.

Markovitz, Eugene. "Henry Pereira Mendes: Architect of the Union of Orthodox Jewish Congregations of America." *American Jewish Historical Quarterly* 55 (March 1966): 364–84.

Marsden, George M. *Reforming Fundamentalism: Fuller Seminary and the New Evangelicalism*. Grand Rapids, Mich.: Eerdmans, 1987.

McGiffert, Arthur C. Jr. *No Ivory Tower: The Story of the Chicago Theological Seminary*. Chicago: Chicago Theological Seminary, 1965.

Monson, Rela Geffen. "The Jewish Theological Seminary and Conservative Congregations: Limited Associates or Full Partners?" In *The Seminary at 100*, ed. Nina Beth Cardin and David Wolf Silverman. New York: Jewish Theological Seminary of America, 1987.

Mosely, John D., and Glenn R. Bucher. "Church-Related Colleges in a Changing Context." *Educational Record* (winter 1982): 46–52.

Nadell, Pamela S. *Conservative Judaism in America: A Biographical Dictionary and Sourcebook*. Westport, Conn.: Greenwood Press, 1988.

Noveck, Simon. *Milton Steinberg—Portrait of a Rabbi*. New York: Ktav, 1978.

O'Brien, David J. *From the Heart of the Church: Catholic Higher Education and American Culture*. New York: Orbus Books, 1994.

Pace, C. R. *Education and Evangelism: A Profile of Protestant Colleges*. New York: McGraw-Hill, 1972.

Parsonage, Robert Rue. "Church-College Relationships: Shaping a Faithful and Viable Future." In *Church and*

College: A Vital Partnership, vol. 2. Sherman, Tex.: National Congress of Church-Related Colleges and Universities, 1980.

———-, ed. *Church-Related Higher Education.* Valley Forge: Judson Press, 1978.

Parzen, Herbert. *Architects of Conservative Judaism.* New York: Jonathan David, 1964.

Patillo, Manning M., and Donald M. MacKenzie. *Church-Sponsored Higher Education in the United States.* Washington, D.C.: American Council on Education, 1966.

Reznikoff, Charles, ed. *Louis Marshall, Champion of Liberty: Selected Papers and Addresses.* 2 vols. Philadelphia: Jewish Publication Society, 1957.

Riesman, David. *On Higher Education.* San Francisco: Jossey-Bass, 1980.

Ringenberg, William C. *The Christian College: A History of Protestant Higher Education in America.* Grand Rapids, Mich.: Eerdmans, 1984.

Robinson, Ira. "Cyrus Adler and the Jewish Theological Seminary of America: Image and Reality." *American Jewish History* 78, no. 3 (March 1989).

———-, ed. *Cyrus Adler: Selected Letters.* Vols. 1 and 2. Philadelphia/New York: Jewish Publication Society of America/Jewish Theological Seminary of America, 1985.

Rodenhouse, Mary Pat, ed. *2000 Higher Education Directory.* Falls Church, Va.: Higher Education Publications, 1999.

Rothkoff, Aaron. *Bernard Revel: Builder of American Jewish Orthodoxy.* Philadelphia: Jewish Publication Society, 1972.

Rozenblit, Marsha L. "The Seminary during the Holocaust Years." In *Tradition Renewed: A History of the Jewish*

Theological Seminary of America, ed. Jack Wertheimer, vol. 2. New York: Jewish Theological Seminary, 1997.

Rubenovitz, Herman H., and Mignon L. Rubenovitz. *The Waking Heart.* Cambridge: Nathanial Dame and Company, 1967.

Sandin, R. T. *Autonomy and Faith: Religious Preference in Employment Decisions in Religiously Affiliated Higher Education.* Atlanta: Center for Constitutional Studies, Mercer University and Omega, 1990.

Schechter, Solomon. *Seminary Addresses and Other Papers.* Cincinnati: Ark, 1915.

———. *Studies in Judaism: Essays on Persons, Concepts, and Movements of Thought in Jewish Tradition.* New York: Atheneum, 1970.

Schmelzer, Menahem, Burton Visotzky, and Micha Oppenheim, eds. *A Bibliography of the Writings of Louis Finkelstein.* New York: Jewish Theological Seminary, 1977.

Schuth, Katarina. *Reason to Hope: The Futures of Roman Catholic Theologates.* Wilmington, Del.: Michael Glazier, 1989.

Seltzer, Robert M. "Kaplan and Jewish Modernity." In *The American Judaism of Mordecai M. Kaplan*, ed. Emmanuel S. Goldsmith, Mel Scult, and Robert M. Seltzer. New York: New York University Press, 1990.

Semi-Centennial Volume: Theological School and Calvin College 1876–1926. Grand Rapids, Mich.: n.p., 1926.

Shargel, Baila Round. *Practical Dreamer: Israel Friedlander and the Shaping of American Judaism.* New York: Jewish Theological Seminary of America, 1985.

Sherry, Paul H. "Church or College: Either, But Not Both." *Christian Century 84* (4 October 1967).

Sklare, Marshall. *Conservative Judaism.* Glencoe, Ill.: Free Press, 1955, 1972.

Sloan, Douglas. *Faith and Knowledge: Mainline Protestantism and*

American Higher Education. Westminster John Knox Press, Louisville, 1994.

Solberg, Richard W., and Morton P. Strommen. *How Church-Related Are Church-Related Colleges?* Philadelphia: Lutheran Church in America, 1980.

Steinberg, Milton. *Anatomy of Faith*. Ed. with an introduction by Arthur A. Cohen. New York: Harcourt, Brace, 1960.

Stoltzfus, Victor. *Church-Affiliated Higher Education: Exploratory Case Studies of Presbyterian, Roman Catholic, and Wesleyan Colleges*. Goshen, Ind.: Pinchpenny Press, 1992.

Strommen, Morton P. "Research Report to the Joint Committee of the Division for Mission in North America and the Council of LCA Colleges on A Survey of Images and Expectations of LCA Colleges. Lutheran Church in America," 1976.

Students Annual. vol. 2. New York: Jewish Theological Seminary of America, 1915.

Tappert, Theodore G. *History of the Lutheran Theological Seminary at Philadelphia 1864–1964*. Philadelphia: Lutheran Theological Seminary, 1964.

Waxman, Mordecai, ed. *Tradition and Change: The Development of Conservative Judaism*. New York: Burning Bush Press, 1964.

Weinstein, J. J. *Solomon Goldman: A Rabbi's Rabbi*. New York: Ktav, 1973.

West, Dan C. "Effective Church-College Relationships and How They Are Made." In *Church and College: A Vital Partnership*, vol. 2: Mission—A Shared Vision of Educational Purpose. Sherman, Tex.: National Congress of Church-Related Colleges and Universities, 1980.

Index

N.B. Page numbers that appear in italics refer to material in the footnotes.

A

C

D

E

G

H

I

J

K

L

N

O

P

R

S

T

U

V

W

Y